Frederick Weyerhaeuser
AND THE *American West*

Frederick Weyerhaeuser, 1907

Frederick Weyerhaeuser
AND THE *American West*

JUDITH KOLL HEALEY

Minnesota Historical
Society Press

The publication of this book was supported through a generous grant from the Atherton and Winifred (Wollaeger) Bean Fund for Business History.

www.mhspress.org
The Minnesota Historical Society Press is a member of the Association of American University Presses.
Manufactured in the United States of America
10 9 8 7 6 5 4 3 2 1
⊗ The paper used in this publication meets the minimum requirements of the American National Standard for Information Sciences— Permanence for Printed Library Materials, ANSI Z39.48–1984.

International Standard Book Number
ISBN: 978-0-87351-891-8 (paper)
ISBN: 978-0-87351-898-7 (e-book)

Library of Congress Cataloging-in-Publication Data

Healey, Judith Koll.
Frederick Weyerhaeuser and the American West /
Judith Koll Healey, Char Miller.
pages cm
Includes bibliographical references and index.
ISBN 978-0-87351-891-8 (pbk. : alk. paper) — ISBN 978-0-87351-898-7 (ebk.) (print)
1. Weyerhaeuser, Frederick, 1834–1914. 2. Industrialists—United States—Biography.
3. Lumber trade—United States—History. I. Title.
HD9750.5.H43 2013
338.7´63498092—dc23 [B]
2012048185

This and other Minnesota Historical Society Press publications are available from popular e-book vendors.

The Way It Is

There's a thread you follow. It goes among
things that change. But it doesn't change.
People wonder about what you are pursuing.
You have to explain about the thread.
But it is hard for others to see.
While you hold it you can't get lost.
Tragedies happen; people get hurt
or die; and you suffer and get old.
Nothing you do can stop time's unfolding.
You don't ever let go of the thread.

—WILLIAM STAFFORD (1914–93)

Contents

Foreword

CHAR MILLER

Frederick Weyerhaeuser was something of a marked man. His reputation as a shrewd investor in high-value timberlands across the country, his extraordinary success in identifying, purchasing, and managing these wooded properties, meant that wherever he traveled local journalists and business interests avidly tracked his movements. His 1894 inspection of the southern pineries, for example, sparked nonstop speculation about his potential purchase of large tracts of land there. As newspaper editorials pleaded with Weyerhaeuser to invest heavily, one of his private correspondents concurred, arguing that any such purchases would redound to the legendary lumberman's profit and be a boon to regional development. All would be good if only "we had a Weyerhaeuser here."[1]

This importuning could get old, and no doubt was a reason why Weyerhaeuser preferred to negotiate out of the public eye. One of these deals produced a staggering result. In 1900, Weyerhaeuser negotiated with his down-the-street neighbor in St. Paul, Minnesota, James Hill, head of the Northern Pacific Railroad, to purchase nine hundred thousand acres of the railroad's holdings in the state of Washington for what in retrospect seems a paltry $5.4 million. The sale—its massive scale and relatively cheap price tag—produced considerable debate. So much so that when Weyerhaeuser headed west in June 1902 to look over his acquisition he cautioned George Long, manager of the company's sprawling forested estate, "Do not advertise our coming any more than you possibly have to. I do not want callers after the style of Black Dan[,] and the less fellows I have calling on me who have axes to grind the more I will enjoy my visit."[2]

Weyerhaeuser's preference for anonymity came conjoined with a desire to hold himself apart. For all his manifold ability to work with others, to develop complex, collaborative arrangements within the usually brutally competitive wood products industry, he liked to keep his own counsel. This personal quality is captured in an evocative photograph snapped while he and his partners in the Weyerhaeuser Timber Company toured the region. One stop along the way was at a major sawmill in Everett, where a photographer caught their image: six men are in the frame, all standing solidly on huge logs floating in Puget Sound, ready for milling. Five of them face one another in a semicircle, seemingly in conversation, most with their backs to the camera. The indisputable head of the eponymous corporation, by contrast, stands several feet to their right: hands clasped behind his back, head bowed as if in reflection; even in close proximity, the self-contained Frederick Weyerhaeuser seems a study in solitude.

These definitive traits are smartly revealed in Judith Koll Healey's new biography of Weyerhaeuser, one of the great industrialists of the late nineteenth and early twentieth centuries. He has been the subject of study before—business historians have probed his corporate dealings; muckraking reporters have exposed what they believed to be his monopolistic ambitions; and in rebuttal his children have written paeans to his virtue. Yet Healey's is the first attempt to integrate his personal and public life: to see the man in his work, to trace how his professional aspirations furthered his family's internal life, and to set him in the larger social context.[3]

Along the way she discovered, as good biographers do, that her subject had something to teach her. Reading Weyerhaeuser's extensive correspondence and journal entries and leafing through letters and diaries of family members, friends, and business associates, Healey received "the unexpected gift of getting

to know a complex, gifted, and interesting character." A self-made man who, not incidentally, helped make America.

That indeed is one of the central themes of this new biographical study. Like so many other German immigrants who came to the United States in the decade before the Civil War, Weyerhaeuser spent several years working a variety of jobs to make ends meet and, in the process, to sort out what field seemed most consistent with his abilities. It is too easy to suggest that his new country's gargantuan appetite for wood in the initial stages of the industrial revolution made Weyerhaeuser's choice straightforward. But it is fair to say that he correctly perceived how significant timber was to the nation's development. In moving to Rock Island, Illinois, a bustling port on the Mississippi River—down whose many tributaries millions of board feet annually flowed—Weyerhaeuser was positioning himself to take advantage of this remarkable opportunity.

His success was not preordained, either, as Healey demonstrates. It helped that he worked hard, very hard. It proved invaluable that his wife and growing family were supportive of his energetic efforts and frequent absences. Like any budding entrepreneur, he took calculated risks, only some of which bore fruit. Perhaps most significantly, Weyerhaeuser correctly intuited that there were two key factors that must be managed if his business—and, by extension, the larger industry—was to flourish.

The first was how to ensure a steady and full movement of sawlogs to sawmills. Resolving this issue was more difficult than it might first appear because, while Weyerhaeuser's base of operations was in Illinois, the timber was located well upstream, in central Wisconsin (and, later, in Minnesota). Add to the problem of distance one of competition: Chippewa and Eau Claire loggers and mill owners had little interest in cooperating with those, like Weyerhaeuser, whom they pegged as downriver interlopers. The brawls that erupted—political, legal, even physical—and the infrastructure over which they battled, such as the flashpoint known as the Beef Slough boom, testified to this fierce struggle for market dominance.

To break this logjam required an innovative conception of how timber was logged and transported. Healey rightly credits Weyerhaeuser with convincing his allies and enemies to lay down the hatchet. After a disastrous 1880 flood along the Chippewa, he set up a partnership called the Chippewa Logging Company, patterned after another he had established a decade earlier that had incorporated his downstream rivals, known as the Mississippi River Logging Company—in both cases, Weyerhaeuser's expansive vision encompassed entire watersheds. As physical features and organizing principles, these riparian systems prioritized the shared interests that accrued to the new companies'

numerous investors regardless of where they lived and worked. In developing these broad-based partnerships, Weyerhaeuser revolutionized the corporate infrastructure that thereafter would shape the timber industry until the
mid-twentieth century.[4]

By rationalizing the business, the new corporation also sped up production
in Wisconsin; predictably, those forests were rapidly cut out. Soon, Weyerhaeuser and his colleagues shifted their attention to the unharvested forests
of northern Minnesota. By the 1890s, with his sons taking important roles in
this expansion and the family itself having moved to St. Paul to be closer to its
new north country operations, Frederick Weyerhaeuser began to think beyond
the current lumberman's frontier.

Correctly forecasting that the next cycle of harvests would occur in the South
and West, sites of vast old-growth forests, he shrewdly recognized that for him
the West made the most sense. Congress's massive land grants to railroads
to stimulate the construction of a world-class transcontinental transportation
grid made it possible quickly to move people, goods, and services east and
west; almost all roads led to St. Paul. Yet those same gifts of public land for the
development of private enterprise meant that the unutilized portions, which
amounted to millions of acres, might be available at a relatively lower cost. Confirmation came when railroad magnate Hill agreed to sell Weyerhaeuser those
nine hundred thousand timber-rich acres for a mere six dollars per. This deal
sealed the corporation's fortunes and the Weyerhaeusers' future.

As Healey details these and many other business transactions, weaves in the
family's internal dynamics, and integrates the impact that war and unrest, economic upswings and downturns, and western expansion and eastern urbani-
zation had on Frederick Weyerhaeuser's commercial opportunities, she nicely
frames his achievements and some of the limitations of his vision.

A gifted administrator of human and natural resources, Weyerhaeuser was
a careful steward of his family's wealth and business assets; a gambler, he
seemed easily able to calculate odds long and short. In this account, Weyerhaeuser emerges as a man of imagination and action, ever forward thinking.

Not all his contemporaries, or later detractors, agreed that Weyerhaeuser's
over-the-horizon perspective was good for the country. William Randolph
Hearst, who knew a thing or two about empire building, lashed out at Weyerhaeuser's fashioning of an enduring "Timber Trust." Other critics likened him
to the generation of robber barons who had grabbed up the nation's natural
resources for personal profit, not social gain. Theodore Roosevelt, in a speech
that son Frederick E. Weyerhaeuser attended, slammed the lumber industry
as unrepentant "land skinners." Even the founding chief of the U.S. Forest
Service, Gifford Pinchot, who was on cordial terms with two generations of

Weyerhaeusers, delivered a kind of backhanded compliment in his analysis of the significance of the Northern Pacific Railroad land deal. "When the people of the West . . . saw huge areas of the finest timberland pass into the ownership of great lumbermen," he wrote in his memoir, *Breaking New Ground,* "they were naturally indignant"—and their indignation brought increased popular support for conservationists' demands for public control of the nation's forests.[5]

Weyerhaeuser was neither ignorant of nor immune to these criticisms. He had his own doubts about the unstated personal costs that came from his vigorous, lifelong pursuit of economic power. He shared some of them with journalist Lincoln Steffens in a wide-ranging, off-the-record interview; his openness and self-questioning left Steffens "thinking how much better a man can be than he thinks he is." That said, Weyerhaeuser had no qualms about mounting an effective defense of his enterprises. In October 1908, he testified before a congressional hearing, arguing that as long as local property taxation annually valued "standing trees," and until there was a full-fledged state and federal policy to reduce the threat of fire to timber resources, there was little economic incentive to pursue more environmentally sound and long-term harvesting practices. However much these circumstances cut into the industry's profitability, Weyerhaeuser asserted, they did not lead his companies to cut and run, as was often the practice among peer corporations. Evidence for this was the ongoing logging on Wisconsin's Black River, still operating fifty years after Weyerhaeuser had begun harvesting there.[6]

Weyerhaeuser, a deeply pious man, was also fully aware that his responsibilities did not begin and end with the bottom line. The German émigré's private philanthropy was robust, including gifts to American universities, churches, and libraries as well as to several cultural and civic institutions in Niedersaulheim, Germany, where he had been born and raised. The family's archives also contain records of Weyerhaeuser's donations of land to the states of Wisconsin and Minnesota for the creation of parks and recreation grounds. And despite his conviction that the free market should determine economic action, he supported federal and state ownership of woodlands, recognizing that the late-nineteenth-century arrival of scientific forestry in the United States—a European import, like Weyerhaeuser himself—would benefit the commonweal.

That his progeny should benefit from his commercial endeavors was never in question. Note the familial metaphor he is reported to have employed to describe the economic possibilities inherent in the 1900 purchase of that impressive sweep of Pacific Northwest forest cover: "This is not for us, or for our children, but for our grandchildren." As had been true in Illinois, Wisconsin, and Minnesota, so would it be in Washington State—Frederick Weyerhaeuser was in business for the long haul.

NOTES

1. O. Henderson to Frederick Weyerhaeuser, Weyerhaeuser Papers, Dec. 29, 1890, P-930, File 20, Weyerhaeuser Family Papers, Minnesota Historical Society, St. Paul (hereafter: W-MHS).

2. Frederick Weyerhaeuser to George S. Long, June 7, 1902, W-MHS.

3. Ralph W. Hidy, Frank Ernest Hill, and Allan Nevins, *Timber and Men: The Weyerhauser Story* (New York: MacMillan Company, 1963); "Bunyan in Broadcloth—The House of Weyerhaeuser," *Fortune* 9:4 (Apr. 1934): 63–65, 170–82; Louise L. Weyerhaeuser, *Frederick Weyerhaeuser: Pioneer Lumberman* (Minneapolis: McGill Lithograph Co., 1940); Frederick Edward Weyerhaeuser, *A Record of the Life and Business Activities of Frederick Weyerhaeuser, 1834–1914*, 5 vols. (St. Paul, MN: Privately printed, 1937).

4. Thomas R. Cox, *The Lumberman's Frontier: Three Centuries of Land Use, Society, and Change in America's Forests* (Corvallis: Oregon State University Press, 2010), 188–89.

5. Cox, *Lumberman's Frontier*, 179; F. E. Weyerhaeuser to C. Davis Weyerhaeuser, Feb. 25, 1932, W-MHS; Gifford Pinchot, *Breaking New Ground*, Commemorative Edition (Washington, DC: Island Press, 1998), 249, 255.

6. Lincoln Steffens, *The Autobiography of Lincoln Steffens, Volume II* (New York: Harcourt, Brace and World, 1932), 365–68.

CHAR MILLER is the W. M. Keck Professor of Environmental Analysis at Pomona College, Claremont, California, and author of *Gifford Pinchot and the Making of Modern Environmentalism* and *Public Lands, Public Debates: A Century of Controversy*.

Chronology

1834   Frederick born in Niedersaulheim, Germany, November 21

1846   Frederick's father, John Weyerhaeuser, dies; Frederick leaves school one year later

1852   The Weyerhaeuser family emigrates to America

1856   Frederick arrives in Rock Island, Illinois

1857   Frederick marries Elisabetha (called Sarah) Bloedel and moves to Coal Valley, Illinois

1860   Frederick forms his first partnership with F. C. A. Denkmann

1867   Frederick buys stumpage in Wisconsin forests

1869   Frederick and Sarah move back to Rock Island

1872   Frederick is elected president of the Mississippi River Logging Company (MRLC)

1880   Frederick's personal leadership resolves the Wisconsin river wars

1890   Frederick enters the Minnesota forests' market with Pine Tree Lumber Company

1891   Frederick moves his family and business office to St. Paul, Minnesota

1900   Frederick organizes the Great Northern Railroad timberland purchase in the West; the company is named Weyerhaeuser Timber Company

1907   Frederick and Sarah celebrate their golden wedding anniversary

1911   Sarah dies in St. Paul, Minnesota

1914   Frederick dies in Pasadena, California, April 4, at seventy-nine

Genealogy of the First Two Generations of the Weyerhaeuser Family

Frederick WEYERHAEUSER
b. 21 Nov 1834
d.   4 Apr 1914
& Elizabeth Sarah BLOEDEL
b. 20 Apr 1839
d. 29 Nov 1911
m. 11 Oct 1857

John Phillip WEYERHAEUSER
b.   4 Nov 1858
d. 16 May 1935
& Nellie Lincoln ANDERSON
b. 30 Nov 1864
d. 26 Mar 1900
m. 26 Mar 1890

John Phillip WEYERHAEUSER
b.   4 Nov 1858
d. 16 May 1935
& Anna Mary HOLBROOK
b.   7 May 1862
d. 23 Apr 1933
m.   7 Nov 1901

Elise WEYERHAEUSER
b. 15 Jul 1860
d. 10 Jan 1946
& William Bancroft HILL
b. 17 Feb 1857
d. 23 Jan 1945
m. 29 Dec 1892

Margaret WEYERHAEUSER
b. 18 Jul 1862
d. 14 Jan 1939
& James Richard JEWETT
b. 14 Mar 1862
d. 31 Mar 1943
m. 28 Jun 1894

Apollonia WEYERHAEUSER
b. 14 Feb 1864
d.   8 Apr 1953
& Samuel Sharpe DAVIS
b.   1 Feb 1858
d.   5 Nov 1951
m. 21 Sep 1892

Charles Augustus WEYERHAEUSER
b.   2 Apr 1866
d. 15 Feb 1930
& Frances Maud MOON
b.   2 Oct 1876
d.   5 Nov 1965
m. 14 Dec 1898

Rudolph Michael WEYERHAEUSER
b. 11 Mar 1868
d. 12 Jul 1946
& Louise Bertha LINDEKE
b. 12 Mar 1870
d.   5 Oct 1952
m. 29 Oct 1896

Frederick Edward WEYERHAEUSER
b.   4 Nov 1872
d. 18 Oct 1945
& Harriette Louise DAVIS
b. 14 Jan 1876
d. 28 Nov 1960
m.   3 Dec 1902

Frederick Weyerhaeuser
AND THE *American West*

Introduction

Frederick Weyerhaeuser was born in Niedersaulheim, Germany, on November 21, 1834. He left school at the age of thirteen after his father's death and emigrated to America with his mother and sisters when he was eighteen. A few years later he made his way to the banks of the Mississippi in Illinois and apprenticed in the lumber business. Soon he owned a mill and began buying timber from Wisconsin loggers, tramping the forests himself in winter, searching for quality timber.

Showing a talent for organizing associates, he gathered other mill owners on the Mississippi and began buying standing timber and sometimes land in Wisconsin. His interest moved to Minnesota, then to West Coast timberlands. Many of his partners were persuaded to follow him, staking their own fortunes on his judgment.

During this time America blossomed. Emigrants from Europe flooded in through New York Harbor and moved west. Chinese came to build railroads that spread like spider webs across the country. Pioneers cleared the land for farms. Farmers and settlers needed lumber for houses, churches, and gathering places as well as for tables and chests, cribs and coffins. The Homestead Act and the aftermath of the Civil War spurred massive change and opened the West to settlement. Frederick's business flourished.

When he died at age seventy-nine in Pasadena, California, on April 4, 1914, Frederick Weyerhaeuser had amassed wealth, much of which he reinvested in new ventures or gave away. But he always counted as his greatest achievement his children. All of his sons worked with him in his various business efforts, and many of his grandchildren and their children to the fourth generation followed in their footsteps. Near the end of his life Frederick said, "A man's success cannot be determined while he lives. At least not until the lives of his children have been lived."

This is Frederick's story, drawn from his letters and notebooks and from the letters and diaries of others, together with newspaper accounts of the time. These sources weave the tale of a devoted family man and an astute business leader, one who was intensely absorbed by timber and lumber. Frederick's story is of a man of character formed by his times but one who also shaped them.

Frederick and Sarah's youngest son, Frederick, known as F. E., compiled a five-volume *Record of the Life and Business Activity of Frederick Weyerhaeuser, 1834–1914*. The work is based on family letters, diaries, and letters from his father's colleagues and partners sent after Frederick's death. This source and others, including all quotations, are referenced in the Notes by Chapter, starting on page 230.

PART ONE

THE NINETEENTH CENTURY— AMERICA MOVES WEST

Westward Ho!

Just remember the Red River Valley, and the Cowboy
who loves you so true.

—*Early American ballad*

WHERE, EXACTLY, WAS THE AMERICAN WEST in the nineteenth century?
Looking back from the point of view of the twenty-first, we tend to imagine the West that Hollywood created for us in the films of the 1940s, a rough
and ready land of natives, ranchers, cowboys, and sheriffs stretching along the
Rocky Mountains from the Canadian border south to Mexico. If asked to name
a locale for the nineteenth-century West two hundred years later, one might
say Montana, Colorado, or even the aptly named Tombstone, Arizona. But the
reality of the nineteenth-century West was something very different. Everything
west of Ohio was the West, a vast area populated by hundreds of Native American tribes. The cowboy in the folk song quoted above lived on the border between Minnesota and North Dakota, where the Red River flows. By the middle
of the nineteenth century, the federal government had begun forcing treaties
on the indigenous people of Minnesota, Wisconsin, and Illinois, opening their
lands to the European immigrants who were surging westward. Young Frederick Weyerhaeuser, born in Germany near the Rhine, was one of those European immigrants.

Until the beginning of the nineteenth century, the land claimed by the newly
formed United States ended at the Mississippi River, which cut down the center of the continent and provided a natural barrier. In 1803, the Louisiana Purchase from the French added a huge block of land from New Orleans north to
Canada and west to the borders of the Spanish lands (much of today's New
Mexico, Arizona, Colorado, and California) and the Oregon Country to the
north. Continental unity was achieved with the acquisition of Texas in 1845 and
the Oregon territory in 1846 and with the Mexican cession at the Treaty of
Hidalgo in 1848.

Henry Lewis, a nineteenth-century English travel writer, described the promise of these rapidly enlarging lands when he wrote: "No person can pass down
the Mississippi and view the immense bodies of uncultivated lands, lying con-
tiguous to its banks, without reflecting on the great changes which time will
produce . . . We can comprehend the great destiny, awaiting only the development of time, in store for this already far-farmed region."

Today a traveler can board the *Jonathon Padelford* riverboat on Harriet Island
across the river from the commercial downtown of St. Paul, Minnesota, and
travel leisurely upriver ten miles to the historic army fort, Fort Snelling, while
listening to stories of Europeans and Americans who first saw this stretch of
river in the seventeenth, eighteenth, and nineteenth centuries and whose names
now label streets and schools and counties: the explorer Father Louis Hennepin;
the French geographer Joseph Nicollet; Henry Sibley, fur trader, congressman,
governor, and military leader, a man of talent who found great opportunity here
but had to fight his Dakota friends and relatives in the Dakota War of 1862; and
Alexander Ramsey, whose greatest challenge as Minnesota's first territorial governor was to get title to the lands from Indians so settlers could come and the
territory might become a state. Watching the densely wooded riverbanks, the
traveler can also imagine the time before white settlement, when the river was
a thoroughfare for Dakota families in canoes visiting Bdote, the place central to
Dakota spirituality, where the Minnesota River joins the Mississippi.

LAND AND IMMIGRANTS

Frederick Weyerhaeuser, born in 1834, arrived in America in 1852 along with
droves of other new Americans. He was part of the thousands of Europeans
who, disembarking in New York Harbor and marching westward, built America. These pioneers, as they came to be called, moved in spurts, stopping for
some years in Pennsylvania or Ohio, then moving on in search of more opportunity. They traveled in coaches and covered wagons first and then on riverboats
propelled by steam. Later they moved on the railroads that were springing up
everywhere.

The eastern seaboard could not offer land enough, nor sufficient opportunity,
for the rising tide of Europeans entering the country. The push for immigrants
to move westward was promoted by many prominent journalists of the time.
John Louis O'Sullivan wrote in 1845, "Our manifest destiny is to overspread the
continent allotted by Providence for the free development of our yearly multiply-
ing millions." Mr. O'Sullivan, possibly himself a recent emigrant from Ireland,
conveniently overlooked the rights of the native peoples already living on the
land and assumed those rights and the land itself for the newcomers. He was
not alone.

Open and available land—as the newcomers saw it—was an important factor in the pressure to move ever westward. The grab for land as a national pastime began even before the Louisiana Purchase. William Priest, an English traveler, wrote in 1796, "Were I to characterize the United States, it would be by the appellation of the land of speculations."

Matthew Josephson, in *The Robber Barons,* described the practice of the time: "The very fathers of the Republic, Washington, Franklin, Robert Morris and Livingston and most of the others, were busy buying land at one shilling or less the acre and selling it out at $2, in parcels of 10,000 acres or more . . . Even before 1800, 'land offices' were opened up, orators harangued the populace and sold shares or scrip, lots and subdivisions to settlers, often without deed or title. Cities like Cincinnati and Cleveland were laid out in the trackless wilderness and 'jobbed.'"

Even Mark Twain, in *The Gilded Age,* found an opportunity to satirize the craze to buy and sell land when his character Si Hawkins, a shiftless pioneer who was always following the frontier to make a deal, says, "But some day people would be glad to get it [the land] for twenty dollars, fifty dollars, a hundred dollars an acre! What should you say to (here he dropped his voice to a whisper and looked anxiously around to see that there were not eavesdroppers) a thousand dollars an acre!"

The phenomenon of immigration rushing like a flood across mid-nineteenth-century America cannot be overstated. In the 1850s, nearly one million Germans emigrated to America. In 1854 alone, two years after Frederick and his family came, 215,000 German immigrants arrived. In the year 1860, just as Frederick was starting his new lumber business with his brother-in-law F. C. A. Denkmann in Rock Island, an estimated 1.3 million German immigrants lived in the United States, many of them in the Midwest. In St. Louis there were seven German-language newspapers at this time.

Much of this immigration was fueled by letters sent home by relatives who had already arrived—what historians call "America letters." Frederick's older sister and his aunt had made the ocean voyage and written home of the opportunities in their new land. Many family decisions to make the difficult boat journey to America were spurred by recent crop failures and political upheavals in Germany in the 1840s. And so it was with Frederick's family.

When the force of immigrant numbers met the limited capacity of the eastern states to absorb them and the greed of land agents eager to sell them land, the massive drive westward was on. Horace Greeley famously said, "If you have no family or friends to aid you, and no prospect opened to you there, turn your face to the Great West, and there build up a home and fortune." A later writer, Gertrude Stein, put it well when she said, "In the United States, there is more space where nobody is than where anybody is. That is what makes America what it is." Indeed, in the nineteenth century, to the European newcomers it must have seemed as though there was nothing but beckoning space in this vast country. For the native peoples, the influx must have seemed surprising and, later, disastrous.

FORESTS AND FARMERS

At the beginning of the seventeenth century, North American forests covered about one billion acres, roughly half the land mass of the current United States. The forests were concentrated in the eastern part of the continent, stretching from the coast all the way to the midwestern region where the prairie began. There were also significant forests in the Northwest stretching eastward into what would become Montana and some scattered forests in the Rocky Mountains.

Although by the nineteenth century much of the forestland had been modified by the indigenous inhabitants, to the eye of the new arrival from Europe the forests unrolled like a benevolent carpet. In the mid-eighteenth century, the vast spread, number, and variety of forests in America would have been breathtaking to a European. From Chesapeake Bay to Puget Sound lay an estimated 681 million acres of virgin forest. The far west alone held 140.8 million acres. In modern terms, these totals amount to over five trillion board feet of lumber. The historians in *Timber and Men* wrote, "the vastness of the woodlands [at this time] led most people to assume that, like the passenger pigeons and the buffalo, they were inexhaustible."

Johnny Appleseed's expeditions would have yielded the sight of untold varieties of timber. If he could have traveled more widely, he would have come across white pine, birch, maple, and spruce in New England. In the Great Lakes region he could have discovered more birch and beech trees, more maple, and also hemlock, oak, chestnut, and, yes, even hickory. Turning southward to the Piedmont he might have wondered at the longleaf pine forests, while the Midwest, especially Wisconsin and Minnesota, held bountiful white and red pine forests. Mississippi and the South grew cypress and tupelo, and the Rocky Mountain region fostered western white pine, fir, ponderosa pine, red cedar, and shimmering aspen. In the western forests, Douglas fir, white fir, pacific silver fir, and spruce covered the hills.

As pioneers moved west to stake their claims, they made clearing the land of timber a priority. Upon taking possession of a plot, the homesteader's first act was to chop down the trees and dig out the stumps. Often he would not leave standing even a small woodlot, which could give shade in the summer and provide firewood. To modern eyes this approach seems unnecessarily aggressive. But considering the pioneers' survival needs, their actions made some sense.

Their first concern was food. Settlers needed to clear their stakes and till the land for planting soon after they arrived, as food supplies were limited. Then there was the additional issue of safety: predatory animals could hide in trees. Logs were needed to build a dwelling. Firewood to warm the pioneers through the hard winters was another immediate reason to harvest the trees in the surrounding forest.

Many years later Frederick Weyerhaeuser described the farmer's perspective, recalling his experience as a young man on a farm: "When I lived in Pennsylvania we cut down the finest kind of trees, oak and chestnut and some pine, and we would make a rolling bee and roll out the logs in piles and set fire to them and burn them up to get rid of them. It was awful mean, and we ought to have been punished for it, but we had to have a patch for crops."

Having cleared the land upon arrival, pioneers had to buy future supplies of lumber from the emerging group of lumbermen springing up all over the Midwest. As Frederick Weyerhaeuser said later in his testimony to Congress, "You have got to have a crib for everyone who is born, and a box to carry him out." The lumbermen, eager to find timber, mill logs, and sell the finished lumber to settlers, turned to the forests that surrounded settlements everywhere. And here the young lumberman Frederick Weyerhaeuser saw an opportunity.

THE U.S. ARMY, RIVERS, AND SETTLEMENTS

Rivers played a crucial role in transporting logs from the Wisconsin forests to mills on the Mississippi in Minnesota, Illinois, and Iowa. But even before logging began in earnest in the mid-nineteenth century, rivers were already of vital importance to the blossoming settlements. And the U.S. Army was the rivers' patron.

The history of the river town of Rock Island, Illinois, illustrates how the West was really won. Before the Louisiana Purchase, mutual benefit had governed interactions between the Europeans carrying on the fur trade and the native peoples in the territories. The French, especially, had worked with the Indians, marrying into powerful families whose labor and food supplies were essential to success in the trade. But when President Thomas Jefferson paid fifteen million dollars to Napoleon Bonaparte for a huge portion of the western continent, the consequences would create drastic change. The U.S. government decided that its official policy would be to obtain all the land from the Indians for its new frontier settlers.

Shortly after that time, the army moved to establish forts along the Mississippi. From Prairie du Chien in Wisconsin, past Keokuk, Iowa, and on down to St. Louis, the government paved the way for settlement by setting up fortified outposts in response to a congressional order to "protect American trade." Among these outposts was one built on a spit of rocky land jutting into the Mississippi in what would become north-central Illinois. The year was 1816. The fort was named in honor of former secretary of war General John Armstrong. The land upon which Fort Armstrong was built still belonged to the Sauk Indians, whose Saukenuk village stood on the river's shore. The native chiefs had only reluctantly assented to the fort's establishment, which was illegal according to the 1804 treaty between the federal government and the Indian nations.

The army and the settlers would eventually be enabled to expand these inroads into Indian country by a new development in river transportation, the steamboat. In 1823 a primitive steam engine flatboat eighteen feet wide— *The Virginia*—made history as the first steam-powered boat to cross the Des Moines rapids above Keokuk. This voyage established that steam traffic could overcome natural barriers such as rapids, and it opened the upper Mississippi to settlement by Europeans, with the army forts as protection. It is ironic in retrospect to read accounts of the arrival of *The Virginia*, welcomed both by the inhabitants of Fort Armstrong and also by a salvo of musket fire from the Sauk and Mesquakie tribes, whose members lined the shores to see the steamboat. They had no idea what was coming.

SETTLERS AND NATIVES

Westward migration of the Europeans pouring into the country eased pressure on cities and towns in the East and provided newcomers the opportunity to build a home and find ways to sustain a family in a short period of time. This phenomenon had its dark side, however. Much of the land was already populated with native tribes who had the philosophy that land should be shared. The Europeans had a different idea of ownership.

Frederick arrived in the former Fort Armstrong, now renamed Rock Island, Illinois, in 1854. He may have had little knowledge of the area's history, but the development of European settlement had formed the frontier culture that greeted him. Scarcely thirty years earlier, the Sauk had lost their village, and many lives, to the encroaching settlers.

The village of Saukenuk was a highly organized community of three thousand, its main road lined with lodges made of arched saplings and logs covered in bark. The central avenue was also used for military drills, games, and social gatherings. Outside the village lay pastures for animals and acres of cornfields and gardens that provided food for the villagers. The Sauk had been promised peace, but despite treaties with the U.S. government, they returned from their winter hunt in 1831 to find their village had been taken over by European squatters. The settlers organized the Rock Island Rangers, a paramilitary company which, together with six companies of U.S. soldiers from the fort, confronted Chief Black Hawk and his people. The settlers burned the village's sixty or eighty log lodges to the ground rather than yield them back to the tribe.

Chief Black Sparrow Hawk, known to history as Chief Black Hawk, was actually a warrior leader rather than an official chief. When the Sauk Indians were caught between the Americans and the English in the War of 1812, the Sauk tribe under Black Hawk sided with the British. The tribe had intended to remain neutral, but when the Americans defaulted on provisions promised to help the natives through the winter, they threw their lot in with the British. Fifteen years later, in 1831, the government had its revenge in taking the village. Black Hawk was a brave leader of his people, but the small tribe was greatly outnumbered by the new settlers and the army.

The ensuing "Black Hawk Wars," as they came to be called, included a massacre of most of the village's men after U.S. troops forced them across a slough onto a small island where the army opened fire, killing 150 tribal members. In just one year the Indians were completely defeated. Of the one thousand warriors who had made their home in the village, only 150 remained when a treaty with the federal government was signed in 1832. The treaty was made between Chief Keokuk of Iowa, General Winfield Scott, and Governor John Reynolds. Black Hawk was taken on a forced "tour" of eastern cities by the government, eventually ending in Washington, DC, where President Andrew Jackson impressed him with the power of the United States. He ended his life with his wife and children in the custody of Chief Keokuk, dying peacefully on the Iowa side of the Mississippi.

Through the treaty of 1832 the U.S. government secured all of the Sauk and Mesquakie land in Illinois plus a strip along the western Mississippi fifty miles wide that allowed continued command of the river. In exchange, the Indians received twenty thousand dollars, forty kegs of tobacco, and "to give a striking evidence of liberality and mercy, the United States government added 35 beef cattle, 20 barrels of pork, fifty of flour and 12 bushels of salt for the use of the widows and orphans of those killed in the war."

It is not known how much of this history Frederick knew when he arrived in Rock Island twenty years later. But as he began his first efforts at logging in Wisconsin in the late 1860s, he must certainly have heard of another, more recent struggle in Minnesota that also involved the natives and the new settlers.

The first attack in what was to be called the U.S.–Dakota War of 1862 occurred on a U.S. government administrative center for the Mdewakanton and Wahpekute bands of Dakota. The uprising of native tribes was preceded by

months of failed payments and the U.S. government's refusal to provide promised food and supplies. On August 18, Chief Little Crow led an attack on the
Indian agency, killing eighteen traders and government employees.

Weeks of warfare followed, with attacks on communities near Redwood Falls,
Granite Falls, New Ulm, and other settlements. Eventually the U.S. Army was
victorious, but not before thousands of both settlers and natives were killed or
forced to flee their homes. In the war's aftermath, 303 Dakota men were hast-
ily convicted in a military court. President Abraham Lincoln commuted the
sentences of 264 to prison, but thirty-eight men (one was pardoned at the last
moment) were hanged in Mankato in December 1862, the largest mass execu-
tion in U.S. history.

Although Frederick Weyerhaeuser did not begin logging in Minnesota until
two decades after these events, he could not have failed to know about them.
They had helped shape the towns and regions where he lived and worked.
Meanwhile, as the settlers gradually took over the land from the native tribes,
they created an increasing demand for logs and lumber to build permanent
towns, farms, churches, and schools.

Not all of the transition from native culture to European was violent. There
are some wonderful surviving stories of early settlers in the Mississippi River
town of Winona, nestled in the bluffs of southern Minnesota. Villagers left
records of incidents where natives simply appeared unannounced at the back
doors of their cottages: not unfriendly, just curious or looking for food. The
settlers were understandably startled to see them.

RAILROADS AND LUMBER

Perhaps the greatest facilitator of westward migration in the nineteenth century
was the railroad. It was railroad development, first in the East, then the Midwest,
and finally all the way to the West Coast, that offered firm support for pioneers
in their new lives. Railroads provided for the efficient shipment of lumber and
supplies that settlers needed.

Railroads were an early development in the building of America. In 1840
there were already nine thousand miles of railroad constructed in the United
States: "Abandoning the river, turnpike and canal, farmers of the West turned
to using the railroad as they would soon turn to using McCormick's reaper." By
1860 there were thirty thousand miles of railroad, and "the settler was part of
the orbit of a national market at which goods circulated at a new speed."

Much of the history of early railroad development is littered with consoli-
dation of resources, bond issues that became worthless, dubious congressional
grants of land and money, and associated misbehavior—stories that make for
lively reading. The industrialists and financiers responsible for these chaotic

years were later termed the "robber barons" (in a 1935 book of that title) for their luxurious modes of living, like the barons who lived on the Rhine River in castles separated from peasants. These American "barons" found and spent money with little regard for ordinary investors, who were left to pick up the pieces from poor management when the railroads (as often happened) went bankrupt.

In 1862 the Pacific Railroad bill was passed by Congress, creating the first transcontinental railroad. Grants and land donations to both the Union Pacific Railway and the Central Pacific Railroad were intended to facilitate a transcontinental connection, one building from the east and the other from the west. The Union Pacific, backed by the financing company Crédit Mobilier—which later failed in a great scandal, staining many "railroad congressmen"—was granted twelve million acres of land and twenty-seven million dollars in thirty-year government bonds at six percent interest, while the Central Pacific, with West Coast former "watch peddler" Collis Huntington and his associate Leland Stanford as principals, was granted nine million acres of land and twenty-four million dollars in government bonds.

This first transcontinental railroad was finally joined six years later, on May 10, 1869, in Promontory Point, Utah, ending a fierce and sometimes violent battle between the Irish workers of the Union Pacific and the twenty thousand Chinese workers of the Central Pacific to "win" the race toward each other.

Following the Pacific Railroad bill, in 1864 Congress passed the Northern Pacific land grant bill, which gave the Northern Pacific Railroad forty million acres of land in the "territories" of the West, nearly two percent of the land mass of the United States. Owner and banker Jay Cooke had arranged to sell four million dollars of bonds to the public for this railroad, secured by its congressional land grants. Horace Greeley, the great promoter of western migration, was a shareholder in Cooke's adventures. His journalistic urgings to "Go West, young man" were designed to increase his own financial well-being.

The 1864 Northern Pacific land grant act set the stage for Frederick Weyerhaeuser's greatest business success some years later, in 1900: the purchase from James J. Hill's Great Northern Railroad of nine hundred thousand acres that opened up the West for major logging and settlement. Hill had created the Great Northern in 1889 and bought the financially troubled Northern Pacific in 1893.

The railroad funding and building decades were turbulent ones for the United States. Jim Fisk, Jay Gould, and Jay Cooke were self-made millionaires who crashed when their bonds became worthless and their railroads failed. Unfortunately, it was the American people, holding bonds individually and through their communities to support railroad building, who eventually paid the price.

But development of the railroads, however disastrously financed and regardless of the self-interest and corruption of certain financiers and congressmen, was a major factor in facilitating westward migration. Railroads provided a timely and affordable method of moving people to their destinations and logs from the forests to the consumer. Railroads were also customers of the burgeoning lumber business, with endless needs for these same logs—for ties, railroad bridges, and boxcars. (Among the customers of Frederick's early partnership years with his brother-in-law F. C. A. Denkmann, the Union Pacific Railway stands out, ordering 950,000 feet of bridge lumber to complete the segment from Chicago to Rockford, Illinois, in 1860.) When the Union Pacific and Central Pacific were joined at Promontory Point, Utah, on May 10, 1869, east and west were permanently linked. The constant migration of people, supplies, and logs for building the West was assured by completion of the first transcontinental railroad.

FORESTS AND CONSERVATION

As Frederick began his lumber career in the mid-fifties, public knowledge of, or interest in, conservation in the United States was nearly nonexistent. This situation began to change in 1864 when George Perkins Marsh published his seminal work, *Man and Nature*. This book captured public interest even in the middle of the Civil War, and the American conservation movement may be traced to this work.

Meanwhile, the demand for lumber was creating a fast-growing industry, and Frederick Weyerhaeuser was at its epicenter. In the 1880s the volume of lumber in commercial trade surpassed that of personal wood usage, for fuel and building homes and furniture, for the first time. The First American Forest Congress was held in Cincinnati in 1882, and four years later Bernhard Fernow, a German immigrant, became director of a national division of forestry, the first federal officer with such responsibility. The value of timber increased five times through the 1880s as demand grew faster than supply, and that trend continued through the 1890s. As timber became more valuable, it made more sense to everyone to protect it.

In 1891 the Forest Reserve Act authorized the president to create, from the public domain, forestlands to be held in reserve for the general public. And in 1892, the same year the Sierra Club was founded under John Muir's leadership, Gifford Pinchot joined the Biltmore estate in North Carolina in the first effort to manage forests in the United States. Pinchot was the first American trained in forestry, having studied at the French National School of Forestry. In 1900, the year Frederick and his associates made their massive purchase of western Washington timberland from James J. Hill, schools of forestry had already

been established by two universities: Cornell and Yale. In 1901 President William McKinley made Pinchot head of the Division of Forestry, later renamed the
U.S. Forest Service.

In September 1901, upon McKinley's assassination, Theodore Roosevelt was
sworn in as president of the United States. He was "all forward motion, ready
to rule by righteousness and a bit of the belt." Roosevelt, who had made the
acquaintance of Pinchot when he was governor of New York, relied increasingly on the forester's advice. Gifford Pinchot went on to play an important role
in the Second American Forest Congress in 1905. Frederick Weyerhaeuser
would decline an invitation to speak at that congress due to illness, and his son
F. E. would go in his place. Pinchot had written the president's speech, but in
a startling departure, President Roosevelt instead attacked the lumbermen who
had invited him to address them.

As the value of timber increased in the 1880s and '90s, government officials became concerned about sustaining the timber supply for the country.
Three years after the Second American Forest Congress Frederick testified
before the Congressional Committee on Pulp and Paper, outlining his ideas on
how to secure a source of timber for the future.

The sweep of events in the nineteenth century that shaped the twentieth century also influenced Weyerhaeuser: the influx of immigrants, the situation of
native peoples, the development of railroads, the growth of logging, and the
corresponding consciousness of the need for conservation formed Frederick's
world. He, in turn, created partnerships with lumbermen and produced lumber, playing an important part in the building of America.

PART TWO

TRAVELS FROM A GERMAN VILLAGE
TO THE AMERICAN MIDWEST

Father and son, October 6, 1846

The boy Frederick Weyerhaeuser awoke as usual before dawn in his small bedroom above the kitchen. He yawned and stretched. He had no reason to expect his life would change dramatically that day. He was nearly twelve years of age and already accustomed to hard work, and he knew the chores that must be done before he set off for his lessons. Since his father had fallen ill with dropsy, he had been dividing his time between helping out on the farm and attending his Lutheran school in the village.

Frederick pulled his woolen jacket over his shirt and ran downstairs, two steps at a time. The night before soft breezes had blown around, but the pre-dawn air might well contain frost. Soon the last of the grapes would be harvested to make the sweet ice wine the neighboring villages so favored.

But his first task, even before breakfast, was to feed his mother's animals. The boy stopped for a moment to poke his head into his father's bedroom next to the kitchen. The older man lay quietly, but at the sound of footsteps he turned his head to look at his son. He managed to produce a wan smile. Frederick gave him a wave and continued out the door.

His father, John Weyerhaeuser, had been a healthy, strong man, over six feet in height. But now he had been ill for some time, and he looked frail in his bed. One day two years earlier he had suddenly been stricken while working in the vineyards. At first the family thought it was the grippe, a kind of influenza, but the illness did not pass. He became weaker and weaker and gradually had to stop physical labor altogether. The family had called the village doctor, who made a serious examination, only to report that nothing could be done. To see such a vigorous man fade before their very eyes distressed Frederick and his sisters. But it was his mother, Margaretha, who was most affected. Frederick could do nothing to comfort her.

When he returned from school that afternoon, his father was gone.

Based on Pioneer Lumberman, *memories of Frederick Weyerhaeuser's childhood as related to his son-in-law William Bancroft Hill.*

CHAPTER 1

An Early Death
Changes a Family

THE THREAD THAT RAN THROUGH all of Frederick's life had two strands: his family and the forest he came to love. These twin forces had their roots in Frederick's childhood. The man who was the catalyst for lumber production in nineteenth-century America began life as part of a small, close family living in a simple rural farming village near the Rhine River in Germany—Niedersaulheim.

On the October day when John Weyerhaeuser finally succumbed to his illness, his son's life changed radically. Frederick, who had not yet had his twelfth birthday, became the head of the household, for he was the only surviving son. A little more than a year later, his school days were finished and the farming necessary for the family's well-being absorbed his entire waking hours. He had scarcely entered his teen years.

Niedersaulheim, as it was known in the nineteenth century, was once a place of some importance in the region. In earlier years stone walls surrounded the village, an indication that it had been used as a baron's fortress. At the time of Frederick's birth those barriers had long since disappeared, and the nobles had been replaced by modest farmers, mostly vintners. In later life Frederick recalled his childhood home: "The town when I was born . . . had a population of five or six hundred. The people were mostly farmers who went forth each morning to till the acres and tend the vineyards of the low, fertile hills near-by. This part of Germany in life and thought is French, rather than German, a land of wine instead of beer. Napoleon was its hero when I was a boy."

The Weyerhaeuser family name was native to this part of Germany, and Frederick's ancestors had lived in or around the village for many generations. The family name, translated into English, means "dweller in a house on a mere, or lake."

Frederick's father, John Weyerhaeuser, was a tall, strong man and a hard worker. He was one of the more well-to-do men of the village as he had been in great demand by other area farmers for his special skill in setting out new vines. He owned fifteen acres of farmland and three acres of vineyards. Like the other villagers, John's family lived in an ample but simple dwelling in town and went out to the surrounding countryside to cultivate vines and produce.

The Weyerhaeuser family house in Niedersaulheim was large, befitting a farmer of some success. The dwelling was formed of stone on the first floor, with the upper stories made of plaster and timber. Frederick later likened his childhood home to the Shakespeare house at Stratford, England, which he had seen in his travels. A sitting room, dining room, kitchen, and bedroom—ample space for a family—spread over the ground floor. In the second story there were four or five bedrooms. A third floor held an attic used for storing grain for the winter. A stable joined the living quarters, housing the family's several cows and small animals. But the pride of the family was a large, detached barn, which was used to store the winepress. Underneath the barn, the wine cellar kept the family's store of home-pressed wine cool during the summers. Frederick later recalled that the family produced twenty-four barrels of white wine annually.

In those years, many women died in childbirth or died young in illness, leaving fathers to fend for their families. Men often remarried, and John was no exception. His first marriage produced two children, a boy and a girl, before the early death of his wife. Both of those children died young, but Frederick later thought he remembered the girl. He estimated that she may have been nearly sixteen when she died. When John's first wife died, he married Katharina Margaretha Gabel of a neighboring town. This union yielded eleven children—three boys and eight girls—of whom Frederick, along with four of his sisters, lived to adulthood.

In Frederick's younger years, while his father was occupied with farming, he was sent to the Lutheran grammar school. A typical day might find Frederick rising early, pulling on his cotton shirt and a wool jacket against the cold northern Germany air, and going down the stairs to the kitchen to take his breakfast before setting out for school. Margaretha would have risen even earlier to prepare hot porridge or to bake bread for the day's meals. After some early-morning chores, the boy would trudge off to the Lutheran school for his lessons.

In Germany at this time there was no "public" or government-sponsored elementary education. The Lutheran and the Catholic churches each ran schools for their parishioners. The Weyerhaeuser family's tradition was Lutheran, so that was to be the children's school experience.

It was not only for his letters, however, that the family sent Frederick to the Lutheran church school. Each Wednesday and Saturday afternoons the students spent several hours studying the Bible and the catechism. Frederick was confirmed in the Lutheran church the year after John's death, participating in a ritual that marks both religious development and a passage out of childhood. These early lessons in the Lutheran religion would stay with Frederick all of his life, although in his later years he attended the Presbyterian church.

With his own formation in the strict Lutheran tradition, Frederick developed firm convictions. However, he was surprisingly tolerant of religious beliefs that differed from his own. His eldest daughter, Elise, later described her father's approach: "Theologically, Father was a fundamentalist, but without any bitterness toward those who did not believe as he did. He was more concerned about practical living than theology, but he felt strongly that Christ must be the center of our lives."

Frederick had a boyhood experience that may have been a catalyst for his strong religious faith. While quite young, Frederick was present when the old stone church in the village was torn down. Coffins had been buried in the basement of the church for years. When the coffins were opened, corpses appeared preserved in their form, but with exposure to air they were suddenly reduced to dust. This dramatic scene made an impression on Frederick. Perhaps it contributed to his attachment to the religion of his childhood, blending as it did the evidence of the transitory nature of life with the spiritual stories and lessons of the Lutheran Church's belief in immortality.

If Frederick were able to look back on this period of his life, he might say that the death of his father, his confirmation in the Lutheran Church in 1848, and his decision to leave school and move to full-time farming formed his passage to adulthood. From this date to 1852, when the family decided to emigrate to America, Frederick oversaw the farm and appears to have managed it as well as any adult might have done.

Frederick's recollections of the time after his father's death:

> From the time I was eight years old I began to work on the farm, outside of school hours. After my father's death, the place was carried on by my mother with the aid of hired men, and I was often excused from school to assist them. A year later, in 1847, when I was 13, my school days ended and thenceforth I was constantly occupied with farm work. Matters were well managed so that the farm yielded enough to pay expenses and support the family and something over. In 1848 I was confirmed in the Lutheran Church.

A year after his father's death, Frederick's life was the same in some respects as it had been before. He still arose early, perhaps even before dawn, and dressed in the autumn chill. He still wore the rough clothes of a farmer and still breakfasted on Katharina Margaretha's porridge. But now he headed not into the center of town to the Lutheran school but out of town into the surrounding fields to work with the men his mother had hired to help run the farm. His head was no longer filled with reading or figures but with the weather, the livestock, the yield of the crops, and the quality of the grapes for the press in the family's cellar. He now had a life different from his former student days and different also from many of his childhood friends'.

Although Frederick later expressed regret for his lack of formal education, he seemed to have absorbed enough from his few years in the village school to facilitate an astonishing life. He read and wrote in both German and English; his penmanship is still discernible today in his many well-composed personal and business letters; his competency in arithmetic is clear in his early notebooks, as is his ability to comprehend situations and design solutions for problems. These skills were useful throughout his life.

In later years Frederick Weyerhaeuser wrote to his daughter Margaret on the stationery of the Grand Hotel Anvers, Bruxelles, Belgium, on June 13, 1894. The Weyerhaeusers had just paid a visit to Niedersaulheim:

> Your good mother and I feel very thankful that after forty years we can go back to the place where we were born and still feel like young people. We ought to praise our maker for it.
>
> Forty years ago almost a homeless boy and now blessed with a family of the best of children, the best loving wife in the world, good health, plenty of good and true friends and more than our share of this world's goods. Thanks to God for it all.

But most of all, Frederick gained enough confidence to meet whatever life presented. He would make good use of that characteristic. For soon the little family undertook a bold move to a completely new situation: they decided to emigrate to America.

Frederick was already successful at farming, by his own account supporting his mother and sisters well. So what happened in the intervening years, from 1846 to 1852, to persuade the family to pull up stakes and move to America? The answer to that question is complicated. Political and economic events across Europe affected even remote farming villages. But events closer to home may have finally prompted the family to seize this life-changing opportunity.

CHAPTER 2

Coming to America
and Moving West

WHAT COMPELLED WAVES OF IMMIGRANTS to come to America in the mid-nineteenth century? They came for at least two reasons. Europe's economic and agricultural situation was dire at midcentury, and families everywhere felt the results. At the same time, many had relatives who had made the journey to America and wrote back to encourage other family members to join them.

Part of the economic strain in Germany had to do with bad harvests, but political upheaval was also causing difficulty. German unification failed in 1848, and by later that year the civil unrest and riots in Paris had spread across Europe, creating further instability. These external factors played some part in the Weyerhaeuser family's decision to emigrate. But other problems, largely financial, were also pressing on them. While Frederick's farm was doing well, his relatives were not so fortunate.

His oldest sister, Katharina, born in 1820, had married a man named Michael Koch. In his later years Frederick described Koch as "a man of some ability." In Germany Koch had been trained as a priest but never ordained. He made nails and eventually ran a grocery store to support his family. Unfortunately, the store fell victim to the general economic distress and failed. In the culture of the German extended family system, the Koch family's financial problems became Frederick's. The burden of helping the Koch family as well as supporting his own with the proceeds of the modest farm strained the family's meager resources.

Shortly before this time Frederick's second-oldest surviving sister, confusingly named Katharina Margaret (as opposed to the oldest sister, Katharina Koch), had emigrated to America with an aunt, Christina Barbara Weyerhaeuser Gabel. Christina's husband, Christian Gabel, had been a soldier in his youth. Christian had often regaled the young Frederick with heroic stories of Napoleon's campaign in Russia. The boy had been particularly impressed by his uncle's recollection of seeing whole regiments standing lifeless, frozen by the terrible Russian winter.

Katharina Margaret had married in America, a man named Fred Ackerman, and settled in Erie, Pennsylvania. She and Aunt Christina sent to Frederick's family glowing letters describing their new homeland. These piqued the interest of Katharina Margaret's mother, brother, and remaining sisters in Germany. Gradually the Weyerhaeuser family members began to turn their attention westward and consider joining their sister and her aunt in the New World.

The family members finally made a decision. They sold their land and divided the proceeds. Frederick and his younger sister Eliza, not yet of legal age, did not immediately receive their portion. Those funds would be sent to them later.

The journey to America was arduous. The family left Niedersaulheim in mid-May 1852, when the weather was just warming. Parting from the village of their ancestors must have been poignant. They faced an uncertain future and surely must have doubted they would ever see their homeland again.

The little troupe comprised Margaretha, Frederick (then seventeen), and his three sisters Katherina Koch (and her husband, Michael), Louisa, and Elisabetha or Elise, later called Eliza. They made the journey down the Rhine to Rotterdam. There they were delayed by the need to find a boat to take them to London. When they arrived in London, there was another delay of several days, but finally they were able to book passage on a sailing ship to New York. Their sea voyage lasted about six weeks.

Frederick Weyerhaeuser later described the decision and journey to his son-in-law William Bancroft Hill:

> For the voyage, we had to provide our own food, as no one would be received on board ship who did not have supplies for fifty days. We baked a lot of bread, baking it twice (Zwieback) and laid in a store of flour, ham and beans, rice, sugar, molasses and a few potatoes. We took a few household articles, and Koch took his tools as a nail maker. This last proved a mistake, for better tools were to be had in the United States . . .
>
> Our fellow passengers were mainly Welch [sic], Irish and English. The voyage occupied about six weeks, and was rather rough at times; but I enjoyed every hour of it, and the harder the wind blew, the happier I was.
>
> We landed in New York early in July 1852.

The sleeping accommodations on board were hard, cramped, and fetid by the end of the trip. Yet when the ship sailed into New York Harbor in the hot July sunshine, excitement must have built in the hearts of the tired travelers as they viewed the skyline. They had finally arrived. This was their new homeland and the beginning of a great adventure. And despite the hardships of the voyage, Frederick later stated emphatically that he "enjoyed every hour of it."

If Frederick were alive today, he might relate to us his astonishment at everything he saw around him when he arrived in the United States of America. The United States at mid-nineteenth century was poised somewhere between the rough colonial culture of the Revolutionary War years and the soon-to-come Gilded Age of wealth, between an eastern concentration of power and people and the great expansion west that would fulfill the country's "manifest destiny."

The New York Harbor was a busy port, and the passengers must have found all the bustle confusing after being confined to the ship. Commerce was booming in New York, and the streets hummed with activity. Frederick was surprised to see the gentry riding in light carriages that moved smartly along, pulled by trotting horses, for in his native rural Germany only heavy, two-wheeled carts were used and horses were expected to walk.

Brownstone houses had just become the fashion, and Fifth Avenue was coming alive with these somber, strong-looking stone dwellings, each one attached to its neighbor. Frederick could not have known that a new, vastly wealthy class was emerging to build these expensive homes. People like Cornelius Vanderbilt and Jim Fisk were accumulating money and property at an astounding rate. In 1848 William B. Astor, son of John Jacob Astor, was already called "the landlord of New York." However, Frederick's shrewd eye would have noted that the bustle of New York City boded well for a newcomer's opportunity in this country.

Upon disembarking in New York Harbor, Frederick, his mother, and his sisters took the train to Dunkirk on Lake Erie and then proceeded to Northeast, Pennsylvania, a small town about fifteen miles from Erie. Perhaps the tired little group was met by relatives at Dunkirk, or perhaps they hired some livery to take them the last few miles. Katharina Margaret and Christina Gabel had both made their home in this little community. Katharina Margaret's husband, Fred Ackerman, was to give Frederick his first American job.

Frederick's new relatives by marriage, the Ackermans, were also an immigrant family from Germany, but unlike the Weyerhaeusers, they had arrived in America with significant resources. However, according to Frederick's later account, they had made poor investments of time and money and were not well-off by the time Frederick and his remaining family arrived.

After failing as a farmer, Ackerman had established a brewery, and it was here that Frederick began working. The little brewery could make fifteen barrels a day, and the beer was sold around the vicinity and all the way to Erie.

Although he learned the brewing business quickly and was often in charge when Ackerman was absent (as he frequently was), Frederick decided work in the brewery was not for him. He later explained that he gave up his plan to make his way in the brewing business when he saw how often brewers became confirmed drunkards. A family story has it that Frederick was known to quip, "I left the brewery when I saw that a brewer was often his own best customer."

At the brewery Frederick was earning four dollars a month the first year and seven dollars a month the second year, plus his room and board. His lot improved somewhat when he left the brewery to take a position on a farm about four miles from Northeast. The farmer's name, as Frederick recalled many years later, was Pickett, and he paid his new employee thirteen dollars a month. Frederick noted later how he was suited to farming work but he lacked some knowledge of how things were done, as the practices in Germany were so different: "My early experience in farming had fitted me for this place, though there was much that I had to learn. I did not know how to plough or cradle grain; and though in Niedersaulheim we kept cows, I had never learned to milk because that work always falls to women in Germany."

During the four years Frederick lived in Pennsylvania, he experimented with various occupations. Many of his efforts resulted only in his identification of work he did *not* want to pursue. While he was engaged in this search for his métier, he stumbled upon the one commitment in his life that would endure: he met Elisabetha Bloedel.

Elisabetha Bloedel, like Frederick, had been born in Niedersaulheim. Her family had emigrated more than a decade before Frederick's. Elisabetha was always called Sarah by her husband, or the German form, *Setta,* and so she shall be Sarah in this story. She was known so widely in the family as Sarah that years later some of her descendants, well versed in family history, were surprised to learn the correct order of her names, Elisabetha Sarah. Still later, upon perusing her birth certificate, family members were even more surprised to see the name written on that document as simply Elisabetha Bloedel, with no mention of Sarah.

John Philip Bloedel, Sarah's father, had been a prosperous blacksmith in Germany. His core business was making iron chains, which were regularly used on the Rhine River. Unlike Frederick, Sarah had been raised in America, as she was only a little over a year old when her family emigrated in 1841. Her father made his living by means of a small factory in Erie, Pennsylvania, where he made axes and other sharp-edged tools much in demand by farmers in that area.

Frederick met Sarah at the Ackerman household when she drove over from Erie with several friends to visit for a few days. Elisabetha Sarah was described by a friend at the time as a tall, graceful, attractive young woman, and Fred (F. E.),

Sarah and Frederick's youngest son, later wrote of how his father immediately began a courtship of Sarah upon meeting her.

We can imagine the quiet German youth, still struggling to learn English, encountering his sister's attractive friend from Erie. It was the first meeting between two strong-willed, quiet people. Frederick may have been coming downstairs when the group of friends arrived in a clap of laughter and friendly, welcoming hubbub. Perhaps he noticed Sarah right away, or perhaps it was later at the dinner table that her grave but friendly face captured his attention. Eventually some conversation took place between the two of them. We only know that after Frederick made his way to Illinois, Sarah followed within the year. Six months later the two were married. Although no letters between the couple in this period survive, there is no doubt that the courtship originated in Pennsylvania after that first, brief meeting.

The four years after Frederick's arrival in Northeast, Pennsylvania, were extraordinary years of change for the young immigrant. He came as a nearly penniless teenager. He tried many types of work, eked out a livelihood, and met and courted the woman he planned to marry. Finally, when he attained his age of majority, he received his inheritance from the sale of his family's German farm. (There is no record of who conserved those funds for him in Germany, nor of who forwarded the payments to Frederick and his sister when they reached legal age.) At first Frederick thought of buying a farm near Erie but finally decided against it, as the location was too isolated for his taste.

At this point, in 1856, Frederick was twenty-two. With his new resources, he now took a fateful step: he decided to move westward. His chosen destination was Rock Island, Illinois, because his father had a cousin who lived near this town. He was migrating to the edge of the American frontier, the volatile and somewhat chaotic area bordering the Mississippi River that would offer him unimagined opportunities.

PART THREE

THE ROCK ISLAND YEARS

A young man finds a frontier town, March 1856

Frederick was tired from the long trip when he stepped out of the farmer's wagon. He had taken the train as far west in Illinois as he could and then, slinging his pack on his back, had begun the walk down the road toward Rock Island. He had been lucky that a passing farmer picked him up and brought him the rest of the way to the town.

"Just wait," the farmer had said to Frederick as he climbed into the cart. "The rails will be laid by the end of this year. Rock Island will have the railroad. Imagine that. People can ride all the way to the Mississippi."

Frederick listened with half an ear to the chatter, but part of him marked the opportunity. If nothing else, maybe he could get a job hauling chain or pounding stakes for the final section of the Rock Island railroad.

He was amazed at his first sight of the Mississippi River as the wagon crested the hill and started down toward the town. He could see the U.S. Army fort, built on a spit of land reaching into the Mississippi, that guarded the town. The river, with the sun playing on the rushing water, appeared to Frederick to have a force of its own. It did not resemble the placid Rhine of his homeland. A steamboat was pulling in past the fort.

He took in the unpaved streets that lined the town, and the bustle of the wagons and horses. As they rode toward the first cluster of houses, he heard shouts as men urged horses on or pushed the cows roaming the mud streets out of the way. Coming closer, Frederick smelled the leather tanners' work and the sharp tang of the blacksmith fires. The steamboat whistle cut the air, alerting the townspeople that mail and supplies were arriving. All was hustle and bustle below him.

"Hard to believe there was no town here fifty years ago," the old farmer was saying. "And thirty years ago it was Chief Black Hawk's village. Now the steamboat arrives twice a week. Why, they just opened a sawmill with two saws!"

Frederick took a long, thoughtful look around. Although he still intended to visit his kinswoman's farm near Edgington, perhaps he would not, after all, stay there. The vitality of this town was inviting. There would be opportunity here.

Based on Pioneer Lumberman, *memories of Frederick Weyerhaeuser's youth as related to his son-in-law William Bancroft Hill.*

CHAPTER 3

◈

Seize the Day

U PON HIS ARRIVAL IN ROCK ISLAND IN 1856, Frederick may have been greeted by unpaved streets and possibly even cows, but he also saw signs of growth and vitality. The town already had a newspaper, the *Argus* (founded in 1854 as the *Rock Island Republican*). Moline, Rock Island's neighboring town, was home to the John Deere plow manufacturer, whose design had revolutionized farming. The John Deere factory had been built in 1848, bringing new employment and jobs to the area. In 1860, within four years of Frederick's arrival, the population of Rock Island would reach 5,130, as compared with 600 residents only twenty years earlier. An additional attraction for Frederick must have been the number of German immigrants. Indeed, there were so many local German speakers by 1857 that a physician from Bavaria was able to found a successful German-language newspaper.

By the end of the 1840s, the river traffic had become lively. The town's situation at the bend of the Mississippi put it in a commanding position for the river's steamboat lanes that served immigrants coming upriver to make their home in the new territory of Minnesota as well as those heading west across the Mississippi for the gold rush in California. The railroads were building at an incredible speed, tying the western outposts to the rest of the country. The Rock Island and Peoria Railroad was completed in 1856. More than twenty-one thousand miles of rail tracks were laid across the country in the 1850s alone.

Frederick's decision to try the Rock Island area was not a random one. At least two motivations can be discerned in his choice. While in Pennsylvania, he had heard from a cousin of his father's about the opportunities in the western Illinois area. This cousin was Mrs. Schneider, an elderly woman who lived in Edgington, a farming community close by Rock Island. The fact that there was family in the area was important to Frederick. He had demonstrated his respect for family ties in his financial support for his brother-in-law Michael

Koch while still in Germany. (Upon arriving in America, Michael Koch had been hired by a foundry manager in Erie, Pennsylvania, and he remained there for some time. The family later moved to Rock Island, where Koch worked for Frederick at one point.)

Shortly after Frederick arrived in Rock Island, he made his way to Mrs. Schneider's home, where he was reported to have enjoyed fried chicken and beefsteak. From Frederick's later recollections, it's clear he moved west with the idea of becoming a farmer. It was what he knew from childhood, and Mrs. Schneider had sent back to the Erie relatives glowing reports on the richness of the prairie soil. However, Frederick noted that after visiting Rock Island and then looking around on the farm, "of the two, I preferred the town." He returned to Rock Island and settled there.

Although he was not tall nor broad-shouldered, all the manual labor and farming that Frederick had engaged in since his boyhood had created strength: "Physically so strong that he easily carried a two bushel sack of wheat, 120 pounds, up a plank into a boxcar, he maintained his health, he used to say, by drinking a quart of buttermilk daily, taking reasonable exercise in the fresh air and sunshine, and above all, refusing to worry. He scrupulously kept the Sabbath and attended church. In time, he joined the Odd Fellows and Masons in Coal Valley and found companionship in these fraternal bodies."

The young immigrant's experience in Pennsylvania had accustomed him to new situations. He had been employed in a brewery and on a farm and was developing some confidence in his abilities. With characteristic energy, he looked around Rock Island for opportunities. The last rails of the Rock Island and Peoria Railroad were being laid into town, and he worked on it for some time, carrying chain for the surveyors. Then he found a job in a brewery again, working there only briefly. As he said later, "I kept an eye out for some other type of employment."

His chance finally came in 1856, when he was hired by three men who owned the town's sole sawmill and lumberyard, located on the banks of the Mississippi River. The name of the firm was Mead, Smith and Marsh. They sawed logs and sold lumber.

The Mead, Smith and Marsh sawmill had been established by three other recent settlers only the year before. Enoch Mead was a Yankee from Vermont and also a Congregational minister. He was the man who managed the capital needed to start the mill. John Marsh, an Irish bachelor, kept the books. Gilman Smith, like Mead, was from the New England states, and he was the machinist of the group, providing the practical know-how.

Frederick had a friend who told him the mill needed a night fireman. He applied for the job and was hired. However, after only one or two days, the partners stopped running the mill at night. Frederick thought he would be laid off, but instead the partners offered him another job, that of tallying and grading the lumber as it came from the mill, before it was piled on the flat, horse-drawn carts. He recalls that the job "was easy as there were only four grades of timber milled at the time: clear, common, No. 2 and sheeting."

The firm's owners seemed to trust Frederick from the start, but no doubt their confidence grew even stronger through observation of their new man's initiative and responsibility. One significant incident, a turning point, remained clear in Frederick's memory into his later years. He tells how he was left alone in the yard while the owners were away: "One day, as I was eating my dinner in the yard, as was my custom, some Germans came to buy lumber. As there was no one to wait on them, I showed the lumber and made a sale receiving $60 in gold. When Mr. Marsh returned from his dinner, I reported what I had done, and gave him the bill and the money; and I was greatly relieved when he approved of my performance. This was my first sale of lumber."

Soon after this incident, Frederick recalls that he "had charge of the yard and the sales, and presently was looking after all the business." Frederick was initially paid eight dollars a week by the Mead, Smith and Marsh firm, but his wages were raised from time to time.

Frederick's initiative was not the only marker of future success, although it was an important ingredient. He also had, from his early days as a farm boy in Germany, the habit of rising early and working hard for long hours. Frederick would do whatever was required to get the job done. There is no doubt that Mead, Smith and Marsh were happy with their new hire. Marsh tried to teach Frederick bookkeeping, but Frederick was never one to care for the complications of accounting. He relied primarily on his remarkable memory. His real gifts were in sales and innovation.

The year of 1856 was packed with more change for Frederick. He thought his job with the mill would end when the cold weather set in, and his plan was to stay the winter with Mrs. Schneider on the farm at Edgington. But Marsh assured Frederick there would be work for him at the firm during the winter months, and so there was. His various assignments included serving as mill watchman, driving horses, and generally making himself useful. In later years Frederick showed his gratitude to his old employers by regularly sending personal checks to Mrs. Mead and Miss Mead, apparently the widow and daughter of his former employer.

As Frederick was gaining confidence in his work, another part of his life was also going well. His friendship with Sarah Bloedel, which had begun in Erie, blossomed in Rock Island. Sarah's older sister, Anna Catherine, had married a man named F. C. A. (Frederick Carl Augustus) Denkmann in 1851, and the couple made their home in Rock Island. Frederick made contact with the Denkmanns (possibly through Sarah) when he arrived and even boarded at the Denkmann home when he decided to stay in the city.

The following spring, in 1857, Elisabetha Sarah Bloedel traveled west from Pennsylvania to Rock Island to help her sister, Anna Catherine. When the Denkmanns first came to Rock Island, they had purchased a small house from John E. Case for $310. With the industry that appears to have marked many German immigrants, F. C. A. cleared the first floor of his house and made it into a grocery store, which his wife ran. He would go out early in the morning and do the buying from the local growers. After he delivered the produce to his home for his wife to sell, F. C. A. would go off to the factory where he was employed full-time as a machinist.

The Denkmanns had a difficult year in 1857. Their son Ludwig, only three years old, fell ill and died at the same time that Anna Catherine was giving birth to a new baby, Apollonia Adelaide. Anna Catherine desperately needed assistance, so Sarah undertook the long journey west to help her sister and, conveniently, to reunite with the earnest young German who had attracted her attention when they met in Pennsylvania.

Just before Sarah arrived, Frederick left the Denkmann house and rented other rooms in the village. Six months later, on October 11, 1857, the couple took out a marriage license. (Sarah's name was misspelled as "Platel" in the official record.) They were married in the Denkmann home, since the house Frederick was building for them was not yet ready. That first house was a two-story frame building, about 16 feet by 32 feet, and cost $800 to build, plus the land at $400. Frederick later admitted this cost was a "squeeze" for him at the time.

Sarah's sister seems to have objected to the marriage, although the cause of her reservation is never clarified in family histories. In later years Sarah's youngest son, F. E., mused that perhaps Anna Catherine thought eighteen-year-old Sarah was too young to marry. Another possible explanation was Anna's own unhappy experience. When Anna married F. C. A., her mother was so disappointed in the prospects the new bridegroom represented for her daughter that she refused to attend the ceremony. Perhaps Anna, like her mother, thought her sister's life as the wife of another German immigrant might not have the brightest future. But Frederick and Sarah were determined.

Just before their marriage, Frederick and Sarah were at an auction, buying goods to set up housekeeping, when Mr. Marsh happened to pass by. He asked if the couple were planning marriage. When Frederick replied they were indeed, Marsh had news for them. He said the firm was expecting to send Frederick out to Coal Valley, a community ten miles from Rock Island, to run its retail lumberyard.

Although it would mean a promotion and some independence, this news was also distressing to Frederick, who had strained his finances to build the little house in Rock Island. However, his flexibility in the face of life's opportunities was soon rewarded when the partners announced that the firm would build him a similar house in Coal Valley, at no cost to the young couple. With that matter settled, Frederick embraced his new opportunity with zeal. Frederick and Sarah lived happily in Coal Valley for twelve years, until a community health crisis in 1869 forced their return to Rock Island.

CHAPTER 4

The Family Prospers
in Coal Valley

AT THE TIME THAT MEAD, SMITH AND MARSH sent Frederick and Sarah to live in Coal Valley, the little town of a dozen houses lay in the center of a region in which coal was just beginning to provide a major economic boost. With the lumberyard's opening, builders and new settlers could come to the village for both coal and lumber, meeting several needs at once.

Roads laced the village and surrounding areas, but getting around on them was often a challenge. When Frederick had to do business in Rock Island, he planned to be away from his retail yard for a full day. On the way he would as likely as not encounter wandering livestock from neighboring farms clogging the road. A winter's round-trip to Rock Island, through the snow, could take five hours of travel time. In the spring, wheels caught in the mud and created blocked roads. Summertime brought better conditions, but even then blowing dust from the unpaved roads, kicked up by horses pulling carts or carriages, was dangerous.

There could be domestic challenges in this underdeveloped rural area as well. The Weyerhaeuser family laundry was initially done in the river. Coal dust would often blow over the clothes as they were drying, to Sarah's consternation.

But one advantage of living in the little community was the proximity of work and shops. Frederick could walk to his Coal Valley yard as early as he liked every day—sun, rain, or snow. One of the best parts of Coal Valley was the sparse settlement and the rich land available at low cost. The family made good use of the broad land that was attached to their house. Their children's early years were spent running and tumbling outside in what must have seemed an endless playground.

While Frederick was expanding his interests and growing his business, Sarah was occupied with a growing business of her own: her family. The children arrived with a regularity that was "quite appalling," as F. E. later humorously described it. John Phillip was born on November 4, 1858; Elise, July 15, 1860; Margaret, July 18, 1862; Apollonia, February 14, 1864; Charles, April 2, 1866; and Rudolph, March 11, 1868. F. E., called Freddie and then Fred, was born November 4, 1872, after the family had moved back to Rock Island.

This growing brood and the management requirements of the household, livestock, and gardens made Sarah's life every bit as challenging as anything Frederick experienced in his burgeoning business adventures. Despite the hardships of living on the frontier, Sarah managed to make a comfortable and healthy life for her family. She was in constant motion, caring for children and extended family, growing vegetables and canning fruits, overseeing the chickens and livestock, and keeping house for Frederick, who was putting long hours into his new work responsibilities.

Pioneer families fared better when they could sustain themselves, and the young Weyerhaeuser family was no exception. Their everyday life included a generous allotment of time and effort to produce most of their own needed provisions. The couple had enough land for their poultry and small livestock, together with a vegetable garden and a modest orchard. Sarah canned preserves and jellies and had enough apples and potatoes to share with the neighbors. When Frederick's youngest sister, Eliza, came from Pennsylvania to live with them, the two women divided the work between them, with Eliza taking on the cooking and Sarah seeing to the house, gardens, and orchard. As the children grew older, they, too, each had responsibilities in the house and garden as well as the care of the small animals.

Sarah, by all accounts, was an exceptional housekeeper. F. E. recalled, "Mother's household resembled an accordion in its power of expansion. She was an excellent manager." As well she had to be, for in addition to the birth of a new child every other year, she helped Frederick with his clerical work and was reported to be generous in her hospitality to family, friends, and her husband's frequent, often spontaneous, invitees for dinner. Frederick himself was quite gregarious, often inviting out-of-town customers, friends, and even employees home with him. Since there were no telephones, Sarah would not have any advance notice of a last-minute guest for dinner, but she seemed to take it all in stride.

A friend of the family later wrote that, unlike some villagers of the time, the couple entertained without regard to background or religion. Although they were Lutherans, they welcomed the Methodist pastors or any of the various itinerant ministers of other denominations who happened to be passing through. The little town had a number of churches: in addition to the Lutherans, there were Methodists, Welsh Congregationalists and Welsh Baptists, and Presbyterians. The few Roman Catholics in the area worshipped in Rock Island.

In spite of the constant activities, Frederick made time for a hobby, and one that might appear odd to the casual observer: beekeeping. F. E. later surmises that his father adopted this pastime because it reminded him of his youthful farming years in Germany. The activity was not without its risks: "Once a helper shook down from a tree a swarm that landed squarely on his head, and he had to spend five days in bed while Elizabeth [Sarah] poulticed his stings." Beekeeping may have been a useful recreation for him in another sense. In the hive, every bee has its job, yet the entire colony operates as an organism. Perhaps their lives taught him something about organizing. One might see that the hive activity was similar to the business model that Frederick later developed with his various partnerships in the lumber and logging business.

Other family members were always welcomed into the Coal Valley household. In addition to Frederick's youngest sister, Eliza, Sarah's father, John Philip Bloedel, made his home with them after his wife died in 1868. Andrew Bloedel, Sarah's brother, also came to Coal Valley and found a place under his sister's roof. Andrew was a carpenter, and Frederick employed him in his various enterprises. Later Andrew wryly noted Frederick's true skills: "He always had ten or fifteen carpenters. He couldn't drive a nail himself, but he knew how to contract and he never had any competition [in that] you might say."

Frederick's mother, Margaretha, lived with the family until the year before her death in 1870, when she went to live with Eliza and her husband, Hugh Caughey. Margaretha, the strong matriarch who ran the farm in Germany after her husband's death and brought her son and daughters to America, is buried in the Rock Island cemetery. She was an invalid for her last years, and part of the duties of John, Frederick and Sarah's eldest son, was to attend to his grandmother's needs. He became a particular favorite of hers.

John had weighed only three and a half pounds when born. He was very delicate, and Sarah feared for his life. During the Coal Valley years, John was given the responsibility for raising the poultry. He was full of creative, if strange, ideas on how to do his job. For example, he had charge of a fine flock of geese, and he decided to paint the tops of their heads a brilliant green so that he could easily identify them.

One family story has it that young John's cousin, Marietta Denkmann, teased him by taking his cat away from him. He responded by grabbing the cat from her, then throwing it back at her face. He had won the battle, but he began to wonder what his father would say about the affair. Perhaps he had lost the war. He made his usual retreat to his grandmother Margaretha, who protected the boy when he was in trouble. In this case she hid him under her bed swathed in three pairs of pants to protect him from his father's discipline for the incident.

Apparently Frederick did not notice the extra pairs of pants, no doubt intended to mitigate any physical punishment on the backside.

John was both kindly and generous by nature. His younger brother Charlie, on the other hand, had inherited Frederick's love of dickering and bargaining. One time John received a newborn calf from his father as a gift. He soon gave it up for nothing to a neighbor, Mr. Dodge, who had persuaded him that he had more need of it than John. When John told his father what he had done, Frederick said, "Charlie would have gotten $5 for the animal."

F. E. remembered his mother as quiet and placid, always with a tender and loving smile for him, her youngest son. But through F. E.'s eyes, we also see a strong woman in her dealings with her energetic and peripatetic husband: "Very rarely, Father went beyond the limit of Mother's patience; in fact, there seemed to be no limit, but when he did, Mother's quiet but firm personality was always master of the situation."

Though Frederick was a devoted husband, his attention was absorbed by his growing business. Because of this divided loyalty, Sarah occasionally had her disappointments with him. F. E. describes a situation that occurred in 1868 when a log raft belonging to the fledgling Weyerhaeuser and Denkmann partnership broke away from the booms in Rock Island and floated downriver along with masses of ice driven by the rising spring floods. Sarah's sixth child, Rudolph, was only a day or two old; nevertheless, Frederick rushed off with his brother-in-law Denkmann to rescue the logs. Sarah could not understand how her husband could leave her side at such a time, but leave he did. The two young German lumbermen followed the logs in a skiff and collected what they could, selling them to the millmen at Muscatine, Iowa, rather than hauling them upriver back to Rock Island. Fred suspects his father was entirely penitent when he returned home. What Sarah had to say to him is not recorded.

Frederick's civic contributions to his small but growing village were considerable. In these he was as active as the bees he kept in his spacious backyard. In addition to being postmaster and paymaster during the Civil War, he was a candidate for the county board of supervisors, a building contractor, a prominent member of the recruiting committee for the Union army, a church leader, and a growing political leader. He joined the Masonic Lodge and was elevated to the position of Knight Templar. In his volunteer capacity as well as his business enterprises, he was an excellent promoter of the little village of Coal Valley during the twelve years he dwelt there.

When Frederick and Sarah moved to Coal Valley in 1857, no more than a dozen houses existed in the village and there were literally no amenities for daily living, not even a grocery store. Ten years later a directory of businesses published in the town newspaper illustrated the astonishing growth: a millinery shop, a shoemaker and a tailor, a saddle shop, a bakery, a livery, and a dry-goods store were all operating. A drugstore, a hardware store, a brewery, and the inevitable several saloons dotted the landscape of the town as well. John Hauberg, Anna Catherine and F. C. A. Denkmann's son-in-law, later wrote that Frederick, as a businessman and participant in the town's organizations, had a hand in all this growth.

As for the couple, even with a growing family they found time to spend together; in fact, they seemed to prefer the quiet life. Robert Lee, a family friend in the Coal Valley years and a business associate of Frederick's, later wrote to F. E.: "The little house that the lumber company built for Fred was the best house in town and Mrs. Weyerhaeuser was always hospitable. Everyone was welcome there. She was and is a splendid woman. She helped Weyerhaeuser lay the foundation of his fortune, if any woman ever helped her husband."

John C. Hill, a longtime friend of Frederick's who contributed many anecdotes to F. E.'s *Record,* recalled how Frederick and Sarah could be seen at night by passersby in the village. They sat in their front room with open doors and windows, she with her sewing and he with his books and ledgers. The couple seemed oblivious to the fact that they could be inviting trouble or robbery. Frederick said later to John Hill, "John, the happiest days of my life were in Coal Valley."

✧❀✧

CHAPTER 5

An Entrepreneur's Adventures

A S THE FAMILY SETTLED COMFORTABLY into domestic life, Frederick's career was moving in new and exciting directions. By 1858, a year after his marriage and resettlement in Coal Valley, Frederick's emerging entrepreneurial skills were becoming apparent. He was not only making a success of the yard but branching out into other avenues of related business as well.

At the end of 1858, December 14, Frederick became a "naturalized" citizen of the United States. His sponsors were Denkmann and another man named John Beitges. In the Rock Island court, Frederick renounced all allegiance to "every prince and potentate, especially to Louis III, grande Duke of Hesse-Darmstedt," the principality in which Saulheim was located.

The Mead, Smith and Marsh lumberyard was the only one in Coal Valley, a village surrounded by both rich agricultural land and valuable coal fields. Frederick set about selling the lumber the sawmill in Rock Island was producing daily, and initially he was very successful. However, the economic downturn of 1858 came suddenly upon the area, and things changed. His customers— farmers and townspeople, builders of schools and churches, boats and barns— needed what he had to sell but often lacked the cash to pay for their goods. Frederick's solution was to barter with them. He would exchange lumber for hogs, horses, oxen, eggs, or "anything they had," as he later said.

He would then re-trade these bartered items to the rafters for logs or to the merchants for stoves or tinware and logging kits, often carrying through an entire complicated transaction solely by barter. For a time, Frederick's initiative and flexibility allowed him not only to keep the Coal Valley concern going but to support his employers' Rock Island sawmill as well.

Frederick was proud of his hard work. He said once that "he never asked any man who worked for him to keep long hours that he was not doing himself." Later he stated to his son-in-law Bancroft Hill, "The secret in this lay simply in

my readiness to work. I never counted the hours or knocked off until I had finished what I had in hand." F. E. reports that in these years his father thought
nothing of driving to Port Byron on the Mississippi River in the small hours of
the morning to purchase lime at the Gates Lime Kiln, returning to Coal Valley
in time to open his retail yard for business before any customers arrived.

Once, F. E. recalls, he challenged his father's recollection of how hard he
worked in his early years. Frederick insisted that while employed by Mead,
Smith and Marsh, he frequently drew pay for seven days' work a week. When
his son pointed out that this practice would be inconsistent with Frederick's
strict rule as a religious man not to work on Sundays, his father had a ready
answer: he said he always tried to get in four extra quarters during the week-
days (a quarter being two hours of the supposed eight-hour day) even though
the regular workday was assumed to be ten or eleven hours at the time.

In this period, Frederick initially focused all his efforts on activities related
to his lumber business. He not only sold the wood (or bartered for it); he contracted for the construction of both private and public buildings. He found a
population ready to buy the barns, schools, and bridges he proposed. Then he
found laborers to do the building under his direction.

An illustration of this process is found in an item describing the fiftieth
anniversary of the Beulah Church building, written on August 8, 1936: "The
church was erected in 1860 and was dedicated August 17 of that year. The cost
of the building, contract for which was let to the late Frederick Weyerhaeuser,
then a resident of Coal Valley, was about $1,600.00. Several of the members
pledged $100 each and paid their pledges by selling corn at 10 cents a bushel."
In this type of business, reputation counted. "Weyerhaeuser became known in
the whole area as a shrewd trader, so honest that immigrant farmers who could
neither read nor write paid his bills without question," a later scholar wrote.

Unfortunately, while Frederick's entrepreneurial skills in Coal Valley were
blooming during this period, his employers back in Rock Island experienced
increasing difficulties. The economic panic of 1857 sent prices for all goods
plummeting. Lumber was no exception. In the fall of 1856, logs from the northern forests sold for twenty dollars per thousand on the Mississippi River. In 1858
Frederick was able to buy them, delivered to Rock Island, for five dollars per
thousand, with a ten percent discount for gold. While this deal was good news
for Frederick's operation in Coal Valley, the fall in lumber prices across the
region was a contributing factor to the failure of the Mead, Smith and Marsh
sawmill in Rock Island.

Although the panic of 1857 presented problems for the firm, it was not
until 1858 that Mead, Smith and Marsh became officially insolvent. The partners might have weathered the financial downturn with the aid of Frederick's

entrepreneurial undertakings but for one significant event: an unscrupulous raftsman perpetrated a fraud on the firm. The story reflects the wide-open, Wild West era in which Frederick was making his way.

The Rock Island firm had purchased a raft or two of logs (a large investment, considering their limited capital) and given their note in payment. The "rascal" (as Frederick later termed him) with whom they were doing business took the note and sold it, then resold these same logs to another buyer in Clinton, Iowa. This criminal event broke the firm. In the frontier environment of that time, Mead, Smith and Marsh had no legal recourse for recovering its money or its logs. The transaction, like the flow of the river, was made on the run. The Mead, Smith and Marsh firm was finished.

The sheriff took possession of the mill in Rock Island so that it could be sold at auction. The capital for the sawmill had originally been loaned to the firm by John K. James, Mead's brother-in-law. When the mill went into receivership, James suggested that Frederick buy the firm's assets (everything but the mill structure) from him. Frederick agreed to do so, but the transaction had to occur primarily on the strength of his credit, since he had little money of his own in 1858. He said later that he "paid James for it [the firm's assets] on account as I could." As part of this transaction, recorded at an auction on February 14, 1859, Frederick was able to obtain a clear title to his home in Coal Valley (which the firm still carried on its books) for the price of $151. Sarah must have been pleased, settled as she was into the large house and expansive grounds with her growing brood.

In the midst of this maneuver, Frederick saw another opportunity. The Rock Island mill stood shuttered while rafted logs coming out of the Wisconsin forests were carried by the Mississippi current for sale to sawmills farther south. These were the same logs Frederick had been buying for the now-defunct firm. Why could he not buy them and saw them himself?

And so he did. He bought a raft of logs sitting idle in the eddy at Davenport, Iowa, across the river, paying five dollars per thousand for them. Then he hired John Potter, an unemployed sawyer of his acquaintance, to saw them for him at the idle mill, paying him two dollars a thousand for the job. (The sheriff's office was willing to rent the sawmill until the auction of the mill buildings could take place.) The savings from this makeshift enterprise, coupled with his other various efforts, would allow Frederick to put together his first partnership.

The young German had done well on his own in Coal Valley. Much to his surprise, he had earned three thousand dollars over expenses his first nine months, and in his second year he made a five-thousand-dollar profit for his work.

Frederick's brother-in-law, F. C. A. Denkmann, was having a much more difficult time making a go of his grocery store project. He had expanded his house to make a larger retail space from which to sell his groceries, but that change didn't make enough of a difference. Frederick had tried to help him by paying some of his men in credit to Denkmann's grocery store, but trade was still not strong enough to turn a profit. Denkmann's solution was to move farther into the western frontier. (On this early attempt to help Denkmann, Frederick's son Charles used to say, with a twinkle in his eye, "Father began working for uncle early on.")

It was rumored that gold had been found on Pike's Peak in Colorado, and Denkmann thought there might be opportunity for him to start over there. He had already purchased a wagon and was loading his family's goods for the journey when Frederick surprised him one afternoon with a visit. The young entrepreneur suggested an alternative to his brother-in-law. He proposed that together they create a partnership to buy the former Mead, Smith and Marsh mill structure, which was mired in debt and scheduled for auction. The holder of the mill mortgage was the same John K. James from whom Frederick had earlier purchased the firm's other assets.

Frederick's arguments to Denkmann were persuasive. Frederick had the retail experience in buying and selling lumber and knew how to contract with others. Denkmann had been trained as a machinist. Denkmann could run the mill, and Frederick could be the salesman and buyer of logs, a plan that promised a great chance for success. Frederick was the younger of the two men by thirteen years, but he was the instigator of the plan. Their discussions were concluded in early May with an agreement. Denkmann was persuaded to abandon his plans to move west and instead to join his brother-in-law's enterprises. The two men became official partners on May 1, 1860.

In 1860 Frederick had been in the Rock Island area for only four years. He was twenty-six years old.

_____ ～❦～ _____

CHAPTER 6

The First Partnership Years
during a Cruel War

F REDERICK'S PARTNERSHIP PLAN HAD ONE PROBLEM: Denkmann had almost no money. But Frederick devised an innovative solution. He would advance Denkmann the funds needed from his own savings. Each partner was to have a stake in the partnership equal to three thousand dollars at the outset. Frederick, in his later years, remembers the transaction in round numbers in his account to Bancroft Hill: "So I proposed to him that we join together and buy the mill. We formed a partnership. He put in his groceries and horse and wagon, valued in all at about $800; and as I put in about $3,000 more than he, I advanced him another $3,000 to put in, for which he was to pay me 10% interest."

The partnership's detailed accounts, offered by John Hauberg, differ somewhat from Frederick's general recollection. According to Hauberg, Frederick put in $4,616.51 (some of it in goods and animals), while Denkmann's total contribution was $1,607.03, including his groceries and wagon valued at $800. The difference for Denkmann was a debt to Frederick of $1,504.74.

There was clarity, however, in the agreement on what they would do: "That they, and each of them will give their attendance and do each of their best endeavors, and to the utmost of their skill and power exert themselves for their joint interest, profit, benefit and advantage and truly employ, buy sell and merchandise, with their joint stock, and the increase thereof, in the business aforesaid."

The partnership agreement was written in English on foolscap, and John Hauberg notes that "[the agreement] was said to be in the hand of Mrs. Denkmann," but F. E. later wrote that "it is evident that Michael Koch [another of Frederick's brothers-in-law] was the author of the Articles of Agreement, in spite of the fact that his name does not appear." F. E. also notes that, given a lack of facility with English, "Father associated almost exclusively [for some time after coming to this country] with men who spoke the German language . . . It is remarkable that the document was drawn up in English rather than German."

A family story has it that once Denkmann and Weyerhaeuser agreed to go into partnership, Denkmann continued to work openly on his wagon for the westward trip, while Frederick maintained publicly that he would never bid on the mill structure without his brother-in-law Denkmann's participation. By this strategy they hoped to get James to accept less for the mill than he might demand if he thought the sale was a sure thing.

John Hauberg's "Comments" in presenting the initial Weyerhaeuser-Denkmann partnership agreement:

If to achieve greatness it is necessary to keep an eye on the smaller details, then Messrs. Weyerhaeuser and Denkmann were destined for the higher brackets . . . The following was drawn up on foolscap . . . said to be in the handwriting of Mrs. Denkmann [later thought to be that of Michael Koch]:

Weyerhaeuser and Denkmann Sawmill stock:
F. Weyerhaeuser put in as his share:
Lumber, frames, doors Sashes, Shingles $ 875.46
Two horses, value one hundred each 200.
One wagon 50.
Three sett [sic] harnesses 75.
Two cows, 25 each 50.
Seven hogs 30.
Corn for the summer 10.
One cable 10.
One log chain 1.00
One brass collar 2.00
Wheat and lime house, Coal Valley 50.
One desk, books etc. 20.
One saw 3.25
One Hand Saw 1.50
One Corn Sheller 5.50
Cash for Logs, Expenses etc. 3,212.80
Total: $4,616.51
Denkmann put in as follows:
Groceries to the amount $ 810
Cash on hand 80
Cash on part payment on Saw Mill 320
One horse, value 100

Two cows, 20 each 40
One harnes 10
One Schiff (or sckiff) 15
Iron 30
One Wagon 35
Sundries 40
Cash received from Weyerhaeuser on his I [?] 36.50
Advance by Expenses in the Mill 39.65
Mead, Driscoll, Kreis and Biddison [?] 30.88
Amount: $1,607.03

To some degree their plan worked. The idle mill, which had previously been sold for much more (once for $15,700 and another time for $17,000), was awarded to the Weyerhaeuser-Denkmann partnership for $3,859.72. The partners paid $500 of their own money down, using credit for the rest of the purchase. The remainder of their pooled capital was to be their business operating fund.

What the two men bought that spring was not exactly title to the mill but a mortgage lien on the property, which would have to be processed through the court system. John K. James signed a document that, in consideration of $3,859.72, assigns all of the rights, title, and interest to the mill and the eighteen town lots adjacent to it to the Weyerhaeuser and Denkmann partnership. But for some time, even after the new partners began operating their mill, the brothers-in-law did not have clear legal title to the property. That was achieved only after fifteen months. That they began their partnership with property still entailed is evidence of their trust in the future.

John Hauberg wrote a description of their situation nearly one hundred years later:

Purchasing a property and knowing the exact date of purchase, with no further worries about securing title is one thing, but to enter into business with a hazard, such as these two men had, must have taxed their nerves, i.e., the partnership agreement May 1860; taking over and starting the saws with a more or less precarious sheriff's sale not coming on until eight months have passed at which it is any creditor's right to bid and be the highest bidder; and after that having to wait another fifteen months before they are sure of their bargain—for by that time the two of them doubtless proved the mill was a good investment—a load must have dropped from their shoulders when the last legal hurdle had been negotiated.

Under date of May 15, 1862, the sheriff of Rock Island County executed his deed of conveyance for the mill-site to Weyerhaeuser and Denkmann. Nobody had interfered with their program of securing title to it.

The elements of this initial partnership are classic Frederick, and he would repeat the formula in various ways over the next four decades, culminating in the enormous land purchase from the Great Northern Railroad in 1900. His method was simple: he found a partner to spread the risk; he secured an infusion of capital from another source; and he used his good credit to finance purchase of the mill and nearby land, preserving much of the capital for running the operation. He built the partnership on trust—that Denkmann would do his share in running the mill and pay back his initial loan. Frederick was not disappointed. The business flourished, and Denkmann was able to repay Frederick within three years.

The family theme continued when another brother-in-law, Michael Koch, was also taken on as a colleague a short time later, but the outcome was less satisfactory. Koch's seminary education made him a first-rate clerk, and he filled the new partnership's needs competently, acting as office manager, communicator, and paymaster. All of the firm's early documents and letters are in his hand. Anthony Koch later remembered the partnership. His father Michael, he reported, "did as much work then as half a dozen men do now. He was timekeeper, salesman and book keeper . . . They were three brothers-in-law and the work of the mill was taken up with all three employed: Koch doing the clerical work, Denkmann as the machinist and Weyerhaeuser good at buying logs and timber."

Alas, an incident occurred that forced Koch's separation from the firm and gave an early indication of Frederick's steely character, especially where loyalty was concerned. Friends had persuaded Michael Koch to run for alderman of Rock Island, and he was elected. However, a thorny issue soon arose in the city council. The Weyerhaeuser-Denkmann sawmill was blocking access of the village fire trucks to the river because the lumber was stacked up in great piles. The city council was asked to make a regulation remedying this situation. Frederick told Koch that he would not tolerate interference in his business, that "he would not stand for it," as Anthony put it later. But Michael Koch was also stubborn, and he believed he "had taken an oath to do what is best for the city." A new law to force an opening in the lumber stacks for the fire trucks to get to the river was voted in unanimously by the city council members.

Frederick was angered. He believed that because Koch worked for Weyerhaeuser and Denkmann, he should have voted in the interest of the company. Soon after this incident, Koch left the firm. Oddly enough, Anthony Koch's memory was that the family was not hurt by this falling out: "They were always friendly brothers-in-law, but never in a business way after that."

Anthony himself had come to live with his aunt Sarah and uncle Frederick and looked upon Frederick as his "caretaker" from the time he was young. He seems to have borne Frederick no ill will for letting his father go, although he did say that if Koch had done things Weyerhaeuser's way, it would have been Weyerhaeuser, Denkmann and Koch.

A "Peppery" Disposition

Frederick Carl Augustus Denkmann was the perfect counterpart to Frederick Weyerhaeuser in his personality. Andrew Bloedel, Sarah's brother, also thought Frederick was "easygoing compared with Uncle [Denkmann]." Philip Bloedel, another of Sarah's brothers, described the two men who had married his sisters in this way: "Denkmann was a go ahead man. Weyerhaeuser was more slow and easy going." In retrospect, *slow* seems an odd term to apply to Frederick, who was already working time and a half at many enterprises. Perhaps Philip intended the description to illustrate the way the two men interacted with others. Where Weyerhaeuser was open and could often tease his children or tell a good story, sometimes on himself, F. C. A. (as he was always called) was unremittingly serious.

Denkmann had been born in Salzwedel, West Prussia, in 1821. Surviving pictures show a man with "small, dark restless eyes" and a "curious" beard that was but a white fringe on his chin. F. E. later recalled F. C. A. as follows: "He was quite a typical Prussian in pride and also in lack of a sense of humor. It was this lack of a sense of humor that got him into many amusing situations."

F. E. also described his uncle Denkmann as being "quick and highly nervous in action, and possessed [of] unlimited and tireless energy" and as having a "peppery" disposition. He was always in a hurry. The Denkmanns' house abutted the sawmill property, so he was well situated, as mill manager, to keep an eye on things. Andrew Rietz, a servant in the Denkmann home, later told this story: "The whistle [for the sawmill] blew at six o'clock in the morning; if it was a weak whistle, Mr. Denkmann knew they did not have the steam up the way they ought to have, and he would be out there in a minute to see what was the matter."

Weyerhaeuser and Denkmann were complementary in ways other than personality. F. C. A. had a machinist's talent and training, while Frederick had already displayed a natural liking for people that led him to sales. Frederick also was a good negotiator, loved to bargain, and was rapidly learning the lumber sales business. F. C. A. seemed much happier to be taking care of the machines than traveling the roads and forests or talking to customers. Given the division of labor, the partnership flourished.

Many family stories about F. C. A. show him as a man of stamina and courage in any incident that put his business at risk. One time Denkmann was watching the mill's muley saw perform when a slab swung around and hit him in the side of the head. A large raw beefsteak was required to assuage that wound, but there were no complaints. Another time he saw a boom holding a raft of loosely tied logs pull away from its moorings and the raft of logs shoot downriver. Denkmann managed to run out on the logs to try and stop them, but he was immediately pulled under by the current. Only his hat remained on the river's surface. Those trying to save him kept following, as they could see him bob up at regular intervals. When he was finally rescued, the first thing he said was, "Where's my hat?"

No matter the extent of his own talents, one may surmise that it must have been hard from time to time for Denkmann to see his younger kinsman forging ahead, with an obvious talent for organizing and selling and for the public life. Some natural competitiveness arose over their lifetime, and Denkmann occasionally gave voice to his frustration.

One such anecdote showing these human feelings occurred at a meeting of the Cloquet Lumber Company in northern Minnesota in later years. When the minutes of the previous corporate meeting were read, Denkmann was offended by the omission of his name, while Weyerhaeuser's had been included. Denkmann had been absent from the earlier meeting, so he was not on the roll of attendees, as Weyerhaeuser was. F. C. A. exploded in anger, saying, "Weyerhaeuser, always Weyerhaeuser, Denkmann not any. I adjourn!" He rushed for the door. The Cloquet Lumber Company president, Mr. Shaw, hurried after him to explain why his name was not read, but Shaw was unable to persuade him to return.

On a later occasion a Michigan lumberman, Ezra Rust, was visiting with Denkmann on a car trip in northern Minnesota. He remarked that Frederick Weyerhaeuser must have amassed a considerable fortune through his efforts in timber over the years. Denkmann's tart reply, with his German accent, was, "I got jus' so much as Fret!"

A DIVISION OF TALENTS

From Frederick's perspective, this initial partnership was a combination of talents. He knew that Denkmann was a good machinist and would contribute on-the-ground knowledge and hard work to the proposed collaboration. Frederick was beginning to understand his own competencies as well. He thought their fledgling company could manufacture about three million feet of lumber a year and eventually hoped it could be ten million, a goal they did, in fact, achieve a few years later.

Denkmann ran the mill, while Frederick was primarily responsible for purchasing logs either at Rock Island or from boom owners on the Black River, the Chippewa River, or the St. Croix farther north. (Frederick was "in the woods" in 1866 when his mother-in-law died.)

Denkmann was responsible for recruiting and managing the mill employees. Reports of the time paint F. C. A. as a tough manager. This characteristic eventually was a benefit to the mill employees, as the business prospered. In 1858 the head sawyers made $1.50 per day at the mill, while seven years later they were making $3.00 a day. But there were hard times in the development of that benefit. Denkmann accomplished this increase in pay by lowering unit costs in the mill and driving his employees to work harder.

Anthony Koch tells another story that illustrates both Denkmann's discipline and his stubbornness. Early on in the business venture, the workers demanded a holiday on Labor Day. Denkmann refused. The men protested and stayed home. The day after they had taken the holiday, no whistle blew to announce the mill's opening. When the men came to work, they found the mill closed. It remained closed until the men begged Denkmann to reopen it. Denkmann said to them, "Nun habt ihr euer Labor Day [Now you have your Labor Day]." No doubt the workers learned their lesson. Things were not all bleak for the men, however. Weyerhaeuser and Denkmann were known for paying them on time and in cash.

While Denkmann worked his team hard instead of expanding his workforce, he made further efficiencies by applying his knowledge of machines to invest the partners' limited capital and credit wisely. He installed an oscillating muley saw and increased sawmill production to twenty thousand board feet daily. He added other mechanical devices, such as edgers, trimmers, and lathe saws. One big purchase was a planing machine that would allow the firm to produce much more finished lumber. The *Rock Island Daily Union*, on January 16, 1868, reported with some wit: "Heretofore, 50 ft was as long a log as W. and D. [sic] mill could handle. They are now putting an addition to their mill which will enable them to saw timber long enough, wide enough and strong enough for a Republican Platform."

In these early years, Frederick was also in charge of finances, which included finding other investment opportunities to increase the firm's capital. In some of the ventures, later described to Bancroft Hill, he did well. Others, especially where he strayed from the core lumber business, might better be termed "good learning experiences."

One of the better investments occurred when Denkmann paid back the initial $1,504.74 he had borrowed to buy into the partnership. Frederick used the funds to buy some more land in Coal Valley, which he later sold at a profit.

F. E.'s description of his father's acuity (or lack of it) in accounting:

> [Frederick] was not a master of the profession for Father never knew
> much about accounting. His records were largely in the nature of single entry
> memoranda; in fact, he depended very largely upon his remarkable memory.

Other choices did not come out so well. His misadventures into the wheat business are a case in point. Weyerhaeuser and Denkmann bought a flour mill for eighteen thousand dollars. This investment appeared to make sense, as the area's population was growing and there was a great demand for flour. Unfortunately, just at this time an infestation of cinch bugs occurred, and the entire region turned to growing corn instead. Frederick's initial solution of shipping wheat from Minnesota was not feasible over the long term. Eventually the mill was closed and left to rot, and Frederick experienced his first major investment loss.

> When Mr. Denkmann paid me the $3,000 he had borrowed, I added $300 to it and bought . . . some coal land in Coal Valley. We kept it awhile, and sold it to P. L. Cable at a good profit. Then with the money I bought Government seven-thirtys.
>
> Coal Valley, when I went there, was a region devoted to wheat. So about 1865, with Denkmann, [Hugh] Caughey and McQuid, I built a flour mill costing $18,000. But wheat presently ran out; the farmers went to raising corn and we had to ship wheat from Minnesota. This made the flouring business unprofitable, and the mill was closed. It was never sold, and finally left to rot down years later. William Eggleston, a distiller, owned a foundry in Rock Island where now the Burlington Depot stands . . . Certain parties tried to buy it for a woolen mill, but could not make the deal. Then they took Denkmann, Eggleston and myself in with them and we bought the property.

Around this time, another of Frederick's projects failed, not through accidents of nature but because of human weakness. A former distiller, William Eggleston, managed a woolen factory. He needed some investment backing. Frederick later said, "[Eggleston's] yearly statements showed he was making money. But I did not believe this. He had poor help and dishonest clerks. His son was taken in, which did not help matters." The business went downhill, and Frederick eventually cut his losses. He was able to retrieve part of his investment by taking some goods and a mortgage on nine houses in Rock Island owned by the unfortunate Eggleston. This experience provided Frederick with early instruction on the relationship between trustworthy help (or partners) and business success.

In the midst of these challenges, lumber sales from the Coal Valley yard and the sawmill operation that Denkmann ran in Rock Island were flourishing. Indeed, the public's insatiable appetite for building materials was increasing by the day. America was on the move.

The Civil War and Great Changes

While Frederick was experimenting with various forms of trade and investing, larger forces were at work that would have a significant impact on his future. The signal American event of this decade was the Civil War, a five-year crisis that changed everything for decades to come, not only in politics and abolition but in land settlement and lumber as well.

In 1862 it became clear to the people of Coal Valley that the Civil War would be a long, drawn-out affair. A company of men from Coal Valley was organized to fight in the Union Army, and volunteers were plentiful as most of the men in that area were described as "of the pioneer type, unattached and venturesome."

Frederick was one of the first to be drafted to serve the North in the war, and he expected to go. However, Andrew Bloedel, who was working for Frederick's enterprises, reported that the men themselves decided Frederick should stay in Rock Island, as he was responsible for creating and sustaining so many jobs. Men could buy themselves out of the service in those days, and that is what Frederick did. A local man, Billie Diesenroth, volunteered as Frederick's substitute. Andrew Bloedel enlisted in the first group, and the formal induction was held on Frederick's front porch. Philip Bloedel, another of Sarah's brothers, enlisted two years later.

Frederick and two other men, A. Donaldson and J. A. Jordan, were appointed as a recruiting committee for Coal Valley. Frederick was elected to the post of secretary. To encourage young men to join the Union army, volunteers from Coal Valley were offered a cash bonus of four hundred dollars at the time of signing—an added inducement to enlist.

The Civil War took the lives of more than six hundred thousand men from the North and the South. The impact was felt keenly in areas as remote as the Illinois-Iowa Mississippi communities. The liberal Germans in Davenport, Iowa, across the river from Rock Island, Illinois, were highly sympathetic to abolition, and when John Brown was hung, the Davenport community lowered its flag to half mast and draped their stores in mourning.

Initially, Rock Island was more in tune with the South. In 1855 the town's major newspaper changed its name from the *Rock Island Republican* to the *Rock Island Argus* in protest of the Republican Party's antislavery platform. However, after news of the firing on Fort Sumter in South Carolina reached Rock Island, even the *Argus* called upon its readers to support the Union.

The Rock Island volunteers became Company D of the Twelfth Illinois Infantry. They fought in the battle of Shiloh and the battle and siege of Atlanta and joined Sherman's March to the Sea. When the war was over, the one thousand men of the Twelfth Illinois Infantry had been reduced to fewer than two hundred. It is not known how many of those men came back to Rock Island. Sarah's brothers, Andrew and Philip Bloedel, survived and returned to their hometown. They lived into the next century, both dying in the same year— 1933. No record of Billie Diesenroth's fate can be found.

John Weyerhaeuser was only six years old when the war ended, but he had memories later described to F. E., his youngest brother, of the celebration when the men came back: "The men came home in open coal cars from Rock Island . . . [John] was a little fellow at the time and very much frightened by the shooting, but did not miss the grand barbecue given to celebrate the occasion. A large steer was provided and fully dressed for the party . . . Speeches were in order, the loyalty and patriotism and sacrifices of our soldiers were extolled by local orators, while the guests partook of the feast, many happy and many crying."

During the war Frederick had responsibilities as a paymaster for the men, and he recounts going from Coal Valley to Springfield to collect money to give to the soldiers' families. This assignment might have been in line with his duties as postmaster, a title he held from 1863 until 1867. He continued to develop his business interests while serving his community throughout the war years.

THE CIVIL WAR AND THE CIRCULATION OF SCRIP FOR LAND

The end of the Civil War was to have a lasting impact on Frederick Weyerhaeuser's future, but in a way he could not foresee at this point. Many of the demobilized men were paid by the federal government in scrip, which they could exchange for property. This action created a burgeoning land rush in the Midwest and the West. Often men used the scrip to homestead new areas, and their need for building materials fed the young business Frederick and his partner were growing. Population in the prairie states was booming in the 1860s: in Minnesota, it increased 160 percent in that decade; in Kansas, 240 percent; in Nebraska, 326 percent. The push westward had begun in earnest.

But the scrip distribution also had some unintended consequences. Many men returning from the war did not want to homestead in the developing regions, and they sold their scrip at a discount, often to newly organized groups amassing capital to buy rich forestland in Wisconsin and Minnesota. The buyers were frequently timberland owners from states—like Maine and Michigan—where logging had depleted the forests. These men from the East saw new potential to expand their holdings into the midwestern forests. The war veterans' scrip was their ticket in.

During this time, the Weyerhaeuser-Denkmann partnership was so successful that the five-year evaluation period cited in the original agreement in 1860 came and went apparently without formal action.

The local newspapers chronicle the Weyerhaeuser-Denkmann firm's progress:

From the *Rock Island Daily Union*, August 2, 1865, five years after the partnership agreement was signed:

The firm of Weyerhaeuser and Denkmann are the largest lumber dealers in this section of the State. Mr. W. has spent some time in the lumber regions of Wisconsin, where he has purchased the finest lot of logs ever brought to this market.

The amount of logs they have purchased this season would surprise many not acquainted with the facts. They number 3,000,000 feet.

A description of the rapidly growing Weyerhaeuser-Denkmann firm from a local newspaper in 1867:

EXTENSIVE LUMBER WORKS

Weyerhaeuser and Denkmann's Establishment

We spent a short time in the above establishment last evening and were no little surprised at the extent and capacity of the works. We apprehend few people in this city are aware of the large amount of lumber that is annually taken from the river in the shape of logs and, having been transformed into the various sizes and shapes necessary for man's use, sent all over the country to minister to his comfort . . .

The works are conveniently located for shipping, having siding connected with the Coal Valley Railroad. They are getting out considerable heavy timber for the Rock River Improvement Company, and are also filling large orders from Iowa. They have now a good lot of log rafts "boomed" near their mill and are still receiving additions. They are selling lumber at $20 per M [thousand board feet].

Just after the war ended, Frederick began a new phase in his business. He had already been active in Wisconsin for a couple of years, buying timber from the loggers working there. In 1867, he made a greater commitment to the lumber business by directly purchasing stumpage (buying the trees for logging but not the land on which they are growing) rather than just buying logs. Two years later, in order to fill a large contract for lumber, he bought several stands of white pine along the Chippewa River in Wisconsin. Frederick was about to enter the fraught world of Wisconsin logging.

PART FOUR

FORESTS, RIVERS, AND RIGHTS

Frederick encounters the Wisconsin forests, October 1867

"Captain, watch out." The young man was grasping the side rail of the small steamboat as it swung close in around the curve. He dodged a leafy branch that hung out over the water. They were leaving behind the Mississippi with its broad reach and beginning the journey up the smaller Chippewa River. The boat gradually moved away from the shore toward the center of the flowing stream, and the motor kicked up a little higher.

"I know what I'm doing, Fred. I've taken this boat upriver before," replied Captain Samuel Van Sant. "But I had to make that close turn there because of the channels. When I get in that far you have to watch out for trees. Some of 'em hang pretty low out over the water."

Fred Weyerhaeuser turned to Van Sant, who confidently steered the boat with one hand and kept a firm grip on his pipe with the other. All the while the captain's eyes scanned the shore on either side for signs of animal or human. Now was the moment to ask the question that had been bothering the young lumberman all morning. "Sammy, do you mean what you said last night over dinner? Do you really think you can design a stern-wheeler that will push the log rafts out in front of it?"

"Already done it, Fred," the captain replied casually. "It's being built right now, while we're up here riding the Chippewa River in the old boat. Ain't that right, Tom?" He inclined his head sideways, still staring straight ahead. His son, almost as tall as the father, nodded his head enthusiastically, but he knew better than to interrupt the flow of the captain's thoughts with his own comments. "It'll be on the river next year. But we're not here to discuss my new boat design, Fred. You said you wanted to take a good look at the Chippewa forests yourself. You said you wanted to see what you could buy for stumpage, not just logs from the rafters downriver. Well, here's the forest, laid out before you. Just look at those trees." The captain made an expansive upward gesture with his right hand. The trail of pipe smoke made a curl in the air.

Frederick's gaze followed the gesture's direction, and he caught his breath. "Good Lord!" It was as strong an exclamation as the young Lutheran could utter and seemed to be more of a prayer than anything.

They had reached a point where the river cut through the Wisconsin bluffs and the thick forests began in earnest. As far as Frederick could see there were carpets of trees, unbroken by trails or fields. It seemed he was entering a world where, at the river's edge, men disappeared and only trees lived. He couldn't see exactly what kinds of trees they were, but he could see their riot of colored leaves and hear them whistling in the late-afternoon breeze. Maple, he thought, or ash. He could see the good size of the trees nearest the river, their tall, sturdy trunks beckoning. He could smell the deep odor of the rich forest floor, moist even now at the end of summer because the dense trees held in the last rainfall. And then he could smell something else: the unmistakable scent of pine. Yes, he was suddenly quite certain. They were approaching the world of the white pine forests the loggers talked about. These forests were waiting for him. They would be his.

Based on Frederick's recollections given to his son-in-law William Bancroft Hill in 1901. This is what Frederick said: "When I first saw the fine timber on the Chippewa, I wanted to say nothing about it. It was like the feeling of a man who has discovered a hidden treasure. If only Weyerhaeuser and Denkmann could control this, they would have an inexhaustible supply of the very best timber in the world."

CHAPTER 7

Frederick Likes the
Forest Life

WHEN FREDERICK FIRST SAW THE WISCONSIN FORESTS, he viewed them as a hidden treasure. His view was accurate, from a European immigrant perspective. The forests were hidden because they were unexplored by the newcomers; the natives knew well the treasure they held, treasure that made life possible. Neither native nor immigrant, however, could have predicted how the timber these forests held would fuel the immigrant colonization westward.

In the 1850s, the spread, number, and variety of forests in America would have astonished any European, and Frederick was no exception. From Chesapeake Bay to Puget Sound there were an estimated 681 million acres of virgin forest. White pine, maple and spruce, birch and beech, pine and cypress, red cedar and shimmering aspen, Douglas fir, white fir, and pacific silver fir: from

White pine was the wood of choice for the settlers:

The exchange of a sod house for a frame home built of Wisconsin or Minnesota pine was a badge of success for the homesteader and the basis of a fortune for many a lumber baron.

White Pine, Pinus Strobus, was a type of large forest tree with a straight trunk up to 40 m. high and up to 1 m. in diameter at the base; young trees with regular whorled horizontal branches, the older ones with strong, irregular, ascending branches forming an open irregular crown . . . White pine grows throughout the region of the coniferous forests, chiefly on clayey or loamy soils. It is also found scattered in isolated groves, especially in sheltered ravines or on the bluffs of the Mississippi River and many of its tributaries as far south as northwestern Illinois and southeastern Iowa. In Minnesota it occurs as far west as Spring Valley in western Fillmore County.

coast to coast the forests stretched. But only in Wisconsin was there the density of the highly desirable white pine tree, the timber that made the best houses, best schools, and best four-poster beds of any wood.

This was the forest Frederick entered when he went seeking to buy his own trees.

A TURBULENT LOGGING SCENE

Frederick's plunge into the Wisconsin timber business was a bold move at an opportune time, for both the population and the economy were fluid after the close of the Civil War. The surviving soldiers went home or joined the waves of people moving west with the frontier. Weyerhaeuser and Denkmann in Rock Island needed ever-increasing amounts of timber to meet the demand of settlers and builders for lumber. Eventually the demand was greater than the supply the firm could obtain from rafters coming downriver. Inevitably, they looked north for their own timber source. In the late 1860s, Wisconsin, not far from Frederick's home in Rock Island, was the liveliest new timber venue in the country. It had gorgeous white pine aplenty, but the logging situation was wild and ungoverned.

At the time Frederick had joined Mead, Smith and Marsh a decade earlier, he learned that there were three ways a sawmill could acquire the logs needed to turn out finished lumber ready for building. (Standing trees are called *timber,* cut trees are referred to as *logs,* and after the milling process the wood is known as *lumber.*)

The least complex option was simply to buy the logs that were sent down the Mississippi from the logging camps. These were obtained from rafters, men who drove large floats of bound logs downriver. To purchase logs in this way the sawmill owner had no need to travel north and deal with independent contractors running the camps. In the early years of his business, Frederick chose this method to supply his mill and yard. Most of the logs he purchased came by way of the smaller Wisconsin rivers, the Menominee, the Chippewa, and the St. Croix being the most important waterways out of the logging forests. The slough that nature designed at Rock Island created a perfect place to unload purchased logs.

Auctions presented another method for mill owners to acquire timber. At these events the lumberman could buy "stumpage," or standing timber rights without land ownership. Some of this timber was still on federal land, while other segments were privately owned by someone who had already acquired title to the land on which it stood. In this method the buyer would get the benefit of the "cut" but would not have to worry about selling the land when it could no longer yield timber. (This practice of selling stumpage led to many "cutover" sections of forest, abandoned and left to regenerate naturally. A large portion of these areas were eventually cleared by settlers for farming.)

The third way to get logs was to buy them from independent camp contractors, men who went into the forest with a small team of between six and twenty men in the fall and sent out logs when the melt came in the spring. In the early years of Wisconsin logging, there were many of these individual contractors, often operating on land to which they had no legal right of entry.

The loggers' lack of title to the land was commonplace because the land situation in Wisconsin was entirely fluid in the years between 1835 and 1860. Ownership fluctuated among the Native Americans, the Federal Land Office, and private speculators from the East who had already bought title to some land. The chaotic nature of this situation was further driven by the failure of the federal government to survey much of the Wisconsin timberland well into the late 1850s.

The process for Congress to clear the Indian tribes' title to this valuable land—that is, to take the land from the Indians and award it to the settlers—was no small challenge. The fur traders came first, long before the lumbermen, seeking access to the rivers and forests. These men would have been in an excellent position to profit from the rising lumber market in the decades before 1850, but few seemed successful in making the transition from fur trading to logging. They might have been too old and set in their ways, or they may have discovered the transfer of logs altogether different from moving malleable furs down the rivers. Nevertheless, some made forays into the upper forests, fuming under government restrictions as they demanded that Indian lands be opened up to Europeans. Fur trader Joseph Bailly may have reflected the less-than-admirable attitude of those who wished to get on with European-American settlement when he wrote Congress to complain that the Indians were standing in the way of progress by holding on to their land.

Settler impatience with federal delays in land surveying: in 1836 fur trader Joseph Bailly wrote the following letter to Congress:

> A few years back the labor of a few Lumbering parties operating with whip saws was sufficient to supply the wants of that market, but now that the country is settling with a rapidity unexampled in the history of our country it requires greater supplies . . . Was it the government's intention to let the whole population of the Mississippi Valley suffer for want of Lumber because a few miserable Indians hold the land?

In fact, in March 1837 three impatient French fur traders (Bailly not among them) attempted to forge their own agreement for a ten-year lease with the St. Croix and Ojibwe tribes to get access to the upper St. Croix lands and timber, but they were foiled by Indian agent Lawrence Taliaferro. More enterprising fur traders would simply work their way upriver, offering gifts to local Indian leaders in exchange for the right to ply their trade. These individual efforts seemed to meet with more success.

Later that same year, those aligned politically with Bailly got their wish: the federal government signed a treaty with the Indians that opened the St. Croix Valley, its rivers and forests, to the European-American pioneers. A wildcat logging rush followed this treaty, shaping the world Frederick was about to enter with his 1867 purchase of Wisconsin timberland. But even more important to Frederick's story, the volatile nature of the Wisconsin forest scene also gave rise to independent mill operators, particularly on the Chippewa River, which in turn led to the Wisconsin river wars later known as the "Beef Slough" conflict. Beef Slough was to present Frederick with his first public leadership challenge, beginning with his surprising election as president of the Mississippi River Logging Company in 1872.

Generally, two types of men were attracted to the emerging logging industry in the early years. One type was the "owner," those who bought the land, primarily men from Maine, Canada, and Michigan with access to capital. The most renowned of the early Wisconsin lumbermen owners were Isaac Staples and his partner Samuel F. Hersey. These men managed to take over the valuable land in the St. Croix Valley area and hold it for several decades. Arriving in 1853, they acquired forty thousand acres of Wisconsin timberland within the next eleven years. Other easterners, mostly of Swedish heritage or Yankees, were attracted by the promise of a fortune to be gained from forestland, but there were few Germans in the ownership group. When Weyerhaeuser and Denkmann expanded their operations into Wisconsin and purchased land, they were an anomaly.

The series of events that led to land acquisition by these initial lumbermen is interesting and complex. After the Indian treaty of 1837, the General (later Federal) Land Office delayed the survey of these timberlands for years. On the St. Croix the lower river lands with their patches of pine weren't surveyed until 1847, and the upper river, with its far more desirable forests of "tall trees," waited until the 1850s. Thus, land could not be purchased even if interested buyers had capital and were looking to buy. This scenario left wide open opportunity for the small, independent loggers, the "wildcats," who simply got a team of men together with an ox and moved into the forests to start cutting trees, without benefit of law or title.

THE LIFE OF A "LUMBERJACK"

These loggers, sometimes called "lumberjacks," comprised the second group of men involved in this growing business. As a type, they were much less refined than the owners. They loved the outdoors and didn't mind living all winter with other men in close quarters without bathing and being deprived of the sight of vegetables from October to May—or they were willing to put up with all of it in order to earn what they needed to one day make their own claim. These men hailed primarily from Maine and Canada, but many were also part of the newer immigrant migration from Sweden and Germany.

The men who managed their camps were cut from the same tough cloth as the loggers, except that they were slightly more entrepreneurial. All anyone needed to open a camp was a yoke of oxen to drag the logs across the frozen snow and enough credit to buy the winter's supply of food. A man could hire a crew and cut a million feet of logs or more in the winter. Many were drawn to northern Wisconsin when word of the opportunities got around. By the 1860s there were hundreds of small camps operating independently.

We know quite a bit about how these men lived and what a hard life it was. They survived primarily on a diet of pork and beans prepared in a dutch oven over an open fire. They drank a lot of black tea. Sometimes there were bunks for sleeping, but often there was just one long bed down the middle of the common room, and they all slept together at the end of their hard day's work. Frederick himself spent many nights with the loggers, sleeping in their common quarters. In later life, William Irvine, one of Frederick's long associates, reported the following anecdote, citing Weyerhaeuser's dry wit: "Weyerhaeuser and I were obliged to sleep in a logging camp bunkhouse. Stentorian lumberjack snores kept both of us awake all night. Finally one of the loudest performers gave a convulsive gasp and fell quiet. Weyerhaeuser propped himself up on his elbow and said [in his German-inflected English] to Irvine, 'Villiam, thank God, *one* is dead.'"

Life was not all toil in the camps, however. In the evening the men had certain recreation. Pipe smoking, singing, and reading were common pursuits. Some would read aloud to the others; surprisingly, the novels of Sir Walter Scott were particular favorites. A Canadian logger, James Johnson, reportedly read aloud in camp, choosing the novel *Jane Eyre,* and the men enjoyed it thoroughly. Upon hearing that the child Jane had been humiliated by one of her teachers, "one of the men shouted out a curse from the bottom of his soul. This was followed by laughter and cheers from the other men."

After the land was surveyed in 1857, the situation became more regulated. Hersey, Staples and Company records provide a good example of what went on in the following years. Isaac Staples oversaw the Wisconsin timber business from his Stillwater, Minnesota, mill site, while Samuel F. Hersey used capital acquired in his Maine lumber business and through his connections in Massachusetts to buy prime lands along the St. Croix River.

The government minimum for land purchase was $1.25 an acre, but the Hersey-Staples partnership did what many others at the time did: bought land warrants (or scrip) the government had issued to veterans of the Civil War (and, earlier, the Mexican-American War). This transaction provided a benefit for the veterans who did not want to occupy the parcels the government was subsidizing for them, and for the buyers, who got forestland at a discounted rate. Some of this land eventually passed to Frederick Weyerhaeuser and his associates.

FREDERICK'S LOGGING EDUCATION

Frederick began spending considerable time in the Wisconsin woods shortly after buying stumpage there in 1867. His forays into the camps stretched into weeks and months until they lasted throughout the entire winter. He established an office in Chippewa Falls, and letters to Sarah and his children on letterhead from that office date from the early 1870s. He immersed himself in every aspect of the logging business from standing tree to lumber sale.

Frederick's letters and comments make it clear that, although he missed his wife and children, he grew attached to the forest life. His friend, riverboat captain Samuel Van Sant, once asked him how he could spend those grueling, freezing, snowy winters in camps with rough living conditions. Frederick's reply was, "Captain, I love the woods life."

Frederick was known to tramp the forests, sometimes "following logs to their source, working his way up the large timbered streams by boat or sleigh or afoot . . . sleeping in river shacks or forest camps and seeing first hand how wooded areas were cruised, how logs were scaled, how trees were felled and what were the hazards of driving logs downstream."

The main Wisconsin rivers, the St. Croix, the Menominee, and the Chippewa, were fed by smaller streams that ran through the various forests. These rivers, in turn, flowed into the "great" river—the Mississippi. In winter the logs were dragged by oxen or horses and men over the snow and ice to the frozen streams, marked, and stacked in orderly rows and piles in preparation for their spring journey. When the weather had warmed sufficiently, the streams swelled and were deemed to have risen to a "driving" stage.

Among the many colorful contributions to American culture that have emerged from the lumber industry, the word *boom* must rank high. Making a sound that the word mimics, the melting rivers rush forward and downward in the northern spring thaws. As men of the time would say, "the river is on the boom." The echo of the boom was good news for the woodsmen. It was the signal that the logs they had cut through the winter months could now be sent down local streams to ever-larger rivers that would carry them all the way to market.

But *boom* also came to mean something else: a man-made device of bound logs anchored to poles set across certain points in the river to stop the flow of logs so they could be sorted according to their markings. Beef Slough boom was one of the largest and most important of these places.

FREDERICK LEARNS TO KEEP TRACK OF HIS LOGS

Sometimes in the winter, individual, freshly cut logs were stacked on the river ice, waiting for the melt to start moving them downstream. In other situations, when spring came and the waters started to move, the logs were dumped into a river at the upstream site. This sort of grand, devil-may-care practice soon proved unworkable, as many logs came to be scattered along the riverbanks by storms or ended up at the wrong mill. So in 1843 a young riverman named Steven Hanks (a cousin of Abraham Lincoln) devised a method of tying logs together in a raft for easier driving. Logs were still run down the smaller streams as singles, but now they were caught as they entered a larger river and tied together. The first raft was about sixteen feet wide and between four and six hundred feet long.

Soon rafts of logs were a common sight on the larger rivers, usually manned by a crew of twenty or so, steering the raft with long oars. The crew lived on board, cooking and sleeping on top of the raft as they traveled. This method of transporting logs was the practice until 1869, around the time Frederick first purchased stumpage in Wisconsin. That year Captain Van Sant created the boat that would revolutionize logging transportation. He gave his friend Weyerhaeuser a ride in the new, stern-wheel steamboat. The rear-wheel design pushed the large log rafts much more efficiently than the old side-wheel models, and it was altogether far superior to the practice of using men to ride and steer the rafts.

Frederick was so intrigued by the stern-wheel steamboat that he hired Van Sant to bring down all the logs from Beef Slough. Eventually there were modifications that allowed for the log rafts to be ever larger, guided and steered by the steamboat. The largest raft recorded on the Mississippi River was 1,550 feet long and 270 feet wide. But there were two problems in the transportation of logs to the downriver mills. One was the uncertain state of the smaller streams coming out of the forests. They might overflow in the spring melting, causing floods and rampages that could toss the logs onto shore or push them farther

downriver than the owners intended. The other problem was getting the logs
to their proper destination according to their brands, which were cut into the
base of the log at the site of the tree's felling.

The first problem was often addressed by man-made solutions. Streams were
widened in places, bends in rivers were sometimes straightened, and often
small dams were erected to heighten the streams and create an easier flow. But
it soon became clear that further assistance was needed, particularly at points
where logs were to be sorted. The boom was created to catch and hold the logs.
The sorting process also included "brailling," or gathering logs into groups
according to their brands. The logs could then be "rafted," or tied together for
the journey downstream.

There was a clear division of labor among the men of the logging camps.
The choppers, or "fallers," brought the trees down with their axes or saws (or
both); the "barkers" stripped the trees of their bark; scalers then estimated the
amount of lumber in each log, using one of forty scales agreed upon at the
time; swampers cleared the paths to the rivers so the logs could be dragged
there; finally, at the river's bank, the sawyers would "buck" the logs with cross-
cut saws into twelve-, fourteen-, or sixteen-foot lengths and put bark and stamp
marks on them to assure that they eventually got to their rightful buyers.

The scalers' work was key in determining the worth of the logs:

> No aspect of logging activities generated more friction and heat than the
> subject of log scaling. No scaler and no log rule could completely satisfy
> everyone. There were about forty different scaling rules in use at one time or
> another in the Lake states. In Wisconsin the Scribner Rule vied with the Doyle
> Rule (called the "Irish" rule) in favoring either buyers or sellers and loggers in
> the measurement.

This last act addressed the second major problem for the lumbermen, that
of identifying the logs. The simple, early solution had been to mark each log
with a carving to identify its owner. Each log had a bark mark and an end
stamp. The bark mark was chipped into the side of the log with a broadax, and
the end stamp was applied from four to six times on each end of the log by hard
blows with a cast-iron marker, somewhat similar to the branding of beef in the
cattle regions. These marks were legal proof of ownership, and the marking
business was highly regulated: all marks had to be registered in the office of the
Surveyor General of Logs and Lumber. There might be several marks on each
log, showing which camp it came from and, sometimes, which logger. Companies, too, might have more than one brand. Over two thousand different marks

were recorded at Beef Slough in one year, and over twenty thousand different marks for all logs that actually entered the Mississippi River.

Such marks were jotted down in the worn leather notebooks Frederick Weyerhaeuser always carried with him as he made his way through the woods and camps of Wisconsin. His notebooks give us a working glimpse of both the life of a lumberman and the methods used to find, mark, and manage the logs downriver to their sawmill destination. Initially, Frederick's brands were simple, but as his partnerships grew in complexity the markings necessarily followed. Each partnership had its own set of initials, including, later, the mark MLC for Mississippi [River] Logging Company.

FREDERICK, MAN OF DETAILS

Frederick kept track of his expanding logging interests in his pocket-sized note-books, the shape of a modern checkbook. He recorded carefully his own debts and his debtors as well as occasional memoranda to himself on his loggers and land agreements. The earliest surviving Weyerhaeuser notebooks date from the 1860s. The books reveal a great deal about Frederick's character. He was a meticulous recorder, but not particularly an orderly one. The notebooks were invariably of brown leather, with a fold-over flap and "Memoranda" stamped on the cover. They were small enough to be slipped into the shirt pocket of a busy lumberman but large enough to contain many brief notes and figures. To judge from the frequency of entries, they accompanied him everywhere.

Like Thomas Jefferson before him, Frederick recorded the minutia of his economic life, but where Jefferson tracked his plantation and home expenses, Frederick made notes of his business affairs. Occasionally the German spelling would intrude on the English, which was his daily language now, used even when writing to himself. In 1860, a typical entry of his notebook listed payment from customers:

James Jana: 21 bushels of corn
W. Priget 12 Bushels of corn
James Glen paid cash $24
Farmer Hana 21 bushels korn
(again in the afternoon . . . 22 bushels of korn)

In these diaries Frederick also kept the same careful accounts of those to whom he owed money. This close attention to detail was to become a lifelong habit.

The early notebooks were simply books of blank pages on which he made his daily scribble, but later the small books were more often calendars. Frederick steadfastly ignored their listing of days and dates as he continued to create notes to himself, sometimes in stream-of-consciousness fashion.

For example, on the page labeled April 13, 1879, he wrote, "Jackson Phillips agrees to cut and put on the ice in the Chipp. River in good workman like manner all timber on s ½ of the S.E. ¼ at $3 a foot." The actual handwritten date of this entry was October 6, '79, which makes much more sense considering the allusion to the oncoming winter and the river ice that would hold the logs until the spring melt.

On the page listed as October 13, '79, Frederick dated his note 4–23–79 and wrote,

Sold John Hookerbrook one horse: $85
25.
Due: $60."

Frederick was a familiar figure in the camps, so much so that the camp cooks felt free to ask him to send or bring back additional supplies. On the same date as John Hookerbrook bought the horse, Frederick was given a long list of needed groceries to pass on to the A. B. McDonnell Driving Company, food staples to be shipped to the Chippewa Crossing camp. The loggers' diet for the winter months was well preserved in this list entrusted to their chief:

20 Bbls [must indicate barrels] Flour
12 Bbls Mess Pork
10 Beef
1 b. C sugar
1 b. Dried apples
1 b. currants
4 kegs lard
4 kegs crystal syrup 2 kegs Jasper
2 kegs Pickles
3 boxes codfish
15 gallons cider vinegar

This list also contained a request for various spices, navy beans, soap, candles, and other necessities. (Pork and beans were known as the "fuel" for the loggers through the long winter.)

Frederick's notes to himself indicate that if a colleague or associate failed to respond to an earlier request, his patience might run thin, as when he reported this conversation to himself on February 21, 1884: "Scaler Hayward told Finstad

Mr. McCord did not grade logs to suit the Chip [*sic*] Logging Co and we had nothing to do w/scaling or inspecting. Finstad has written but received no answer. Also for scale cards and reports and lumbermen pencils. Money." The cryptic mention of *money* bore no elaboration.

Sometimes a note of self-questioning was apparent, as in March 22, 1884: "Why did we buy Kinyon poor logs when he did not break last years rollway." Whether this question was for Frederick himself or for some underling who would be grilled on the purchase is unknown.

In April 1887, Frederick had the following expenses, somewhere in Wisconsin:

Basket .15
Breakfast 5.25
Dinner 2.60
Poster .50
Telegram .60

Frederick often listed and drew the marks that identified the logs of his business enterprises. From time to time odd notations on some transaction would appear, such as the following on the inside cover of an 1881 bank book: "some of the deposits are also in a previous book which is mislaid or lost," as if to remind himself that he had lost some records.

Occasionally he would use the notes as a method for thinking through some transaction and in this way document his negotiations, such as this interesting series on May 18, 1876:

Bought the French Lumber for $6 net, agreed to take all what is not rafted for the Mississippi Rive [*sic*] Co."

They will let me have their rafted Lumber at 5.75 net. I'll not agree to take them.

The next day, May 19, 1876, he did reach some agreement.

Agreed with the French Lumber Co to match their Logs for $100.
Payment of $1,000, 2–3 × 4 months. [Must refer to terms]

March 16 has this hopeful note, "F/X Armstrong good," then a series of markings, followed by this note: "Some rott [*sic*], some not. Fair. Flambeau. March 17."

Frederick also made notes to himself on his contractors, especially when displeased. On March 18, 1884, he wrote this ominous note:

Get rid of Josie as soon as possible. Do not pay him any more money until the logs are out of the Little Jump and Josie Creek. He has a great many logs skidded which he will not haul. Josie is a bad egg. Did Charlie Viles drive Little Jump? If not, how much money did we keep back?

And should anyone doubt that Frederick was paying careful attention to the quality of what he bought and from whom, this note on March 26, 1884, puts that question to rest:

Peter Truax: Logs poor. Will cut. Upperlanding good. W. J. Young good. Swift poorly graded. Fred Leonard logs ever so much better than last year. Fowlds claims his contract does not provide for quality.

An unknown wag wrote the following parody of Joyce Kilmer's poem "Trees"; his theme was a scaler's sorting of ragged logs into the number three category rather than number five.

I think that I shall never see
Such lousy looking # three
Each board was full of big spike knots
With ships in dressing, too, in spots
And on each edge there was some wane
And there were worm holes, too, and stain.
Each piece was checked for several feet
And just to make my joy complete
The stock was crooked, too, and green.
Such lumber I have never seen!
It looked like number five to me
And only God could make it three.

A memorandum from the same notebook illustrates his careful partnership distribution records: "Peter Musser ⅛, Peter M. Musser ⅛, Dimock Gould and Co. ¼, Sauntry and Tozer ¼, F.C.A.D. ⅛, F. Weyerhaeuser ⅛." A later comment indicates that this memorandum refers to a purchase made on the St. Croix waters. (Note that "F.C.A.D." refers to Denkmann, who participated in this particular partnership, along with the Mussers.)

FREDERICK'S LIFE ON THE ROAD

These early entries show the care Frederick took to record his many financial and business dealings as he was traveling. This level of detail became increasingly necessary as the complexities of his many partnerships multiplied, especially as he was so often "on the road." This practice may also have contributed to his reputation as a fair man, one who had the trust of his business partners and employees.

However, the notebooks don't tell us anything deeply personal about Frederick. An entry may reflect a bit of impatience with a log supplier, but his willingness to carry grocery lists for the camp cook indicates a connection to the men. We see his concern for quality timber and reminders on his debts and debtors. But we don't know from these notebooks if he was ever lonely while spending long weeks in the North Woods away from his family. We don't know if he had doubts about his own abilities or if he ever wondered if he had chosen the right path. For any personal reflections, we have to rely on the letters he sent to his wife and children from the Wisconsin forests in the 1870s and on the anecdotes that his youngest son, F. E., later compiled from family recollections and letters from his father's business associates.

These initial Wisconsin years provided Frederick with the opportunity to get to know the forests and to learn the lumber business from top to bottom. But the lumber situation was already changing even as he was learning. Tensions in the Wisconsin timber industry over river rights that were to culminate in the Beef Slough conflict were brewing when Frederick made his first foray into the Wisconsin timberlands in 1867. By 1871 the conflict was well on the way to becoming a full-blown logging war. And Frederick found himself thrust into the middle of it. With little more than ten years in business, the young German had his first major leadership challenge.

CHAPTER 8

--------------------------- ⸙ ---------------------------

The Wisconsin Logging Feuds
Breed Bitterness

FREDERICK, STILL A YOUNG THIRTY-SIX YEARS in 1870, was acquiring experience and gaining confidence. But the next decade would test his mettle in unexpected ways. The first indication that such a test was in the offing came from the hostility he encountered from local sawmillers and Wisconsin landowners as he moved deeper into the Wisconsin forests to get his logs. War clouds were gathering as locals began an organized defense against men like Frederick who had mills on the Mississippi and wanted to take their logs out of Wisconsin forests. At issue was not only timber that local mill owners believed belonged exclusively to them but the volatile aspect of the rivers that fed into the Mississippi and were the chief transportation for logs. Tempers were especially hot up and down the Chippewa River in mid-Wisconsin.

A CLASH OF LOGGING INTERESTS

The hostile interactions began in earnest in 1869 with low rivers that created a mammoth logjam. Fights began among individual lumbermen: owners, loggers, and river drivers. They took place on the rivers, in meeting rooms, in the legislature, and eventually even in the courts. The conflicts were not resolved until eleven years later, in 1880, when the capricious rivers flooded, causing chaos for everyone involved. That year, when all parties had suffered huge losses, Frederick engineered a solution that made partners out of his competitors. In so doing, he opened a new system of cooperation on the Chippewa River.

The decade between 1870 and 1880 was a formative one for Wisconsin forest logging and not an easy one for lumbermen engaged in the business. Until the 1860s most of the timber cut in Wisconsin came by way of the Black and St. Croix rivers, somewhat to the north and center of the state. Meanwhile, the forests rich with timber in the Chippewa Valley to the south were literally captive to the Eau Claire and Chippewa Falls sawmill owners. These men had constructed booms that stopped all logs coming downstream at Chippewa Falls and Eau Claire, near the main Chippewa River sawmills. Nothing could get through.

To understand the conflict between the Mississippi lumbermen, Frederick and his many partners, and the Eau Claire and Chippewa Falls lumbermen is not an easy matter. Three distinct groups were involved. Frederick and his colleagues had mills and yards on the Mississippi. These men eventually formed the Mississippi River Logging Company, known as the MRLC.

The second group comprised the Wisconsin millmen, organized by Thaddeus Pound and J. G. Thorp and originally titled the Chippewa River Improvement Company. They had acquired a charter from the Wisconsin state legislature in 1866. This charter's main purpose was to control the Chippewa River and the logs it could deliver to their mills. (It was this group that O. H. Ingram would later lead as chief liaison with Frederick's group.)

The third party was composed of owners whose organization was titled the Beef Slough Manufacturing, Booming, Log Driving and Transportation Company. These were primarily men from Michigan with capital to invest in Wisconsin logging. The principals of this group of partners were James H. Bacon from Ypsilanti and Francis Palms from Detroit.

The balance of power would move from one to another of these three groups depending on their shifting alliances. All were interested in how they could dominate Wisconsin logging or at least participate freely in the growing industry. Some were determined to keep newcomers out. Others were determined to get in. Throw in the unstable nature of rivers, which can flood one season and dry up the next, and the mix was a recipe for inevitable conflict.

Shortly after the Civil War ended in 1865, the lumber mill owners at Eau Claire, notably from Knapp, Stout and other, smaller firms, purchased land at the mouth of the Chippewa River that included the Beef Slough. Their objective was to control the river and forestall interlopers—men who had mills on the Mississippi downriver like Frederick Weyerhaeuser from Rock Island and the Lairds and Nortons, cousins in the family lumber business from Winona, Minnesota.

The Beef Slough, a side channel at the mouth of the Chippewa River where it flowed into the Mississippi, was a natural holding place for the logs that traveled downriver from the forests and an ideal place to construct a boom. Beef Slough was named after an incident that occurred in the late 1820s, one that involved a young lieutenant named Jefferson Davis.

There are two versions of the story.

According to an article on the history of the name in the *Rock Island Argus* on June 27, 1888, Davis led a small party of men north from Prairie du Chien,

Wisconsin, driving a herd of cattle, three to four hundred in number, for distribution to men at the posts upriver. When the small group got to the slough,
they forced the cattle to ford it. Unfortunately, the cattle became mired in the
mud, and the entire herd drowned.

Another version, retold by F. K. Weyerhaeuser in an address to the Newcomen Society in 1951 (and published that year by the Princeton University
Press) entitled "Trees and Men," relates that Zachary Taylor was the colonel
who sent Jeff Davis to Menomonie, Wisconsin, in the fall of 1829, to cut timber
for use at Fort Crawford. In the spring of 1830, a raft loaded with cattle was
floated down the Chippewa River, and it was mistakenly piloted into a channel
blocked by driftwood. All the cattle drowned in both versions of this story, and
the event was immortalized by the name Beef Slough.

It's understandable that the raft of cattle might be sidetracked into the Beef
Slough, for it is a stretched-out, narrow network of lagoons and lakes that
creates an elongated side channel to the Chippewa just where that river opens
into the Mississippi. The slough meanders for twenty-three miles alongside its
parent river until it finally opens onto the Mississippi nine miles south of the
mouth of the main Chippewa River. But if the slough had proved an unfortunate trap for the cattle, it was clearly an ideal place to divert the logs that came
downriver from the Chippewa forests.

In this enormous holding channel, logs could be sorted according to their
markings, brailled, rafted, and then sent out onto the Mississippi. If the lumbermen did not use the slough, the logs coming down from the camps would
have gone directly into the Mississippi, a much larger and faster river than the
Chippewa. There was no chance of catching or holding loose logs in a river like
the Mississippi. Using the slough to sort the logs was the only reasonable way
the Chippewa could become a major logging river and the only way the Chippewa forests could be harvested by those not holding mills on the Chippewa.
Whoever controlled the Beef Slough would control the right to log the Wisconsin forests.

The violence and struggle for control of the Wisconsin logging business
began before Frederick became involved. Initially the Chippewa mill owners
and the Michigan lumbermen were aligned. This arrangement ended when
the Wisconsin mill owners realized that the Michigan owners were going to
improve the slough, thus inviting in outsiders. The Wisconsinites tried to stop
the Michigan partners from action by appealing to the legislature.

They were partially successful. However, in 1868 one of the senators friendly
to the Michigan group slipped into a routine power bill a rider that allowed
any one of the owners to act as if he were alone. Thus, Francis Palms could
sell his stock to a new company, called simply the Beef Slough Company. The

Wisconsin owners, sensing a threat to their monopoly on the river should the slough be developed, created a raft of slabs and logs to seal the entrance to the Beef Slough. The Beef Slough Company applied to the legislature for relief, but in the meanwhile, being practical men, they had their workers tear apart the slabs and logs sealing the slough entrance so logs could get through while the politicians dithered.

The Michigan men had contracted for some fifty million feet of lumber to be taken out of the forests that winter of 1868–69, and Black Dan and his brother Big John McDonald began the drive down to the Beef Slough with a crew of 125 men. (Black Dan McDonald will reappear in Frederick's life at a later date in an entirely different drama.) At Jim Falls on the river, the Beef Slough Company men were met by some of the Chippewa River Improvement Company managers, who proposed to stop the drive. A brawl ensued, and there were some injuries. The McDonald brothers were stopped again at Eau Claire, Wisconsin, where there was another brawl, and later, on the Menominee, the manager of the Knapp, Stout firm was thrown into the river by the Michigan men's drivers.

After this, the Michigan men of the Beef Slough Company, possibly operating on the ancient principle that the enemy of my enemy is my friend, established a relationship with the Mississippi lumbermen, including the Mussers of Iowa, Frederick Weyerhaeuser, and Lorenzo Schricker.

Rivers and Logjams Make Things Worse

The Wisconsin lumbermen had already become suspicious of the interlopers from Minnesota, Illinois, and Iowa when, shortly after the end of the Civil War, these men began their logging operations in the central Wisconsin forests. Then, in 1869 what came to be known as "The Big Log Jam" occurred. The rivers were low that year due to a lack of snow. When spring came, there was not enough water rushing on the Chippewa to bring down the logs that had been cut in the winter. An estimated 150 million feet of logs piled up behind the Union Lumber Company's boom above Chippewa Falls. The Union Lumber Company was the powerful owner of the "Big Mill" at Chippewa Falls. They also owned timberlands, dams, and logging outfits.

In this disaster, logs choked the river from its base to as high as thirty feet above its surface. Hundreds of men had to work all summer to loosen the jam.

William Irvine later told the story of standing with Wisconsin's lieutenant governor, Thaddeus Pound, Frederick's competitor in the lumber business. The two men had come out to view the flood's damage when they spied a lone figure tramping determinedly up the river on the opposite side. Pound turned to Irvine and said, "There goes Weyerhaeuser, looking for his logs." And it is no wonder Frederick wanted to see the damage for himself. His logs and, literally, the future of his fledgling lumber business were scattered on the banks and eddies of a Wisconsin river. It may have been at this point that Frederick realized the Wisconsin situation was too big for one person to solve.

THE MISSISSIPPI RIVER LOGGING COMPANY ORGANIZES

Soon after this disaster, Frederick began to contact his fellow lumbermen on the Mississippi and talk seriously about creating an association that could deal with the problem of getting logs out of the Chippewa forest. He envisioned a loose-knit organization that could work in everyone's favor, as Mathew Norton, his colleague from Winona, later reported in his monograph *The Mississippi River Logging Company: An Historical Sketch*. Frederick first made common cause with the chief lumbermen of Davenport, Iowa, across the river from Rock Island, Lorenzo Schricker and Elijah Swift. Weyerhaeuser had already begun buying logs from Wisconsin in partnership with Schricker in 1869. Gradually others were brought into the conversation, including the Laird-Norton family group of Winona. Mathew Norton was to become one of Frederick's close and lifelong friends.

As a result of Frederick's efforts, a meeting of lumbermen on the Mississippi who were logging in the Chippewa Valley was called at the Briggs House in Chicago on December 29, 1870. After considerable discussion, the group agreed that Beef Slough was potentially the very thing that could open up the Chippewa River and its daughter forests for use by the millmen outside of Wisconsin. All who attended wanted a stake in the Beef Slough arrangement. The stock for their common effort was fixed at one million dollars, a huge sum in those days, and nearly all the millmen on the river agreed to subscribe. The Mississippi River Logging Company (MRLC) was born.

From the original accounts, it is clear that subscriptions were taken on the basis of the amount of logs each mill would require the slough to handle, counted in the millions of log feet. The largest shares of stock were taken by W. J. Young and Co. of Clinton, Iowa (four), and C. Lamb and Sons, Clinton, Iowa (six), with Weyerhaeuser and Denkmann at four shares and their increasingly close associates, the Laird-Norton cousins in Winona, also at four shares.

Lorenzo Schricker was elected president of the newly formed company. He was authorized to go to Chippewa Falls and buy logs, which he did successfully that year on the company's behalf. Others took officer roles, while Frederick was content with an at-large position on the executive committee.

The Mississippi lumbermen would develop strong social bonds as well as identifying and promoting their common business efforts. Mathew Norton was later to write about the MRLC as an association: "The members of this

Company were more like brothers in their intercourse one with another than would be found in most organizations for profit and the promotion of business. A very kindly feeling and brotherly affection grew up among them, busy as they were with their everyday work and life; and it was a joy to them when they could from time to time meet one another and laying aside even for a brief hour the cares of business, enjoy a season of social intercourse."

These new partners leased the Beef Slough boom from the Michigan owners, who already were finding that running the slough brought more trouble than they had anticipated, given the ruckus that had occurred with the McDonald brothers and the Knapp, Stout firm manager who was tossed into the river. The MRLC partners took a two-year lease with the hope that they and others could successfully bring logs all the way down the Chippewa River and onto the Mississippi. The boom itself, however, was in a sad state of disrepair, and the new lessees were understandably reluctant to invest money upgrading a property they didn't own.

But the MRLC men had a larger problem than a rickety boom: the Eau Claire and Chippewa Falls mill owners' vociferous objections to outsider logging increased. They refused to have the interlopers' logs running past their mills on the river, and they employed a variety of methods to slow or stop them.

The Chippewa Falls–Eau Claire mill owners had a history of creating a fuss, with heated rhetoric, when anyone other than their men became involved in the Wisconsin forests.

Some years earlier this group of mills, with other Wisconsin plants, had been strong enough to check federal prosecutions for the illegal cutting of timber on government lands and to force the dismissal of John W. Wilson, the commissioner of the General Land office, who had taken measures to protect the nation's property. When Cornell University and various investors previously noted [Philetus Sawyer and James Jenkins of Oshkosh, Wisconsin; Francis Palms of Detroit; T. B. Walker of Minneapolis; and Isaac Stephenson of Stillwater] had purchased their extensive holdings, the Chippewa millmen had screamed at "absentee capitalists seeking to wrest control of the government pine land from them." Now, on the first appearance of the Mississippi River lumbermen, they muttered ominously of "invaders" and asserted that Chippewa logs should be converted into lumber in the valley where they were cut, and not "stolen" by "aliens" to provide jobs in Illinois and Iowa.

The MRLC leadership was in a quandary. There was no other way to get the logs down from the forests but the Chippewa River. What could they do? The seemingly intractable problem of the Eau Claire and Chippewa Falls mill owners' animosity worsened, and less than one-third of the MRLC-purchased logs made it all the way downriver to Beef Slough that first year, 1871. When the

MRLC commissioned the Laird-Norton cousins to inspect the river, they were "discouraged to see so many of their logs scattered along the way, in the bays and on the banks of the river."

But Frederick was not yet ready to abandon the plan. As Mathew Norton later wrote, "Mr. Weyerhaeuser, however, was not inclined to give up an undertaking which seemed to him to have merit, and with great forethought and determination, decided on a new course; so when the Beef Slough parties were inclined to abandon the enterprise, he with Mr. Schricker and Mr. Elijah Swift, leased the boom for two years to see whether they could put new life into the project."

Because Frederick recommended it, the Mississippi River group decided to continue operation of the slough for another year. He decided it would be better for the MRLC to have entire control of the business of the Beef Slough, so he volunteered to transfer his personal lease on the land to the Mississippi River Logging Company. His associates followed suit, and as a result Beef Slough belonged entirely to the Mississippi River Logging Company, with no individual owners.

The company associates met for the third time at the Huff House in Winona, Minnesota, on September 5, 1872. Representatives of the MRLC had been negotiating with Francis Palms of Detroit to buy his interest in the land around Beef Slough. The main purpose of the annual meeting was to agree to this important transaction. Unfortunately, President Schricker was given to imbibing in the local saloons a little too freely, and he arrived at the meeting late and somewhat tipsy.

The minutes of that meeting relate a heated exchange between Lorenzo Schricker and W. C. Clark of St. Louis. Clark, annoyed at Schricker's tardiness and condition, roared an objection against the Davenport lumberman. "You can't chair this meeting," he shouted. "You're drunk."

Schricker shouted back the ultimate defense: "Schricker knows more drunk as Clark knows sober." However, his colleagues did not agree with that assessment, and the result of this comical drama was that Schricker was replaced with the young German immigrant who had been the quiet leader organizing in the background. Frederick Weyerhaeuser was then only thirty-eight years old, but he had earned the trust of his partners, and he brought order to the group when they elected him the new president.

TEN YEARS OF WRANGLING ON THE RIVERS OF WISCONSIN

The Mississippi lumbermen's efforts were occasionally rewarded with brief truces in the years after 1872, but opposition from the Wisconsin parties always returned. The argument over the river's use was complicated by the fact that the Wisconsin legislature issued conflicting charters to the MRLC and their Wisconsin opponents as to the building of various dams and improvements to help the flow of logs down the Chippewa. The ongoing divisions were further confused by shifting alliances among the three involved parties and, to complicate the scene further, the occasional intra-Wisconsin competition between the Eau Claire lumbermen and those from Chippewa Falls.

One such project—to raise the level of the river—is credited in particular to Frederick. He suggested a dam above the town of Chippewa Falls to the MRLC group when it met in Alma, Wisconsin, in 1875. The river levels were changeable, and often logs were stranded. By holding the water with the dam and letting it out at key times, all the lumbermen would be more certain of enough water to carry the logs downstream. The group agreed with Frederick, and construction on Little Falls Dam began; it was completed in three years. (Note: This Little Falls in Wisconsin is not to be confused with Little Falls, Minnesota, where Frederick's group later had operations called the Pine Tree Lumber Company.)

The following spring, Little Falls Dam underwent its first critical test and passed with flying colors. As heavy rains came, one hundred million feet of logs were carried over the dam when it opened its gates. By June, four hundred men were busy assembling, daily, four million feet of logs into rafts. When the work was finished that August, the Beef Slough boom had "turned out" almost 250 million feet of logs. At its height, Beef Slough had as many as 837 raft-boat departures and was said to be one of the busiest of the Mississippi river ports.

That year, 1875, was also when the Dells Improvement Company, a rival of the Wisconsin mill owners, received legislative approval to construct a dam farther downstream near Eau Claire. The Mississippi River Logging Company associates were alarmed at this plan, perhaps because of the proposed toll of thirty-five cents for every thousand logs to be processed at the dam. MRLC employed a variety of methods, including litigation, to fight the proposal, but all proved futile. The legislature approved the charter for the Dells Dam.

Meanwhile, the once-powerful Union Lumber Company of Chippewa Falls, owned by a group of Pennsylvania lumbermen, was in deep financial trouble and, after some attempts to raise money through securities, offered to sell their entire "big mill" property in Chippewa Falls to the MRLC. Frederick and his associates declined the offer at that time, believing the price was inflated.

Members of the Union Lumber Company then began to make themselves a nuisance to the Weyerhaeuser associates in the hope that the latter would find it cheaper to buy them out than to fight continuous battles in the legislature, in the courts, and on the rivers. The Union Lumber group first made trouble in 1876. The Laird-Norton group discovered that U.S. Army engineers were making a survey of the Chippewa River as a preliminary step to improving the stream for navigation by steamboat traffic. This presaged disaster for the logging industry, as increased steamboat traffic could eventually prevent logging traffic. The Chippewa was a river full of sandbars and not suitable for boat navigation of any kind. The lumbermen had built dams to raise the water levels and increase the chances of good flow for their logs. But the Wisconsin lumbermen saw an opportunity to involve the legislature and create another barrier in the face of the Mississippi men trying to take their logs out.

At issue through some of these fights was the serious topic of loose logs and the rights of steamboats versus the rights of the logging companies to send their logs downriver to the booms. The Union Lumber Company took advantage of this situation and went to court to gain an injunction against the MRLC, citing "loose logs and obstructive river installations."

The MRLC countered with its own helpful depositions, including one from Captain E. E. Heerman, who operated his steamboat the *Monitor* on the river.

The perspective of the *Moline Review* on the Beef Slough affair, December 20, 1879:

> The Mississippi River Logging Company owns some 50,000 acres of pine lands in Wisconsin and on the Chippewa River and its tributaries. From this tract the Company cuts a portion of the logs which are sawed at our mills, and the balance are bought from contractors and owners of the other timberlands, with the provision that all these logs shall be delivered on the banks of the Chippewa.
>
> The Chippewa is comparatively a small stream. It is navigable for small boats as far as Eau Claire, about 100 miles from its mouth, in good stages of water. Along its banks numerous saw mills have been erected whose owners have for years been trying to prevent our Mississippi River saw mill men from getting logs down the stream . . .
>
> In order to facilitate the floating of logs down the river the Chippewa Improvement Co. [now aligned with Frederick and the MRLC] has constructed at its own expense, various dams and booms. The sawmill interest on the river has brought suit against the Company for thus obstructing the channel . . . If the saw mill men of that section could put a stop to that practice competition in the lumber trade would practically cease; the Wisconsin choppers would get lower prices for their work; the owners of stumpage would get smaller margins; the mills on the Mississippi would be placed at a disadvantage and the entire lumber interest of the Great West would be placed in the control of a few mill men on the Chippewa.

He indicated that he had never had any trouble navigating the river, and he supported the Weyerhaeuser group's position. Unfortunately, a year later, in August 1878, the Chippewa was quite low and Captain Heerman's boat struck a submerged log. The captain was furious and switched sides, filing a federal suit against the Weyerhaeuser partners in January 1879.

Eventually the courts ruled that the captain was not "especially damaged," and even if he had been, the logging companies had as much right to the river as the steamboat traffic did. At the time, the Chippewa steamboat traffic was very light, precisely because the river could drop precipitately with the capricious snows or rains. The Weyerhaeuser group contended, in this lawsuit, that rail traffic was gradually becoming the choice for shipping and that the role steamboats had filled early on in that regard had lessened considerably.

In a December 1879 decision, Circuit Court Judge Romanzo Bonn had this to say on the issue of the right to transport logs: "The question is: Which interest shall be subordinated to the other; which has the 'peculiar and sacred right' to navigate the Chippewa: logs or steamboats? A good deal might depend upon the relative importance of these different interests, to the welfare of commerce and the public good. The vast importance of the logging and lumbering interests on the Chippewa River sufficiently appears from the bill of complaint." The judge concluded that both logs and steamboats had freedom of the river under the laws of Wisconsin, and he dismissed the case.

There were some moments of grace in this ongoing drama in Wisconsin, mostly exhibited by Frederick, but the conflict always seemed to resume after brief respites. One such moment occurred in 1879 when Frederick agreed to his competitors' request that he hold back logs on the high river because the Dells Dam could sort only ten million feet of logs a day. Again in June of that year he accommodated the Wisconsin millmen when the Chippewa fell so low that a jam formed at the Dells. At their request, Frederick released enough water from his Little Falls Dam to break the jam.

Frederick also helped his Wisconsin competitors in July of that year when he directed that water should be held at Little Falls Dam until the Wisconsin owners could repair their broken boom at Eau Claire, which had been disabled by rain. Even the local newspaper, the *Chippewa Herald,* which had often opposed the Mississippi "interlopers," noted that "a spirit of accommodation pervaded the entire operations of the managers of the Little Falls dam."

The final resolution of the feud between the Mississippi lumbermen and those in the Chippewa Valley came as a result of the great flood of 1880, a calamity for all who were working in lumber coming from the Chippewa forests. And the cooperation that resulted was a direct result of Frederick's efforts.

CHAPTER 9

Frederick Emerges
as First Among Equals

THE RIVERS OF WISCONSIN were notoriously troubled in the spring of 1880. By May 6, even the *Rock Island Argus* carried the news: "The Captains and rafters say they never saw a season of disaster to rafters as this has been so far. Some of the skippers and wheelmen who have never known what accidents were, in their calling, in ten years of experience, are getting their fill of trouble this spring. What with high water and hard winds, they have had their rafts beached on islands, knocked to pieces against bridges and bad luck, generally."

A RIVER ON THE RAMPAGE AND LOST LOGS

Early in June 1880, a week of heavy rains suddenly and dramatically raised the river to a level twenty-four feet above its low-water mark. The river at this height took on enormous power, sweeping away everything in its path. Not only the logs that had already been put in for driving downriver but those on the banks waiting to be put in were sucked under the expanding waters. The river went on a rampage, pushing 150 million feet of logs along and ignoring the dams and booms that had been painstakingly constructed over the past fifteen years on the upper Chippewa. The raging force crushed everything, its power increased by the solid logs it had appropriated as it rushed onward.

When the roaring flood beat like a drummer against the Dells Dam at Eau Claire, the outcome was uncertain. Then the river finally broke through and plunged over the dam. It was now an unstoppable, battering force that crashed into the bridge below and charged downriver. Houses, barns, shops, and bridges broke before its force. Two sawmills were washed away.

Of the 150 million feet of logs reported to be carried on this force of nature, 110 million of them belonged to the mills at Chippewa Falls and Eau Claire. And they were all headed inexorably downriver to Frederick's Beef Slough. The wreckage was astounding. Most of the logs made it to the Beef Slough, but many were tossed on the riverbanks on the way, some as far as three miles from the river. The Wisconsin mill owners lost more than a million logs in this disaster—logs that now belonged to Frederick as they had finally come to rest in his slough.

A log exchange agreement was possible, but the Wisconsin men knew that the MRLC often charged for holding and/or sawing logs that belonged to other firms. The Wisconsin millmen—Ingram and Wallace, Shaw and Barnard—fully expected that a time of retribution for their years of harassment of the "invaders" had arrived.

FREDERICK'S LEADERSHIP CREATES A NEW COALITION

The Wisconsin owners chose a young attorney from Chippewa Falls named Rouget J. Marshall, later a circuit court judge, who had previously performed intermediary services for Frederick as president of the MRLC. They charged him to approach Frederick and propose a log exchange. They must have been apprehensive at the cost.

However, even as the disaster was happening, Frederick had not been idle. He had already dispatched three steamboats and sixty men to begin to salvage the logs that had been scattered and to bring them down to the slough. He then called a meeting of all owners whose logs were involved in the catastrophe. (The exception in this invitation was the Chippewa Lumber and Boom Company officials, who, Frederick remarked in his understated way, "had kept aloof.")

Frederick had Marshall draw up a legal agreement in which all the logs that had washed into the Beef Slough would be credited to their owners and those owners upstream would be given fair value in trade with MRLC logs that were still upriver. In other words, everyone would be made whole in this agreement and at no cost.

The Wisconsin men were astonished, Marshall said later, "by the utter absence of the downriver parties of any disposition to selfishly use their position of advantage to drive a hard bargain." They resolved to administer the agreement in the same spirit of fairness in which it was made. When the season ended, the upriver firms, which had been in danger of ruin by this natural disaster, were in better shape than they had been before it happened.

Mathew Norton, a key member of the MRLC, wrote in his 1915 account of events,

> In the Spring of 1880 there was a great flood on the Chippewa River, taking out the Little Falls dam and scattering the logs of the Company from one end of the river to the other. The dam at the Dells just above Eau Claire also went out,

and the logs of the Eau Claire men, stored there in great quantities, went with the general mass as many as could be taken care of into Beef Slough and very many of them down to the mouth of the Mississippi. Of course this great flood, taking away the stock of the mill men on the Chippewa, put them in very bad condition; but an arrangement was made by them with the Mississippi River Logging Company to exchange logs so that their mills might have a supply of logs; and the [MRL] Company in addition purchased a very large amount of their logs, paying them in money so as to relieve them from the embarrassment which otherwise would have fallen upon them.

Later that year, on November 22–24, 1880, at the Grand Pacific Hotel in Chicago, nearly all the parties who had been feuding for more than a decade drew up an agreement for a new, common enterprise that eventually became known as the Chippewa Logging Company, later called the Chippewa Lumber and Boom Company, or CLBC. In this company, stock was taken out by eleven members of the MRLC group, including Weyerhaeuser and Denkmann, the Laird-Norton group, and the Mussers of Iowa. They were joined by six of the Chippewa Valley firms: Empire Lumber Company (O. H. Ingram's company), the Daniel Shaw Lumber Company, Northwestern Lumber Company, Valley Lumber Company, Eau Claire Lumber Company, and Badger State Lumber Company. Although these six Chippewa Valley firms did not represent the entire valley's lumber interests, they produced the great majority of the Eau Claire area lumber.

The organization of the MRLC and later the CLBC appeared to some to be on the order of "combinations," what we might now call corporations, or "trusts." It's true that both the MRLC and the CLBC had "stock" held by various individuals and partnerships. However, Frederick did not view these organizations where lumbermen worked together to get the logs down rivers as "trusts" since every mill independently set its own pricing for its market.

He gave an interview in Winona, Minnesota, later printed in the *Rock Island Argus* on September 29, 1888, to explain his views.

"Weyerhaeuser Talks"
"Declaring There Are No Lumber Trusts in Existence"
   The Great Lumberman Gives Some Interesting Explanations and Information—Rumors and Their Origin

   When Frederick Weyerhaeuser, of this city, was in attendance at the meeting of the Chippewa Lumber Company in Winona recently, he was queried a great deal in regard to the great lumber trust which he is alleged to have formed . . .

Mr. Weyerhaeuser talked freely and it may be well, right here, and in order to put an end to all the rumors that are afloat, to quote Mr. Weyerhaeuser's own words upon this alleged trust. In response to an inquiry about the report [of the trust's existence] he said:

"Certainly there is nothing new [in these reports] . . . so far as our operations go there is no trust in existence . . . I can best explain it to you, perhaps, by the use of a familiar illustration. Let us suppose that you, in Winona, own a cow, and that each of a dozen of your neighbors own one. Those cows have to be driven daily to and from the pasture. But instead of each owner hiring a boy to perform that task separately, for the sake of economy and convenience, you all combine to employ one boy, who can just as well tend a dozen cows as a single animal. Now that is precisely what, in principle, we of the associated logging operations do. For the sake of convenience and economy—and it is justifiable in every detail—we combine to act jointly getting our logs into the streams, floating them down to the booms, and otherwise handling them in transit, just what each firm was formerly wont to do on its own account at a much greater cost of time and money than is now found to be necessary.

"Look, for example at the Beef Slough Booms and the convenience that they provide. No one firm could make the investment necessary to their construction or operation. But a dozen or 15 or 20, uniting to do so, find the burden comparatively light, while each member of the organization derives about as much benefit as if he were the sole owner. It is an economy of effort and expenditure that inures directly to the advantage of the consumer, for, depend on it, if each manufacturer had to bear the expense of handling his own logs as they are now handled, he would be compelled to add the larger part of it to the price of his lumber.

"This is so plain that no business man, even with the most limited experience, can fail to see how it operates. But, mind you, when the logs whose cost is thus cheapened by associated efforts are delivered at the mills, all combination ceases and the rivalry between the various manufacturers begins. You see how it operates here in your own city of Winona.

"Your neighbors Messrs Youmans Bros. and Hodkins, the Laird Norton company, Mr. Horton of the Empire company and Messrs Hamilton and Hayes of the Winona Lumber Company work together up here, and wisely so, but once in their own mills they become active competitors with one another."

The results of this reconciliation were immediately apparent. As the historian Chuck Twining put it in *Downriver,* the story of the Orrin H. Ingram Lumber interests: "Whether officially members or not, all parties engaged in logging activities within the area soon came to realize that a conflict of interests was no longer possible on the Chippewa."

For this new consortium—the Chippewa Logging Company (later called the Chippewa Lumber and Boom Company or CLBC)—a new way of doing business was installed. All of the logs taken out of the Chippewa Valley would now go into a pool, and members would receive logs from the pool in proportion to the stock owned. Although all would work together, the MRLC members would retain a slight advantage as they owned a slight majority of stock.

The signal outcome of this fateful flood was that Frederick was clearly in command of the new merger. He received authorization from the group to arrange for any timber purchases on behalf of the organization with no requirement to consult other members in the process. It is no accident that many of his business associates not only accepted Frederick's leadership but sought it. In his quiet way he made decisions that others trusted would be to their benefit.

FREDERICK, FIRST AMONG EQUALS
WITH STRONG PERSONALITIES

Many books and biographies of these early lumbermen, Wisconsin and Mississippi River alike, have been written. Their often outsized personalities created sometimes prickly relationships, even after the generally cooperative outcome of the great flood was achieved. But many fast friendships were formed among these men as well.

One of Frederick's closest personal relationships was with Ed Rutledge of Eau Claire, Wisconsin. But there is ample evidence that another business partner, Mathew G. Norton of Winona, became a close and lifelong friend. Before he died in 1915, Norton wrote the definitive history of the Mississippi River Logging Company, beginning with its formation in 1870. In the work, he is strong in his praise of Frederick's talents as the catalyst for the MRLC and its many successes and Frederick's primary role in ending the Chippewa River conflicts. Letters between the two men survive in which business news and meeting notices vie for attention with the personal and family notes, increasingly interjected as the men aged.

One such letter, dated December 1892, was written after both Norton and his cousin and business partner William H. Laird had been to St. Paul and visited with Frederick in his home. (Sarah continued her open hospitality to Frederick's business partners and employees into her last years.) Upon returning to Winona, Mathew Norton wrote to Frederick thanking him for his concern for Norton's wife, who had taken ill during the visit. The tone of the letter is one of a correspondence between brothers. Mathew mingles the personal with business news: "Looks like the 'Whitney' option will bear fruit . . . Sauntry doing the best he can. There is a delay in prepping the estimates of the land."

Drawn together by common business interests, the men had formed a personal friendship that lasted all their lives.

The Laird and Norton family (several branches of a Scots immigrant family from Pennsylvania) had come to Winona in 1856, about the same time that Frederick had arrived in Rock Island and that railroad builder James J. Hill had moved to St. Paul from Canada. The connection with the Laird-Norton group that Frederick had begun in the formation of the MRLC was to run down several generations in both families and have an important impact in building the strength of the Weyerhaeuser Timber Company, later established on the West Coast.

However, not all the men were always friendly. Norton may have been a closely tuned associate, but other strong-minded lumbermen frequently tangled with Frederick. O. H. Ingram, an original competitor of Frederick's and a powerful force in Wisconsin lumber history, was one of them. He ultimately became Frederick's associate in the Wisconsin-Mississippi cooperative lumber efforts, but unlike the many who left warm private letters or public testimony to Frederick after his death, Ingram apparently carried little personal affection for his erstwhile opponent-turned-partner. Yet he acknowledged and acceded to Frederick's advancing leadership position during the period of merger between the formerly warring factions. He had to accept that it was Frederick who arranged the terms of the new organization, in which the old MRLC members would retain 60 percent control and the Chippewa Valley–Eau Claire interests would be limited to 40 percent.

Frederick was emerging in these years as a complex personality. Two stories, later related to F. E. by George Lindsay of the Lindsay and Phelps Company in Davenport Iowa, illustrate Frederick's human characteristics. Lindsay had spent considerable time with Frederick in the Wisconsin woods when he was a young man, and his memory of some interactions with Frederick was quite clear.

The first story concerned a show of strong temper, unusual for Frederick. Mr. Lindsay had arrived at the Wylie House in Fifield, Wisconsin, and made his way to an upstairs bedroom. He overheard Frederick grilling another man in the next room. The unfortunate victim was Mr. Hinz, an officer in the Fifield bank, of which Frederick was a prominent shareholder. Lindsay reports that Mr. Hinz had enriched himself by mishandling accounts, leaving small stockholders much the poorer and being clever enough to avoid criminal prosecution.

Lindsay, who reports of the hotel's "partitions being not of paper but almost," was an unwilling witness to the exchange. Frederick listened patiently until Hinz was done. Then Frederick began talking, "gradually working up to a louder and louder voice and finally a violence of temper that was so unlike and so beyond anything I had ever known in him, before or since, that it actually frightened me in fearing that he might overtax himself."

This episode stands in contrast to another of that period, also reported by Lindsay. The second scene also took place at the Wylie House, a short time after the first. Lindsay came back to find Frederick marking time while waiting for the eleven o'clock train to St. Paul. The lumbermen were talking of various things when two young boys entered the hotel. These boys were selling fire lighters and said they hoped to raise $2,300 to start a woodworking plant at Wausau, Wisconsin. Frederick became intrigued with their project. He told the boys to come back after they had sold what they could of their fire lighters around town. When they returned at ten o'clock, Frederick put his face quite close to theirs as he talked to them.

He then related to Lindsay that the boys were not drinking, although the only places open at that hour where the boys could be selling were the saloons. Frederick disappeared for some minutes. Lindsay finally went to look for him, for train time was approaching.

> At that time I was but twenty-five years old and he [Frederick] had reached the height of his career. As I entered the dining room he had evidently been writing and, rising slowly and walking toward me with bowed head, his eyes looking at something in his right hand, he raised his eyes and with a really shame-faced expression, he extended his hand so that I might see two tickets and two lower (not upper) berths for Wausau, Wisconsin and a check for $2,300. He, in a most humble voice, asked me, "George, do you think I am foolish?" This man whose judgment was sought and accepted by thousands, found himself sentimentally uncertain, fearful of his judgment, seeking reassurance from the only source at hand, a twenty-five year old boy.

Many years later Lindsay asked William Irvine if he knew what had become of the boys who had been the recipients of Frederick's generosity. Irvine made inquiries at the Wausau bank and discovered that "these two boys" at that time were each worth $150,000. Apparently, Frederick had not misjudged their abilities.

Perhaps Frederick was able to show trust because others showed it to him. It was this trust that the newly merged group had given to Frederick when it deputized him to make financial transactions in their name without consulting others. And it was this kind of unique authority bestowed by the Chippewa Logging Company, implying trust without reservation, that so irritated Chippewa lumberman O. H. Ingram.

Ingram was a strong personality and no doubt saw himself, also, as a natural leader. Born in Massachusetts, Ingram came into the Wisconsin lumber business through Canada in 1857, the same year Frederick and Sarah moved to

Frederick valued logs, not money. The following letter from Mr. William Carson of Burlington, Iowa, addressed to F. E. Weyerhaeuser and written on August 5, 1925, illustrated this fact, as well as described a lesson learned well by a young lumberman.

> When I was called to Eau Claire many years ago to operate the Valley mill at that place, the Valley mill was short of logs and was compelled to borrow nine million feet from the Chippewa Logging Company, or the so-called pool. After the Valley Company had borrowed the logs and before the time for settlement, logs [price] advanced $2 to $3.00 per thousand. Being young, anxious to accomplish everything possible in my new position as manager of the Valley Lumber Company, I telephoned to Chippewa Falls and made an engagement to see Mr. Weyerhaeuser.

> I told him I had come to settle for the logs borrowed for the Valley Lumber Company and that I had a check for the amount to deliver to him. He asked me at what price I had figured the logs, and I told him at the price prevailing at the time the logs were borrowed. Mr. Weyerhaeuser, when talking to one, looked very straight and steadily into one's eyes and when he appreciated the fact that this youngster proposed to make some $2.00 to $3.00 per thousand on nine million feet of logs from the Chippewa Logging Company, his eyes commenced to dance as they did when he was amused.

> He said: "Young man, what did the Chippewa Logging Company lend you?" I said: "Logs." and he said: "We want logs back, we do not want money. We have plenty of money."

> Even the young man immediately saw the point, put his check in his pocket and wrote him (F. W.) an order for nine million feet of logs on the Valley Lumber Company's credit in the pool.

> Mr. Weyerhaeuser apparently gave the young man credit for endeavoring to do the best he could for his company and he was very appreciative of the amusement he had enjoyed and after that he was always most cordial and kind in his reception of me.

Coal Valley. He formed a company with Donald Kennedy and Alexander Dole, later called Ingram and Kennedy Lumber. Eventually Ingram consolidated his holdings and partnerships into the Empire Lumber Company. He wrote his memoir in 1912, and in it he talks about how the MRLC won its fight to open the Chippewa River. F. E. later writes that in this work Ingram "singularly does not mention the generosity of the Mississippi group in freely sharing with the Chippewa River lumbermen the benefits derived from pooling most of the logs in the river."

Ingram was a leader among the Wisconsin lumbermen, and he served on the executive committee of the newly formed Chippewa Logging Company with W. J. Young of Iowa and Frederick Weyerhaeuser. Whether because of Frederick's experience, his force of personality, or his generally positive outcomes, the group usually heeded the young German's advice. But, while most of the associates willingly took Frederick's counsel, Ingram chafed under the strong Weyerhaeuser leadership style, as did a few others. In 1892, a decade after the Wisconsin timber wars' resolution, a man named Will Tearse wrote to Clarence Chamberlin, saying, with some irony, "I suppose after Fred told you what he was going to do about it, you all went quietly out of the door to take the train for home."

But Ingram himself was known by others for his own autocratic behavior. His biographer, Charles Twining, writes in *Downriver:* "It should be noted, however, that Weyerhaeuser was simply the strongest among a group of men in which strong personalities were hardly the exception. Ingram, for example, was accustomed to dominate most of those with whom he associated and this included many who must have resented his authority just as he resented Weyerhaeuser's. One-horse loggers would occasionally mutter angrily concerning their treatment at the hands of 'Rule or Ruin Ingram' and business partners would complain of O. H.'s autocratic tendencies. Clearly at times it must have been difficult to be a Christian businessman."

The friction between the two men could not have been too severe, for they appeared side by side in a picture taken a decade later on one of Frederick's trips to look at southern timber. Despite the outsized personalities involved, all managed to work together—in the spirit of fairness—for their mutual benefit for some years.

Frederick's rise to leadership seems all the more curious given that he was a reticent public speaker. In a letter to one of his grandsons, Fritz Jewett, Frederick acknowledged that he had been "ashamed" of his English all his life. He never lost his German accent and never cared for public speaking. Yet, his self-knowledge with its ironic edge understood that he had other leadership qualities. F. E. reports that Frederick once said of one of his partners, a man who was gifted in speechmaking at their business meetings, "I would give a thousand dollars to be able to make such speeches as _____ can; but" he added after a reflective pause, "somehow they usually do what I recommend anyway."

The events surrounding the flood of 1880 showed Frederick at his finest: his leadership abilities coupled with his innate sense of fair play solved a problem that could have plagued his operations and those of his confederates for another two decades. He became, in a sense, master of the situation that had been handed to him. He could have chosen another path after the flood, but he took the high road, and the MRLC and its Wisconsin competitors prospered because of it. The festering conflict among the lumbermen on the Chippewa was now put to rest. Or so it seemed.

The *Moline Review Dispatch,* August 22, 1890:

> Big Litigation
>
> Some that is in Prospect Against Frederick Weyerhaeuser, The Mississippi and other Logging Companies Resulting from the Flood in 1884. [Not to be confused with the flood of 1880, after which the Chippewa Logging Company was formed.]
>
> The great flood in the Eau Claire region in 1884 seems about to result in some big damage suits in which the plaintiffs will probably be the city of Eau Claire, the county of Chippewa and a large number of individuals whose claims will aggregate over $1,000,000 and the defendants will be Frederick Weyerhaeuser and other stockholders of The Mississippi River Logging Company, the Company itself, The Chippewa Logging Company, the Chippewa Log Driving and Improvement Company.
>
> At the time of the flood in question, the Little Falls Dam went out and a solid wall of water swept down the valley, the Chippewa rose to 28 feet above the low water mark at Eau Claire and over $1,000,000 of damage was done . . . By direction of Mr. Weyerhaeuser, an effort was made to hold back the waters until it was too late to avert disaster.

FREDERICK'S REACTION WHEN
HIS HONOR IS QUESTIONED

This history of Frederick's success in creating the merger of interest between the Wisconsin and Mississippi lumbermen makes all the more peculiar an episode that occurred within a few years of the Grand Pacific Hotel meeting. Around 1885, a couple of Frederick's colleagues became embroiled in a disagreement with him, and, when he would not succumb to their pressure, they insisted he was self-serving. He felt the charges were unfounded, but their actions had a severely negative effect on his state of mind. F. E. wrote about the situation in his *Record,* basing his account on Frederick's personal diaries, while historian Charles Twining took an alternative view of events in *Downriver,* his book on O. H. Ingram. Two different perspectives emerge from these accounts.

In *Downriver,* Twining alludes to events that had to do with the sale of some land while Frederick was chairman of the Chippewa Lumber and Boom Company (the CLBC; the Chippewa Logging Company had been renamed by this time). Frederick owned a great deal of Wisconsin timberland, most, if not all, of it with various partners. Any transaction he made relating to these lands had a potential conflict of interest as the men bought and sold timber and land among themselves. He could meet himself, in the form of his holdings, coming and going in this business.

At the time of Twining's story Frederick was both chairman of the newly formed CLBC and also owner of some land the CLBC wanted to purchase. Frederick's way of dealing with his dual role as a partner in the sale group and as chief of the buyer group was to assign William Irvine, mill manager for the CLBC, to handle the negotiations for him. Thus he took himself out of the negotiations to avoid a conflict of interest.

Twining criticizes Frederick's action because "Ingram and Irvine both knew that Weyerhaeuser could not remove himself. His interests were too wide spread, too large to be avoided, even if such avoidance were desired." Twining also writes, "Weyerhaeuser apparently gave considerable attention to the creation of an image of honesty and fairness." Twining does not say, however, what else Frederick ought to have done or could have done in the situation. Removing himself and turning negotiations over to Irvine was at least an attempt to put one layer between himself as owner of land and himself as chairman of the Chippewa Lumber and Boom Company, buyer of the land.

Item in the *Rock Island Argus*, July 16, 1888:

The Price of Lumber
Mr. Fred Weyerhaeuser Tells a Senate Committee What he Knows About Certain Things—Interesting Information

Last Friday evening Mr. Fred Weyerhaeuser of this city was before a Senate committee in Washington, D.C. where he passed through the ordeal of examination on Indian tradeships. The committee inquired with great minuteness into all details of lumber transactions between the Indians and the companies represented by Mr. Weyerhaeuser.

He testified, in effect, that he had purchased from the Flambeau and the Court de Oreiel [sic] about 100,000,000 feet of lumber during the past year, and about as much the year before . . . The companies never purchased directly from the Indians, but always through middlemen . . . There was, the witness explained, a waste of from ten to fifteen per cent in logs between the reservation and the mill, due largely to decay. The average transit required three years.

He also gave his testimony before the committee that the Indians received the value of their lands. These purchases caused the introduction of the new forestry bill—that is the bill regulating the sale of government lands, classifying and increasing the value of timber lands over agricultural. It provides that the timber lands of the United States must be sold in the same manner as the Canadian timber lands—at auction to the highest bidder."

The Lac Courte Oreilles Band of Ojibwe would see things differently in 2012:

> The federal government quickly provided a mechanism for the lumber interests to invade the Lac Courte Oreilles Reservation, which was considered the wealthiest site for virgin timber anywhere in the north. During the period of 1884–1888, the majority of virgin timber on the reservation was removed, and the tribe, through its individual allottees, had received 7–1000ths of one percent per board foot, which, according to historian James Clifton, "must have been one of the best timber bargains of the century." By 1890, nearly all of the prime timber had been cut, while the logging of the hardwood had been delayed until 1904.

This episode looks much more complex, however, in excerpts from Frederick's diaries, as quoted by his youngest son, F. E., in his *Record*. From his early days at the sawmill in Rock Island through the formation of the MRLC to the Grand Pacific Hotel meeting, Frederick's public career had followed an upward trajectory, his confidence appearing to grow with each new victory. Or at least that was the external picture.

But the private thoughts recorded in his journals portray a man trying for fairness as he makes good deals but a man also highly, perhaps overly, sensitive to any criticism of his ethics. The land in question was part of a parcel in northern Wisconsin that lay in the Chippewa watershed. Frederick owned one-third interest and the Laird-Norton enterprise owned two-thirds. After negotiations, presumably conducted by William Irvine, that parcel of land was sold to the Chippewa Lumber and Boom Company at the January 14, 1885, meeting.

The minutes record that Mr. W. J. Young of Iowa seconded the ratification of this sale. Immediately after that vote Young urged Frederick (as chair of the Chippewa Lumber and Boom Company and on behalf of that company) to authorize the purchase of another set of land parcels that Young himself owned. These parcels were units of land that extended from Shell Lake, Wisconsin, all the way into Michigan. Frederick was not interested in recommending that the CLBC buy these land bits because they were not a cohesive package; they were too scattered to be valuable.

After this meeting, Mr. Young, who was known to be "a man of violent temper," wrote a letter to Frederick accusing him of urging the purchase of his own lands but denying Young the opportunity to sell his. E. S. Youmans, perhaps at

Young's instigation, subsequently demanded an audit of the books of the CLBC and the MRLC and the land transactions of both companies involving their members. It was unusual in those days to audit books of these consortia, and Frederick seemed to feel this was done in part to embarrass him as chair, a vote of "no-confidence" in its way.

Frederick left a series of entries in his notebooks evidencing tremendous anxiety around and preoccupation with these accusations. His notes suggest that he felt he had done much work for the companies (MRLC and CLBC) for nothing, when others had been paid well. One such entry series reads as follows:

> 1) Get the land back. 2) History of land trades. 3) Talk to MRL Company. 4) Beef Slough Company. 5) Same salary as Schricker [the former president of MRLC; under this note appears the word *resign*]. 6) Read letter—not give name. [This may refer to Young's accusatory letter to him.]

A subsequent entry reveals real suffering of mind and spirit: "Leave you hope God may bless you all, may you prosper and NEVER FEEL AS I HAVE FELT FOR THE LAST FIVE WEEKS."

The Chippewa Lumber and Boom Company board of directors meeting in December 1885 was full of drama. Purchase of the Weyerhaeuser-Laird-Norton lands by the CLBC was re-ratified. Frederick resigned as chair, but his resignation was not accepted. Ingram and Young both resigned from the executive committee, but their resignations were also rejected. It appears that all the men kept their offices and the group went forward much as before, with Frederick as chair.

As in the case with Ingram, the animosity between Frederick and Young could not have been longstanding, as many years later Frederick invited Young and his family to accompany him on a trip to Alaska. As F. E. notes in the close of this section in the *Record,* "Father never harbored ill will toward anyone. He used to say "If you forgive, you must also forget.""

"Some Unhappy Incidents," as the heading for this story appears in F. E.'s *Record,* reveals much about Frederick personally: that he valued his good name above all; that he was as human as anyone else who has put in hard work and wants to be appreciated; that he was not afraid of a good fight but also that he was extremely sensitive to any challenge to his honor.

It was not only, as Twining opined, that Frederick was concerned about the *appearance* of fairness. He seemed too deeply troubled by an accusation that he actually acted unfairly, especially as he had tried to remove himself directly from the negotiations over this land. Many letters written upon Frederick's death, and to F. E. years later from men who knew his father, testify to Frederick's actual fairness. But what was little known was that the charge of unfairness was privately devastating to him.

As the Wisconsin chapter in Frederick's life wound down, he would recover and seek new challenges elsewhere. But the sadness in the midst of his many leadership victories here cannot be denied. In these years he began to turn to travels and to family in a way he had not done for the previous twenty-five. Perhaps he had begun to see that public leadership and the conflicts it engenders carry their own price.

CHAPTER 10

Meanwhile, Sarah Keeps the Home Fires Burning

F REDERICK FACED BIGGER TROUBLE than unreliable river flow and hostile Wisconsin mill owners in 1869, just before forming the MRLC. He and Sarah had enjoyed more than a decade of happy family life in Coal Valley as Frederick was building his business, but a dramatic event suddenly uprooted the family from their idyllic home.

A HASTY MOVE TO ROCK ISLAND

In later years Frederick's son John recalled the June day that his father arrived home early in the afternoon to announce that a mysterious illness was spreading through the town and many children were rapidly falling sick. An epidemic of scarlet fever had invaded the valley. Sarah agreed they must leave, and they began preparations immediately. John remembered how Frederick gathered the children quickly and they all scrambled to pack their belongings in boxes. Within hours the family was boarding a railcar on their way to Rock Island. Frederick's fear of the contagious disease was well founded: his younger sister Eliza and her husband, Hugh Caughey, would lose two children to the epidemic. Their graves are in the Chippiannock cemetery in Rock Island.

The family was able to make this move quickly because Frederick already owned a small house in Rock Island. He had initially purchased a lot and had expected to build a house on it, but the failed woolen mill venture took so much money that the project was put on hold. Eventually he traded the lot for a small house on Third Avenue, which he then rented out. He had expected to continue living in Coal Valley, but the epidemic changed his plans. By paying his renters a bonus to move immediately, he secured the Third Avenue house for his family on short notice.

Frederick's original idea had been to stay in Rock Island only through the summer heat and then return to the house in Coal Valley in the autumn of 1869, in time for the apple harvest. When Frederick asked his brother-in-law Hugh Caughey to manage the lumberyard in Coal Valley, it was only seen as a summer assignment. The Caugheys followed the Weyerhaeusers to Rock Island in 1870.

Frederick's mother, Margaretha, was too fragile to travel, so she remained behind in Coal Valley with Eliza when Frederick and Sarah moved to Rock Island. She died the following year, the same year Frederick formed the Mississippi River Logging Company. She did not live to see his worldly success.

The Family Settles on the Hill in Rock Island

Sarah and the children lived in the Third Avenue house for six months. They made do, but they did not like it nearly as well as the extensive property and orchards in Coal Valley. Their new dwelling was in the middle of a crowded street with other houses close by, and the restrictions were hard on the children, who were used to land for running and playing. Fortunately, this living situation did not last long. By autumn Sarah and Frederick decided that the family would remain in Rock Island permanently. At that point Frederick bought a house located at 3052 Lee Street, later called Tenth Avenue, that is known to this day as the "House on the Hill." (Both the family and Augustana College, the recipient of the property in later years, use this name.) Demonstrating his developing negotiating skills, Frederick acquired this larger house and surrounding property in a good deal: he traded the small house on Third Avenue plus an additional seven thousand dollars for the larger property and promptly moved his family there.

The family, which now numbered six children (Freddie was not yet born), was moving into the home they would occupy for the next two decades. Here, the young people would undergo transformation from high-spirited children into adulthood. The eldest, John, was only eleven years old at the time of the move, Elise, nine, Margaret, seven, Apollonia, five, Charles, three, and Rudi but a baby. The growing family was ready for the expanded space.

The larger Rock Island house, surrounded by land, space, and trees, was an ideal place to grow up. The boys had orchards to play in, chores like caring for the many animals and picking apples, and most of all, room for their high jinks, many of which are recorded in young Freddie's adult recollections. The girls were occupied with household tasks and their schoolwork, but they, too, found plenty of time for play outdoors.

The entire property comprised twenty acres of land, including a fruit farm. There were three acres of grapes and many hardwood trees, including sugar maples, oaks, and elms. Shelter and land for horses, cows, chickens, and pigs abounded. On this working farm, hogs were slaughtered once a year. Vegetables were grown in the gardens, and all the young people were expected to do their share of the work. The house was a large, two-story brick affair, with a decorative cupola on top that survives to this day.

Living conditions were still primitive in 1869. Water was not supplied to the "hill" by the city, so a hand pump was installed in the basement to fill the home's water tank, which resided inside the cupola. F. E. later described it as a "rather terrifying force pump" because of the racket it made when operated. He noted that when the water levels dropped, any of the sons who happened to be around was pressed into service to operate the pump so the family would have running water. He dryly adds, "One would hesitate to become responsible for the excessive exaggeration which would immediately develop if any one of the boys were to testify on the amount of time he had handled the operation of this pump."

There were plenty of sleeping rooms, but they were chilly at night; only the front living room was heated, with a large, coal-burning stove. Like other houses of the period, there were open registers in the ceiling so the heat would rise to warm the bedrooms as well. In the evening, as the children were growing up, the entire family would gather in the well-heated front room after dinner because it was the best refuge from the fierce cold of the snowy Illinois winters.

Later, as the children grew older and began their serious schooling, two long desks ran the length of this room. Frederick used one (his letterhead contained the address of this house through the eighties as "The Office of Frederick Weyerhaeuser") and the younger boys—Charlie, Rudi, Freddie, and their cousin Albert Caughey, who lived with them while a student—frequently used the other for their schoolwork.

The surviving marvel of the place is the dining room. In 1888 the room was enlarged and rebuilt, festooned with astonishing carved cherrywood throughout. Over the fireplace a near-perfect La Farge stained-glass window still adds light and grace to the heavier, adorned walls. The woodworking is a masterpiece of fine, artisan carving. In one small section of the room alone, the section under the arch, someone has counted 2,450 leaves, 75 large flowers, and 54 small flowers. The elegance and density of this project reminds one that the Victorian Age reached as far west as Rock Island, Illinois. It is certain that Sarah had a hand in the final design, as she was not a person to yield such important work in her household to others.

The commission of the elaborate woodworking in the dining room appears to run contrary to the couple's usual conservatism. However, there is an explanation. Sales at a company Weyerhaeuser and Denkmann owned, the Rock Island Sash and Door Works (later known as the Rock Island Millwork

Company), had fallen dramatically one year, leaving some expert wood-carvers with little to do. Frederick employed them to carve an amazing number of leaves and flowers into the cherrywood walls of the dining room rather than laying them off.

Shortly after the elaborate carving task was completed, Elise, Margaret, and Charles made a trip to Europe and brought home a cuckoo clock as a gift for their father. Frederick, who was not above making fun of himself, insisted he would teach the bird to say, "Here comes the fool who built this room."

SARAH OVERSEES A LIVELY FAMILY

F. E. may have described his mother's house like an accordion, but a more apt metaphor would be a merry-go-round with Sarah at the controls in the center. Sarah organized the family chores, plucked the chickens, and oversaw the gardens and canning. The house and its surrounding lands lent themselves to her cheerful and firm direction. The space allowed the lifestyle of a small farm, and the work required in keeping up that operation was enormously influential in the lives of the children.

All were expected to work, taking care of the small animals, helping with garden and orchard upkeep, and working the previously mentioned water pump. Apple paring was a seasonal requirement in autumn, and everyone pitched in so that Sarah and Eliza could make their famous apple butter. This cheery product saw the family through the long winters. The treat was made in a huge copper pot that young Fred remembered vividly in later years.

One year there was a near disaster: one of Charlie's horses broke through the fence and ate many of the already pared apples. (Charlie's name figures in many of the more colorful episodes that took place as the children were growing up.) The good news was that apples were still available on the trees, so apart from the fact that the children had to pare a new batch of apples, not much was lost.

The neighbors were welcome to take apples and grapes, and the young, growing Weyerhaeuser boys and their friends and cousins were allowed to sell all the grapes they could pick. Other than that, the food grown was for the family or those to whom they gave their produce.

On one occasion when Frederick and Sarah were gone from the house, the man in charge of the little farm decided to make wine, and when Sarah returned she found several barrels of fermenting grapes in her cellar. One family story teases Rudi by saying he became quite tipsy in the sampling of it.

It was not, however, forbidden to have wine in the house. When company came, homemade wine was frequently served as a special treat. Frederick was not above joking about such things. One time he was meeting with one of his longtime associates, W. J. Young from Clinton, Iowa. Mr. Young was a teetotaler and would not enter a bar, so the two men went to a soda shop. The soda fountain man took one look at Mr. Young, who must have appeared tired that day, and immediately offered to serve him a whiskey. Frederick thought this turn of events was hilarious.

During this time, the family sometimes accompanied Frederick on steamboat trips when he had business upriver. One such occasion gave rise to another family story involving spirits. Sarah and the children went along with Frederick to Wabasha, Minnesota, a town on the Mississippi north of Winona. Frederick was to meet some elected politicians whose help he sought in the Wisconsin river traffic situation, and the meeting was to take place in a saloon. The children found a soda pop stand where Rudi was reported to have overindulged in the sweet drink. That evening the young people chided their father for drinking beer in a saloon, whereupon Frederick "promptly agreed not to drink beer in a saloon so long as the boys drank no pop in the future."

STRONG SARAH, WIFE AND MOTHER

Sarah was enormously energetic, generous, and even-tempered in the midst of great activity. But as Frederick was increasingly occupied with the Wisconsin timber business, she was alone much of the time. Fortunately, in addition to the children, she also had women friends in the town. They would share the traditional morning "kaffee klatsch," a great excuse for women to gather informally during the day, practiced in neighborhoods around the country. Many of the Rock Island women were of German heritage, and their company gave Sarah a chance to revert to her native language in conversation. When Frederick was away he did his best to stay in touch with his wife. The letters he wrote to Sarah from Wisconsin in this period, in the German language of their childhood, were extremely affectionate and newsy. Hers, in return, often gave him details of life in Rock Island.

The following letters between Frederick and Sarah were written in German during this period. They were translated from old to new German by Katharine Annaheim and from German to English by Barbara Berghofer, both residents of Niedersaulheim.

April 26, 1874
My dear husband:
I received your two letters on Wednesday the 22nd and I thank you with all my heart for your congratulations and good [birthday] wishes that you sent me. It would have made me glad if you had been at home.

Several of our good friends were here in spite of the rain which we had all morning, and all had a nice present for me. Lizzie, Maggie and Loni all had their picture taken as a present. I had it framed right away.

Mrs. Wadsworth sent a fine scarf up on the 20th. I thought it was a mistake, but they said it was alright. Therefore, I think it was you who ordered it. Thank you very much again. You couldn't have made me happier than with such a beautiful scarf. I won't wear it before you get home . . . We are all happy and well and wish the same for you.

Your loving E. S. Weyerhaeuser

April 29, 1874
Dear Friedrich:

I have just received your letter of the 27th. I'm sorry to have aggrieved you because of not writing earlier. Maggie Reimers was ill last week, so that she had to stay in bed, this is not enough as an excuse for not writing and if I could write as well as you, I would write more often. I and Mrs. Denkmann were in Davenport and at Mr. Staby's in order to buy some flowers. Staby has a nice choice of flowers and how beautiful he decorates everything. The two sawmills are doing well . . .

Mrs. Denkmann says they are building a German bank in Rock Island and that they want to have the corner part . . . Sarter works in the garden and helps Andrew [nephew Andrew Bloedel, who lived with the Weyerhaeuser family].

I want to close and hope that you won't stop writing even if I don't write so often. I and the children send our best regards from all our hearts and hope that you will come home soon. Otherwise the cakes that I got as presents for my birthday will get dry. I will keep them. Please forgive my bad writing. Once again my best regards and I will always remain,

Your loving, Sarah E. Weyerhaeuser

May 17, 1874
Beloved Sarah,

I received your letter of the 14th of this month on Saturday, the 16th. I'm very sorry to see from your letter that you are worried because of me and I think I'm well and thanks to God I am healthy and well and am feeling quite good. I'm only longing for you and the children so that I am glad to be able to think that I can figure out the week, if not the day, that I am planning to be with you, the 27th of this month so that is in one week . . .

You should have got a letter from me last week, at least I wrote it to you. On Saturday I didn't have time, as I traveled for 52 miles on very bad roads and had to work for several days . . .

I thank you for wishing me luck for the drive. Mostly, thanks to God, it went quite well and so far we had had continuous dry weather, almost no rain, but when you read this almost all our sawmills up to four miles from here will prosper . . .

I'm closing now with regards to you, the children, the Reimers, brother-in-law Leifer, my friend Andreas as well as all our friends.

With all my heart, your loving, Friederich Weyerhaeuser

(Letters from the family archives, St. Paul, MN, translated in 2010.)

Elise recalled childhood memories of her mother in this diary entry written shortly after Sarah's death:

I have said very little about Mother's character. She was just as strong as Father, though in a different way. She was quiet, reserved, dignified; and all who came in contact with her felt her strong personality. She was devotion itself to her husband and children. We sometimes forget the many lonely winters when Father was in the woods, and the burden of running a family of seven children was upon her shoulders. She was energetic and capable; and when prosperity came, she did not lose her head. She had extraordinary common-sense; but she was a true German wife in her subordination to her husband's wishes. She was so sincere, so honest and true, that I have heard father say of her, "Mother cannot tell a lie or deceive."

Elise also told of Sarah's support when Frederick read the Bible to the entire family after supper in the evening: "He used to get less tired than the members of his family, who would slip out, one by one; but not so mother, she remained faithful to the end."

Frederick's absences increased in length in the 1860s as he was working industriously in the Wisconsin logging camps or organizing the Mississippi River Logging Company. One winter he covered fifteen hundred miles by sleigh in the Wisconsin forests. At this time a wen grew on Frederick's nose. This small growth considerably altered his appearance, and not for the better. When Frederick returned after a particularly severe winter in the snow and ice, the wen had disappeared, frozen off in the forest frost. Sarah was pleased to see his original countenance restored, although she was concerned at this evidence of the rigors of a North Woods winter.

Frederick's wife had a mind of her own. Sarah also appears fearless in many surviving anecdotes, often braving the unknown. In the spring of 1875, she made her way north to meet Frederick in Chippewa Falls, his Wisconsin winter headquarters, taking a boat up the Mississippi to do so. She traveled to see Frederick and so that he would not have to leave the "drive," the spring rite of getting the logs downriver out of the forests. John was then seventeen years old (close to the same age as Frederick when he came to the United States). He was already working for his father, but he remained protective of his mother. He wrote Frederick that he did not like the idea of his mother traveling upriver alone. She, however, had insisted to her son that Frederick would not have asked her to come "if it was not right."

On September 12, 1888, the *Rock Island Argus* carried the following article describing Frederick Weyerhaeuser:

> Do you want a pen picture of Fred Weyerhaeuser, honored citizen at home and a lumber king or citizen of the Mississippi Valley? You do? Well, imagine a man about five feet, ten inches, broad shouldered and somewhat portly in bodily presence. Clothed in a neat fitting suit of gray, with trimmed hair and beard—a clean man from boots upward, a remarkable man from his roof downward. A figure with a well formed head and broad expanse of brow, eyes deep set and twinkling with intelligence and good nature . . . A man whom you would say ties closely to the sweet felicities of home life, who makes home a citadel and a sanctuary, who loves his family and above and beyond all else would promote their happiness.

A strong, calm personality is evident in many stories that family members later recalled and recorded of Sarah. One not to be forgotten is that of Frederick and Sarah fishing on a lake in Wisconsin. With them were Frederick's associate and friend Mathew G. Norton of Winona and his wife. During the entire day's fishing expedition no one had caught a single fish—that is, until Sarah felt a tug on her line. Her opponent turned out to be a large muskellunge—and a great fighter. Sarah was equal to the task of reeling in the fish, but Frederick became so agitated at her struggle that he nearly fell out of the boat. Without relinquishing her advantage, Sarah, who was winning over the fish, calmly advised Frederick not to get so excited.

One of the most endearing stories about Sarah and her children was recounted later by her youngest son. In 1877 Frederick gave the children a black pony named Pat. He always insisted it was an Arabian pony. Sarah, reluctant at first, eventually warmed to the idea of driving Pat while he was harnessed to her little phaeton, which had a single seat. Her son Fred remembers her as somewhat stout in those days, and the phaeton and pony were quite small, but he said no one dared tease her about her appearance when driving as she was quite sensitive.

One night her son John, riding a lively pony himself, attempted to pass her to get to the gate of the family farm first. Sarah entered into the spirit of the challenge and urged her pony on. Pat's Arabian blood was stirred. The children, who were watching the race, realized with horror that one of the gates was fastened and that the little phaeton might not fit through the narrow remaining space. But Sarah, seeing the problem, managed to drive her pony and phaeton through the one open gate. The boys measured the distance and discovered not two inches to spare. John pronounced his mother a very clever driver. Sarah's skilled performance was the hit of the day.

While Sarah remained occupied with raising the children and meeting with her friends and relatives for "kaffee" in Rock Island, Frederick was also forming friendships. But whereas hers were centered in her home and domestic relations, his were with some of his many business associates.

The letters and private papers that survive from this period, and F. E.'s many memories later recorded, show that the family was prospering despite Frederick's absence and that there was genuine love between Frederick and his wife. As the children grew, relationships changed. But the house on the hill would remain, in the family's lore and history, a wonderful and nurturing place for the children of this immigrant family.

CHAPTER 11

The Children Grow Up in the "House on the Hill"

URING THE TWO DECADES THAT FREDERICK was off dealing with the Chippewa River mill owners, riding sleighs through snow-laden forests, and shepherding his logs downriver, the years were passing in Rock Island. The family prospered under Sarah, and the children grew into adults, with many adventures along the way.

THE YOUNG WEYERHAEUSERS GET AN EDUCATION AND FIND WORK TO DO

John Phillip appeared the sensitive one, attuned to his mother's loneliness during his father's long absences in the Wisconsin forests and attentive to his grandmother. He took care of the animals and, as the eldest, was given responsibility over the others. A series of letters to his father and mother in the course of the litigation between the Mississippi River Logging Company and the Chippewa River mill owners attests to his growing interest in his father's business.

John seemed attached to both Sarah and Frederick from a young age. In 1877, when his parents planned a Thanksgiving trip to the "Valley," John wrote that he would like to go with them. He showed his affectionate nature when he wrote to his youngest brother in 1877 on the occasion of Freddie's fifth birthday: "I congratulate you very much, my little Fred. I hope you may live to be a hundred years old. How is the little pony? Do you ride much?" When Frederick had to miss the birthday celebration for Sarah in April 1876, being still on the Chippewa River for "the drive," John wrote him an encouraging letter about the affair: "She [Sarah] was more pleased with your kind letter of congratulations than with all the valuable presents presented to her by her many friends."

When he was nineteen, John left home to attend Jennings Academy—a business college located in Aurora, Illinois. He remained in school there only one year. Then he began to work in his father's business. His letters to his parents show that he was excited by the prospects that lay ahead.

For his first assignment, John went to stay with his aunt and uncle Denkmann and work in the family business in Rock Island. He slept upstairs in a room over the office and took his meals with "his warm admirer," Aunt Denkmann—Anna Catherine Bloedel, Sarah's sister.

The Denkmanns' son-in-law, John Hauberg, later wrote of John that he was a "likeable youth" but, at this point in his life, still too young and immature for the serious demands of an executive position. However, Frederick was impatient and "could not wait for John's maturing." When Frederick came to visit, Anna Catherine frequently castigated her brother-in-law for what she considered his stern treatment of his eldest son—despite the fact that at this point John was a young adult and had been working industriously in his father's business for several years.

While John may have been the sensitive child who attempted to play liaison between the parents, Elise, who signed her letters to her father affectionately as "Lizzie," was enormously practical and put this talent to use as an advisor to her parents on her siblings' education. Initially the Weyerhaeuser children attended the local German Lutheran school. However, the Rock Island German grammar school was less than satisfactory academically, except in the areas of Bible study and the catechism, which were emphasized. Equally unsatisfactory was the school's leadership, Headmaster Herr Selle, who was often seen imbibing a bit too freely from the keg of German beer at the school picnics.

Elise saw these problems and persuaded her parents that the younger children should transfer to the Rock Island public schools, which were far superior to the parochial schools in academics. It was at this time, also, that the children began attending the Presbyterian Sunday school rather than following the Lutheran tradition. Elise set the standard for the family and broadened the children's development socially and academically. As she grew older, her mother and father increasingly paid attention to her quiet counsel.

Elise had a good friend in Rock Island, Martha Cook, who attended Wellesley College outside of Boston. Although sending young women to eastern schools was not common in the Midwest at this time, Elise persuaded her parents to allow her to enroll at Wellesley in 1878. After graduating in 1882, she worked in settlement houses in New York City. There she met her future husband, William Bancroft Hill, who was engaged in the same kind of work. Later Elise returned to Wellesley to earn a master's degree in German history and literature.

When Elise came home to Rock Island, she wanted to find a way to continue the work of helping others that she had done in New York City. Her hometown efforts did not always bear fruit, however. One such experience provided her with a valuable lesson in human nature.

Elise had finally focused her helpful energies on an Irish woman, Mrs. Murphy, who appeared in need of assistance. Elise persuaded Sarah to engage the woman in housekeeping, and she also set Mrs. Murphy's son to cutting trees on the edge of the property. (This latter activity dismayed Frederick when he came home to find some of his best trees had been put to the ax. Fortunately, F. E. later recounts, the boy was not energetic enough to have done much damage.)

Letter from John Weyerhaeuser to his father, as written, January 29, 1871, when he was thirteen years of age, a testament to the inadequacy of the Lutheran grammar school education:

> Dear father I sat myself down to write you a few lines to let you know that we are all well and we hope you are the same. This morning it is very cold and we all staid from school, it is 21 below zero. The shottind society hat a maskarade and Fred Denkmann and I went to see it. We did not now it till after we were at school, and so send and mother did not no of it and we did not go to comfermand stoond and the preacher gave us a good scholding . . . There was an acidend hapiend at Coal Valley in behind town by the swich . . .

Letter from John Weyerhaeuser to his father, May 5, 1875, in which John has matured and his spelling very much improved:

> I was very anxious to hear from you and to know how the drive was getting along . . . By the time you receive this letter Mother will be at Chippewa Falls. She is coming on the boat. I did not like the idea of her going alone, but she said if it was not right you would not have asked her to come.

Elise then looked around the little town of Rock Island for others in need and found that another Irish woman, the elderly Mrs. O'Flaherty, was ill and her house was in a sad state. She tried to hire Mrs. Murphy to help clean the little house, but Mrs. Murphy drew the line at this. "What, do you think the loikes of me is so low as to wurrk for the shanty Irish?" she is reported to have informed Elise in her Irish brogue. Elise was taken aback by this response, and her surprised expression was "quite as humorous as the incident," her youngest brother later recalled.

The year 1882 marked Sarah and Frederick's silver anniversary. Elise was the only daughter able to attend the festivities in Rock Island, as Apollonia and

Margaret were away at college. Freddie, still a child at the time, remembered not only that "there was a large amount of silver surrounded by a patriarchal looking group of bankers whose gift it was" but also that "it was an exceedingly happy day for father and mother, many of their friends coming to join with them in their celebration of the event."

After Elise, Margaret was next in age, and her childhood nickname of "Maggie" fit her well, for she was always informal and expressive. Margaret had a particular affection for her father, and he for her. Many years later, her father wrote the following to her on letterhead from "The Grand Hotel in Bruxelles": "Margaret, you have always been more than a kind, loving and dutiful daughter to us. And your good mother and I shall always remember it."

Margaret first attended the Grant School in Chicago, then followed Elise to Wellesley. She was a student there from 1881 to 1885. Poor eyesight prevented Margaret from completing all her course work, but she is listed as an "adopted" member of the Wellesley class of 1886 in their fifty-year reunion booklet. Each member of that class was asked to contribute a poem or piece of writing. Here is Margaret's, with all of her fun and quickness evident:

> You asked for something original
> But how shall I begin?
> As there is nothing original in me
> Except original sin!

The youngest sister, Apollonia, was frail and later struggled with health problems that caused her to leave Wellesley for a period of time and attend the Grant School, closer to home. "Lonie," as she was called by her family, became Frederick's faithful correspondent in her childhood years. It was Apollonia and her husband, Sam Davis, who eventually moved into the house on the hill after Frederick and Sarah relocated to St. Paul. The Davis couple invited the entire family back for the festive fiftieth anniversary celebration of their parents' marriage in 1907.

Charles, next in age and called Charlie when young, was a fine athlete, although his younger brother, F. E., muses in later years that Charles's "interest in athletics and perhaps his successes [at Phillips Academy Andover] also interfered with his scholastic work." Charlie was a first-rate baseball player. That reputation helped assign him credit for the broken window in a vacant house on the north side of Tenth Avenue, although F. E. implies that the true blame belonged to Rudi. Charles was exceedingly handsome in his younger years. While at Andover, a description of Charles in the football lineup picture called him "a man with an iron jaw."

After Andover, Charles attended Augustana College in Rock Island. He later had the same arrangement as John, working for his uncle Denkmann as an assistant bill clerk and sleeping over the office. He was reported to be very unhappy when he discovered that his father had been paying his salary through Denkmann: Charles wanted to prove himself on his own. Eventually he had a chance to do just that when he was put in charge of the Pine Tree Lumber Company in Little Falls, Minnesota.

Rudolph, whom the family called Rudi, appears to have been one of the more experimental of the children, having many youthful adventures: drinking so much sweet soda when the family was visiting Wabasha that he became ill; testing the wine in the family cellar when his parents were away; and, quite possibly, being the true culprit of the stone-throwing incident involving the vacant house. Rudi, like Charlie, attended Phillips Academy Andover, but he went on to Yale and graduated in 1891. He, too, worked for his father's enterprises, taking charge of the Cloquet, Minnesota, operation after college.

F. E., or Freddie, as he was known when he was a boy, came last and was born after the family had made its dramatic move to Rock Island. In later years, he was the collector of many letters and anecdotes about the growing family in his *Record of the Life and Business Activities of Frederick Weyerhaeuser*.

Freddie was, perhaps, the child most closely attuned emotionally to his mother. F. E. recounts a revelatory memory of an incident in his childhood. One spring day Frederick returned to the family home after a long winter away in the northern forests. The young boy spied his father coming around the corner of the house. He recalls that his first impulse was not to run to greet his father, feeling slightly hostile on behalf of his mother, who had been alone with the children for many months. While Sarah may have understood the need for Frederick's long absences, the child only knew his feelings of the moment.

FREDERICK AND HIS CHILDREN

Frederick had a fine sense of irony and humor in dealing with his children. His many notes sent home while he was away in the North Woods were written in an affectionate tone, often gently teasing them. Early letters between him and Margaret are especially touching. One letter to ten-year-old Maggie addresses her solemnly regarding her correspondence with him—or rather, the lack of it.

April 26, 1874 Chippewa Falls, Wisconsin
My dear Maggie:
I know a man not a thousand miles from this place who has a wife, three girls and four boys somewhere down in Illinois in a town called Rock Island. The

mother, the three girls and one of the boys can write very well, and one of the
boys, his name is Charlie, can print first rate, so the man goes to the postoffice
[*sic*] every day and looks for letters and when he comes back he always says,
"Wieder nichts, wieder nichts," which means no letter from home. Are you not
sorry for the man? He likes his wife and children very much and writes them
often. Do you think they like him and do as good children should do?

Now, if you were one of those little girls you would write to your father sometime and I hope you will for I expect a letter from you soon.

This Sunday is a fine, warm day, the first we have had this spring. The water
in the Chippewa River is rising slowly. The prospects for a log drive are better
than they were a few days ago. I will be glad to see the new logs go to Beef
Slough soon and send some to your Uncle Denkmann at Rock Island.

I am well and hoping yourself, your mother and all of you are well and happy,
Your Father, F. Weyerhaeuser

P.S. I will write to Lonie next. She will be glad to get a letter from me and she
will answer it, too.

In another letter written from Chippewa Falls some years later, April 10,
1885, Frederick asks thirteen-year-old Fred a question about a Greek myth he
had earlier shared with his son.

My dear son Freddie:

I hope you and your good mother arrived home safely with the little boys
after having had a good and pleasant time in the big city of the West [Chicago].
I met Mr. Peter Musser in Hudson, Wisconsin according to agreement and
have reached here the day before yesterday in the evening, but have been very
busy ever since. This morning I went up to Paint Creek to see what shape the
logs are in which the big flood last fall put on the banks. Please tell John to get
ready to start up the sawmills for we soon will open up Beef Slough. The ice is
about ready to go out on the Chippewa River.

Enclosed I send you the man's [Diogenes] name, the one who used zu leben
in dem Fass [literal translation: "You live in a barrel"; metaphorically, to live a
simple life]. You will remember I asked you about him last Sunday. I send you
man, Fass and dog. With much love, Father.

(A footnote in F. E.'s account, which quotes this letter, indicates that Diogenes
of Greek myth fame is supposed to have lived in a "tub" and gone about with a
lantern looking for a "man." His dog was always with him.)

Years later William Irvine, secretary to the Chippewa River Logging Company,
witnessed a family exchange at the breakfast table on the subject of another

dog. It began with Sarah complaining to Frederick that something must be done about Charlie's dog, which had become quite wild.

> SARAH: "He is getting so cross. Yesterday he nearly tore the clothes off the delivery boy and it is getting so people are afraid to come to the house."
> FREDERICK: "Charlie, get rid of that dog. Have that dog killed."
> CHARLIE: "Yes, Father." [A moment passed]
> CHARLIE: "You know that preacher who is building that church downtown, he wants to see you. He says you are away so much he can't find you at the office and he is afraid to come to the house on account of the dog."
> FREDERICK [without missing a beat]: "Charlie, keep that dog!"

THE YOUNG WEYERHAEUSERS, GROWN UP, TRAVEL ABROAD

In May 1888, all grown up, Charles, Elise, and Maggie made a voyage to Europe. (This trip provided the opportunity to buy the cuckoo clock for Frederick.) They wrote chatty letters, full of news of their travels. Charlie, in particular, wrote many descriptions of the beauty he saw interlaced with commentary on the current political situation. He even included a teasing reference about dogs to his father—perhaps referring to the unruly dog of his childhood. An irate Maggie wrote on October 14, 1888, of her experiences: "Lizzie and I bought some grapes of an Italian woman and we got so mad because she cheated us out of 20 centimes or about 5 cents. It wasn't the money. What provoked me so is the idea of being cheated . . . We received John's letter in Lucerne. He is splendid to write me so often."

The many letters home are a testament to family relationships as well as a record of foreign adventures for the younger generation. The following letter written on September 2, 1888, by Charlie from Munich to young Fred at Phillips Academy Andover was full of affectionate, brotherly counsel:

> Dear Brother Fred:
> Since you are now man enough to go off to school alone, I will have to quit calling you 'Freddie' as I always have in writing to you.
> Freddie, I know that it will be useless for me to give you any advice about how to act and what you should or should not do, as I know you are as much of a man as I am but still I will say a few things . . .
> Don't think you know something and . . . not study. You remember how I got left just that way in German. I never felt so ashamed of anything in my life before. So, my dear boy, study every lesson as if you had never seen it before . . . so we will all try to be "men among men" as Father says.

The Rock Island years were good to the family, despite the hard work and ordinary difficulties the family faced and despite Frederick's extended absences when he directed his attention to the Wisconsin timber challenges. Without those absences we would not have the letters between husband and wife, father and children that provide a family record. The family members, especially the young women, had also been good to the community, volunteering in churches and schools.

An editorial that appeared in the Rock Island papers when the family moved to St. Paul in 1891, expressing the loss to the community of the daughters' volunteer work:

> With great regret we record the removal to St. Paul of Mr. Frederick Weyerhaeuser and family. Though doubtless [the move is] advantageous to them in many ways, Rock Island experiences a loss she can ill afford. Mr. Weyerhaeuser's family, especially the younger people, have been identified with Broadway [Presbyterian Church], as worshippers and workers, almost from its inception . . . They will be greatly missed in every department . . . The young ladies have for years been among the most efficient teachers . . . A large number of scholars have passed under their instruction and are deeply lamenting their departure.

But the Rock Island years were bound to end as Frederick continued to expand his business. The next move for the family, or for those left at home, would be to Minnesota.

PART FIVE

THE ST. PAUL YEARS— CROWNING ACHIEVEMENTS

Frederick wonders if young Fred has learned to negotiate yet, 1900

"Am I walking too fast for you, Father?" The tall, blond young man turned as he spoke to the shorter man beside him. They were coming to the top of the hill that led to downtown St. Paul.

The shorter, gray-haired man at his side cast a quick glance upward as he kept pace. "I'm not old yet, you know," he replied with the slightly inflected accent he had never lost since coming from Germany. "I'll let you know when I can't keep up."

"Yes, Father," the younger man said, the corners of his mouth twitching. After a moment, he continued, "I was wondering how your discussions with Mr. Hill were coming along, on the sale of that western timberland."

"Well, when I can catch him during the few times we are in St. Paul at the same moment, I should say they are progressing."

"Are you getting any closer on price?" F. E. asked his father, knowing that he shouldn't probe further if the reply was terse.

"Yes, yes, I think we are," Frederick muttered thoughtfully. "Hill is down to seven dollars an acre, and my associates have gone to five dollars, which is quite a bit up for them."

"And who will give?" F. E. wondered, knowing both his father's stubbornness and the feisty nature of their neighbor, James J. Hill.

His father looked up at him once more, this time in amusement. "Why both of us, Frederick. We'll strike a compromise. Neither of us would want to swallow the whole difference." He paused, then grinning added, "Don't you know how to negotiate yet?"

Based on F. E.'s recollections of conversations with his father. See Frederick's dialogue with the younger Fred when he works in Cloquet and first comes to his father for advice on buying land without help (see page 134).

CHAPTER 12

Minnesota's Forests Call

CHANGES WERE COMING to Frederick's Wisconsin logging business in the late 1880s. Although the Chippewa Valley timber wars had been resolved, thirty years of vigorous logging efforts had thinned Wisconsin's glorious white pine forests that Frederick had so admired when he first saw them. Regeneration of the land that had not been cleared for settlement would take years. Frederick and his Mississippi River partners needed new forests now to supply the increasing public demand for lumber.

THE NEED FOR NEW FORESTS

Ever tuned to the possibilities for his next venture, Frederick turned his attention to the neighboring Minnesota forests. But at first, surprisingly, he did not find many of his associates in accord with his planning.

In 1888 some of Frederick's partners began to discuss the possibilities of Minnesota timber. David Joyce, an MRLC member and lumberman from Minnesota,

---

Rock Island Argus, August 29, 1888:

The Latest of Weyerhaeuser

The latest is that Frederick Weyerhaeuser has purchased between $3,000,000 and $4,000,000 worth of lumber in the Eau Claire, Wisconsin lumber district, including those of the Eau Claire Lumber Company. Mr. Weyerhaeuser has for some time made his headquarters at Chippewa Falls and has given especial attention to his Wisconsin interests . . . It is now learned upon good authority that Mr. Weyerhaeuser stands behind the Eau Claire, Mississippi and Lake Superior, a recently organized corporation composed of Eau Claire lumbermen who propose to build a [rail]road from Superior . . . to Winona . . . This gives an outlet to the Southwest markets.

---

suggested to the MRLC board members that they might want to buy an inter-est in the St. Paul Boom Company. An appointed committee looked into it but took no action. Then, in November 1889, Frederick brought the topic of Minnesota back before the directors with a proposal from Edwin C. Whitney of the St. Anthony Lumber Company to buy 330 million feet of timber on the Pine River along with a controlling interest in the Mississippi and Rum River Boom and half interest in the St. Paul Boom Company. The total price for the deal was $1.3 million.

This offer was significant. Such a purchase would establish Frederick and his associates in a new region and provide an important new source of pine to replace the dwindling Wisconsin supply. But the partners declined the offer. Instead, they passed a motion not to entertain the purchase of any pine that had to be manufactured above St. Anthony Falls and thereby closed off MRLC consideration of any activity on the upper Mississippi.

⚓︎

There were several reasons for this decision. For one, most of the pine in north-ern Minnesota was Norway pine, inferior to the splendid white pine taken out of Wisconsin forests. But the age of the individual MRLC associates could have figured into their reluctance to expand operations as well. Many had become quite wealthy and were getting on in years, looking toward retirement. Their reasoning may have been, "Why start a new effort now?"

For other partners the venture might have seemed too risky. Memory of the troubles in Wisconsin was still very much present for most of them. Minnesota operations could generate similar problems. By initiating activity in this new area, would the MRLC be opening itself to the same fights with local mill own-ers that had plagued them in Wisconsin?

Frederick, however, remained attentive to the Minnesota prospects. While he could not persuade all of his MRLC associates, a number of close friends expressed interest in taking on the new territory with him. These included his good friend Mathew Norton from Winona and Norton's cousin William Laird, Peter Musser and his son Drew from Iowa, and longtime associate F. C. A. Denkmann. It was natural that the Minnesota forests would capture Freder-ick's interest. The Minnesota pinelands were larger than Michigan's by one-tenth and were one-third larger than those in Wisconsin.

The lumbermen would discover that there were four groups of forests in Minnesota. The first to be cut lay on the western bank of the St. Croix River, across from the active Wisconsin forests. Then there were stands of timber along the Snake and Kettle rivers in the northern Minnesota basin that included the Rum and Swan rivers. The third group of great timber offerings was adjacent to the St. Louis River, which flowed into Lake Superior on the eastern border and which had been part of the magnificent Northwest Passage of historical and literary fame. Still farther to the northwest were the timber reserves associated with the Red River Valley. From these Minnesota forests Frederick hoped to create his next source of supply for the seemingly inexhaustible demand of the westward-moving population.

In 1890, when Frederick and his associates made their entrance into the Minnesota market, the young state had only 1,310,283 inhabitants. St. Paul, where Frederick moved both his family and his Chippewa Falls headquarters in 1891, had 164,000 residents.

Sometimes the paper got it wrong. Item from the *Moline Review Dispatch*, April 12, 1889:

> A dispatch from Duluth to the *Chicago Herald* says: "Fred Weyerhaeuser, the lumber king, is about to start a saw mill to employ 400 men, just outside of Superior, Wis. on Allouez Bay, the mouth of the Nemadji river. He owns every other section for many miles along the Chicago, St. Paul, Minneapolis and Omaha railway, and also 40,000,000 feet of pine along the Nemadji and tributaries.

(Note: There is no record of this mill ever opening.)

Two major lumber centers eventually emerged from Frederick's efforts in Minnesota. The first to be developed was the Pine Tree Lumber Company in Little Falls, formed in 1890 and using the central and north-central forests as a source. The second, a few years later, would take advantage of the forests near the St. Louis River in the northeastern part of the state. That operation was based in the village of Cloquet.

PINE TREE LUMBER COMPANY, LITTLE FALLS

The Pine Tree Lumber Company, the first to be formed by the Weyerhaeuser associates in Minnesota, purchased 212,700 acres in eight counties on June 24, 1890. The owners were the Mussers (father and son) of Muscatine, Iowa, the Laird-Norton group from Winona, and Weyerhaeuser and Denkmann. A small amount of stock was reserved for the sons of Weyerhaeuser and Musser— Charles and Drew, respectively. The sons, now partial owners, were sent by their fathers to run the Pine Tree Lumber Company mill at Little Falls.

The company began operations on May 18, 1891, under Drew and Charles's leadership. These young men could not have presented more of a contrast.

Drew (later known as R. D.) Musser was slight of build and careful of practice; Charles Weyerhaeuser, on the other hand, was powerfully built, athletic, assertive, and spontaneous. He was expressive and explorative while Drew, who preferred accounting and detail, had a much more reserved personality. With such complementary talents and interests, they presented a formidable team.

The two younger men got on well despite, or perhaps because of, their differing personalities. Evidence of their close association remains in the neighboring baronial homes they built on the banks of the Mississippi, larger than any other houses in the little community at the time. When the Pine Tree Lumber Company ceased operations after thirty years, Charles Weyerhaeuser moved his family to St. Paul, where the rest of the Weyerhaeuser family lived, while the Mussers and their descendents remained in Little Falls for another three-quarters of a century. The mansions still sit side by side a hundred years later, like two dowager sisters. Drew Musser's daughter, Laura Jane Musser, eventually owned both houses and lived in one of them until she died, childless, in the late twentieth century. Her charitable trust gifted the buildings to the city of Little Falls, along with funds to operate the houses for civic purposes.

In 1936, R. D. (Drew) Musser wrote to Charles's younger brother F. E. about that partnership. He cited the fathers' friendship as an important reason for establishing the Pine Tree Lumber Company and sending their sons to co-manage the operations.

Although Frederick's practice was not to interfere with the business he had delegated to his sons, on occasion he was called in to help with a particular situation. Some of the same problems Frederick had encountered in Wisconsin resurfaced in Minnesota. All the logs for all the companies had to come down the same few rivers along with local owners' logs. In June 1892, A. C. Akeley, another area lumberman, appealed to Frederick for help. Pine Tree Lumber Company had to hold all the logs coming downstream from various cuts so the firm could pull its logs out before releasing the rest. Akeley complained that his logs were being retained too long.

Frederick's reply was calm and reasoned as he reviewed the situation in the correspondence. He reminded Akeley that the previous fall he, Frederick, had suggested that all lumbermen send down a larger number of logs while the waters were high, as a hedge against possible spring drought, but the log owners (including, presumably, Mr. Akeley) refused to do so. As Frederick had projected, the spring waters were low and the winds were high, delaying the drive downward. Frederick added that he thought conditions had improved somewhat at the time of his written letter to Akeley and that the logs were moving much faster. This exchange seemed to calm Mr. Akeley.

Frederick was, in fact, known for his nuanced interactions, especially in business matters that he conducted in his own inimitable style. An article in the *Rock Island Argus* on February 15, 1888, entitled "Pumping the Lumber King" described an attempt to get Frederick to make a commitment on a certain matter. He proved too canny for those who sought to nail down his views.

> Mr. Weyerhaeuser is a good deal of a diplomat, and perhaps that is one reason why he is popularly known as "Bismarck." He never expresses an opinion until it is ripe, and is seldom entrapped into a declaration of his purpose until he is ready to act. Some years ago, while litigation was in process between the city of Eau Claire and a logging corporation of which Mr. Weyerhaeuser was president, a prominent lumberman of that place was deputed to "draw out" Mr. Weyerhaeuser and contrive to place him on record upon a certain point of considerable importance. The lumberman accordingly constructed an ingenious letter which was carefully conned by others and so devised as to require a specific answer, and to which a distinct reply, committing Weyerhaeuser on one side or the other, seemed to the writer unavoidable; but weeks passed without bringing an answer. Never before had Weyerhaeuser been known to thus neglect a business communication. At last the writer of the letter encountered the celebrated lumber king. "Did you receive a letter from me, Mr. Weyerhaeuser?" "Yes, Sir. I think I have it in my pocket now." "Well, why in the name of Cadmus didn't you answer it?" "Well," replied Mr. Weyerhaeuser, "the fact is, my clerks have been so very busy—haven't had a minute to spare, and I write such fearfully bad English myself, that I thought I'd better wait and see you"—adding with a grim imitation of a smile: "Sometimes I have spells of not being able to write English at all. This is one of 'em. Often I wish it was that way all of the time. I prefer to talk." Talk he did, and the deep laid plot [to get him to commit himself on paper] had failed.

In 1895 there was another occasion for Pine Tree Lumber Company to call on Frederick's diplomacy. From 1892 to 1896, a long recession resulted in a precipitate fall in the sale of lumber. From 1893 to 1896, Pine Tree had issued directives to its loggers to slow the amount of timber cut by contractors in the woods because the market demand had been so reduced. But since the contractors were paid by what they cut, there was little incentive to comply with this order. Finally the loggers reluctantly made some reduction in 1893–94, but in 1895 heated correspondence between Pine Tree Lumber Company officials and the Swan River Logging Company brought Frederick and his diplomatic talents back to Little Falls.

Letters and memoranda were exchanged between loggers and lumber companies. Strong words were used, some of them coming from the two young partners at Pine Tree Lumber Company. Frederick's ability to harmonize the interests, especially to reassure the Swan River group, whose members seemed to resent the tone of the Pine Tree office memoranda, was called into action.

Perhaps it was on this visit that Frederick's very young granddaughter remembers seeing him. Sarah-Maud, daughter of Charles and his wife Maud Moon, was no older than four years at the time. She recalls being told to be quiet as her grandfather was taking a nap. Following that advice did not prevent her curiosity. She peeked into the room where the elderly Frederick was stretched out on the sofa. What impressed her was that he had spread a white handkerchief over his face while asleep and his deep, rhythmic breathing raised it up and down. The scene stayed with her into her last years.

No doubt Frederick had need of that nap. He was known to be an indefatigable worker. Not all of his efforts came to fruition, but he was never one to brood over any lost opportunity. A case illustrating that point entailed iron ore as well as timberlands.

At issue was the price of land in northern Minnesota to be sold by Charles Davis of Saginaw, Michigan, to the Weyerhaeuser partners. (Davis and Frederick would eventually be linked by the marriage of Davis's daughter Harriette to Frederick's youngest son, F. E.) The partners were interested in forty-five thousand acres of stumpage. A disagreement arose over title because the timber cruisers—men who rode through the forest and assessed the value of the stumpage—had difficulty fixing their compass and therefore claimed they couldn't properly assess the timber's value.

Davis became convinced the compass problem indicated the presence of iron ore under the surface. At his final meeting with Frederick in June 1892, Davis tried to negotiate the sale of mineral rights as well as timber, at a much higher price. Frederick wanted to buy all rights, but his associates disagreed. Finally Weyerhaeuser and his partners bought only the timber rights.

Years later, in 1905, Frederick was watching a Great Northern Railroad train loaded with iron ore coming from the mines in the same area. He counted fifty-two cars. He then turned to his companion and remarked whimsically, "and to think we could have had that land for one hundred thousand dollars." The companion to whom he spoke was Harriette's brother, C. H. Davis Jr.

THE ST. LOUIS COUNTY/KNIFE FALLS VENTURES

After the Pine Tree Lumber Company venture was well on its way, Frederick turned his sights on the St. Louis County forests and a northern enterprise in which he had an investment interest and which needed his attention. The business was located in Cloquet, Minnesota, which had originally been known as Knife Falls.

Knife Falls had already established a colorful history as a lumber town in the 1880s. By 1886 the town had been renamed Cloquet and had four operating mills. The town banned liquor, but one enterprising man had purchased land on an island opposite the town and did a "land-office" business, developing a little suburb complete with saloons, brothels, and a jail.

Small wonder the mill workers needed some recreation. At the time they were laboring six days a week from spring to fall for fifteen cents an hour. When the snow began, many of them departed for the logging camps, where they could work on the following year's mill supply and earn more money.

The village's original name, Knife Falls, was apt. The St. Louis River would have been an ideal venue for shipping logs cut in the great forests of the watershed were it not for one factor: the ledge of pointed slate that crossed the river like a knife, causing it to descend for 573 feet over fourteen miles and end as a meandering, quiet stream at Fond du Lac, Wisconsin, eventually flowing into Lake Superior. When the water was running high, the logs could easily pass over the falls, but when water was low, they continually became ensnared on the slate edges, creating jams that could back up for miles.

The owners of the Knife Falls Boom Corporation (formed in 1871 and taken over by the Knife Falls Lumber Company in 1879) devised a solution to the problem of the slate barrier interfering with passage of the logs on the river: they centered the logging operations above the falls and used rail for transportation. The St. Paul and Duluth rail line was being finished at the time, and it provided an alternative to the river. This solution might have worked were it not for the river's capricious nature.

In 1883 the water remained low on the river all spring, and few logs were able even to get to the boom above Knife Falls. This predicament caused a loss of sales needed to pay the company's debts. Frederick, who had made a twenty-five-thousand-dollar loan to the Knife Falls Lumber Company (or their contracting loggers), feared for his investment. He knew he needed either to take over the company or to bring in other investors to share the risk with him.

He contacted George Shaw of Renwick, Shaw and Crosset in Davenport, Iowa. After a visit to Knife Falls, George Shaw got his partners to agree to the purchase of the rapidly failing Knife Falls Lumber Company. In 1883 a corporation was formed with Shaw's firm, Weyerhaeuser and Denkmann, and four other investors. Shortly thereafter George Shaw bought out his partners in Davenport and became the dominant stockholder in the new venture. He moved to Cloquet and became president of the Cloquet Lumber Company.

An opportunity for greater involvement in the area appeared when Frederick's third son, Rudolph, who was manning the Weyerhaeuser offices in the German National Bank in St. Paul, answered a long-distance telephone call from Chicago. On the other end of the line was a Mr. Bacon, and he had an offer for Frederick.

While a "long-distance" telephone call from Chicago to St. Paul was not ordinary at this time, the offer Bacon made was even more unusual and signaled Frederick's growing reputation in the Midwest. An article in the *Rock Island Argus* on August 15, 1888, illustrates this point, with the accompanying headlines, "Great Is Frederick: The Influence of Mr. Weyerhaeuser upon the lumber business of the Northwest and the importance of his every move."

> Mr. Weyerhaeuser's record in the lumber business for carrying out every plan which he has once conceived are too well known to need comment . . . R. Knox, a prominent Chicago lumberman, says "By the way, I knew this man Fred Weyerhaeuser years ago. I was born and raised at Rock Island and remember him there as the proprietor of a little saw mill on the Mississippi, buying a raft occasionally and working it into lumber. After being away from Rock Island for fifteen years I returned to find Weyerhaeuser worth millions and now the head of a $60,000,000 lumber trust.
>
> George B. Shaw of Eau Claire, Wisc. states that "it requires a great deal of standing timber to supply all the mills which Weyerhauser and his associates control. He is constantly buying pine lands. His purchases are relatively larger and attract more attention therefore than the purchases of the smaller lumber companies and Weyerhauser is buying for the future, but so far as I know, there is not the remotest idea of a trust in his operations.

Bacon's telephone call to Rudi concerned some land in northern Minnesota. C. N. Nelson, a large landowner, was ill and wanted to divest himself of his lands and retire. He owned six hundred million feet of pine, two mills, a commissary, a hotel, and the St. Louis Boom and Improvement Company, as well as the Knife Falls Boom. His lands also held iron ore deposits. He wanted to sell all the land, but Bacon wanted only the mineral rights. He thought Frederick might be interested in the timber part of the sale. Indeed he was. Purchase of this land would open up for Frederick and his associates a toehold in the northwestern Minnesota timber business.

Frederick immediately took an option and contacted George Shaw. Would Shaw be willing to take a partial interest position on the newly available properties? When Frederick named the asking price, Shaw's answer was swift: a resounding yes. Other partners were recruited, including the Irvines, Mathew

Norton, Artemus Lamb, and Ed Rutledge. Frederick then sent Rudolph, recently graduated from Yale College, to Cloquet to manage the new part of the business. Rudolph later said, "My only instruction [from Frederick] was to keep out of politics."

Coupled with Charles's position in Little Falls, Rudolph's new assignment indicated Frederick's willingness to assign his sons significant responsibility in his diverse interests. Rudolph was somewhat concerned that his fiancée, Louise Lindeke, might not take to the North Woods. The rough and ready village of Cloquet was a far cry from Louise's gracious upbringing on Summit Avenue in St. Paul. Rudolph need not have worried. After their marriage in October 1896, she traveled happily north with him and became known as a charming hostess and excellent housekeeper for all the years they lived in Cloquet.

A pattern was emerging in Frederick's family: the expectation that the sons would work in the business in the same way that all the children had been expected to pare apples for the family's winter store. The idea of family participation was a hallmark of the Weyerhaeuser business interests for many years.

Initially Rudolph had some assistance from his father's associate William Irvine, but soon he was running what was now called Northern Lumber Company himself. In the fall of 1896, the youngest son, Fred (F. E.), was sent to assist his brother.

Frederick had a certain philosophy about taking his sons into his business. F. E. later quoted a letter from Archibald Stewart of Ottawa, Canada, dated 1935. He recalled a conversation he had with Frederick years earlier about this topic.

> Your father and I were speaking of Ingram and he spoke of the unfair treatment this man gave his son in not associating him at all in his business. I said that I had noticed that and was sorry for the boy. Now your father said: "When my son Fred is through college he will take up our business and I intend he will not be running to me for advice, but must take full responsibility and if mistakes are made and losses incurred which I might not have made it will happen during my lifetime and I am willing to stand it."

F. E. later told another story about a conversation with his father on this topic early in his career, in which the lessons about responsibility were made quite personal, although delivered with some humor. Rudolph had assigned his younger brother to buy a sixty-million-foot (of timber) forest holding from a Detroit landowner for the Northern Lumber Company. Young Fred, unsure of his abilities in this situation, traveled to St. Paul to consult his father. The conversation F. E. later reported went like this:

FREDERICK: "Buy it."

F. E.: "But I must take William Irvine with me . . . I have never bought any timber."

FREDERICK: "You can't begin younger, can you?"

F. E. "Then I certainly must take our attorney, N. H. Clapp with me."

FREDERICK: "Why?"

F. E. "I have never drawn a purchase contract, and I may need his help."

FREDERICK: "I thought you graduated from Yale College. And you cannot draw up a purchase contract?"

By the end of the late 1890s, Frederick and his associates had amassed an interest in many acres of forest both in the central and north-central part of the state. The Pine Tree Lumber Company, the Cloquet Lumber Company, and the Northern Lumber Company were flourishing. Three of his sons were now working in the Minnesota business, with significant responsibilities.

From F. E.'s *Record*, a memory of the impromptu mention of what became the Northern Pacific land purchase:

In later years Fred would walk or ride with his father to the office downtown. He remembers in 1899, on one of those journeys home at night, his father saying to him, almost casually, "Mr. Hill wishes me to buy 1,000,000 acres of timber lands owned by the Northern Pacific Railway Company. He asks $7 per acre. I think $5 an acre is all we should pay."

Frederick, with his energy and willing partners, had opened up much of Minnesota to lumber production. But he was not content to settle down. He once more turned his attention to new ventures. The South and the West beckoned.

CHAPTER 13

The Family Moves to St. Paul, and Frederick Turns Westward

A s Frederick was building his Minnesota timber business, great changes had come about on the family front. Not only were the children growing into adults ready to take their place in their father's businesses, but Rock Island, the place where they grew up, would no longer be their hometown. In 1891 Frederick decided to move his Chippewa Falls office to St. Paul, Minnesota, and a few months later Sarah followed. The children were grown, and only Fred, who had not yet finished college, and Margaret, who lived with her parents when her husband, Richard, was overseas, were home on a regular basis, although Elise and Apollonia—both married in 1892—spent some time with their mother.

Starting a New Life in Another River Town

Frederick and Sarah moved their home base from Rock Island to St. Paul for several reasons, but a large part of the consideration for Frederick was distance. The MRLC leadership position required his time in northern Wisconsin, and his burgeoning business in Minnesota made a longer trek for him to Rock Island. Even with improved travel conditions, it was not a trip one could make easily for a weekend visit with Sarah.

Other factors figured in his decision as well. The Minneapolis–St. Paul area, located near the Mississippi headwaters, was becoming increasingly important because of its shipping potential. Railroads, too, were being built through the twin cities and rapidly replacing the river as a method for shipping finished lumber. F. E. also notes that "there may have been more agreeable associates" in St. Paul than Frederick was finding in Rock Island. There is some evidence that Frederick's longtime partner and brother-in-law, F. C. A. Denkmann, was becoming increasingly irascible in his older years and perhaps made things difficult for Frederick on a daily basis.

Finally, it was becoming clear even at the outset of the nineties that the forests of Wisconsin and the Great Lakes region (except for Minnesota) were cut over and that new sources of timber had to be found. Protests against further timber cutting were already being heard even as Frederick was obliged to look for new forests. At the time of his move, he had begun exploring opportunities in the West and the South.

There is one other reason for Frederick's decision to move his offices out of the Eau Claire–Chippewa Falls area. The *Moline Review Dispatch* of October 3, 1890, included an article titled "Weyerhaeuser Power":

> An Eau Claire, Wis. dispatch says that Frederick Weyerhaeuser has caused it to be given out that unless the big suits for flood damage against him and his co-partners are withdrawn he will remove the headquarters of his companies from the Chippewa Valley to St. Paul. The Chippewa Logging Co and the Chippewa Lumber and Boom Co. are located at Chippewa Falls, and the Mississippi River Logging Co at Eau Claire. The two latter companies saw lumber. A representative of Mr. Weyerhaeuser said that Mr. Weyerhaeuser would not turn another wheel nor cut a stick of lumber more in the valley if the suits are not abandoned.

The outcome of these lawsuits is not known, nor is it clear why Frederick "caused [this news] to be given out." Was he already planning the move for the reasons cited above? Was this news simply a public relations ploy? Was it even accurate reporting? The article indicated that all operations, including the mills, would be moved if the suits persisted, but in the event only the business office was relocated to St. Paul.

When they arrived in St. Paul, Sarah settled into her new community as easily as she had done in Coal Valley and Rock Island. Soon there was evidence that she was developing a lively social life with other women of the city. An 1894 letter from Sarah to Margaret describes a luncheon given by a Mrs. Davis. It was described as "very informal," but nevertheless every woman mentioned in the letter is referred to as Mrs.—not by her given name.

Within two months of their arrival, Frederick and Sarah had purchased the Olive Culbertson house on the northeast corner of Summit Avenue and Arundel Street. They enjoyed the bustle of the growing city, which was much larger and more cosmopolitan than Rock Island.

Two years later the couple found a slightly larger house a few blocks down Summit Avenue from their home on Arundel. Next door to their new house at 266 Summit, in a much grander mansion, lived James J. Hill with his wife, Mary. By the time the Weyerhaeuser couple moved in, Hill was the owner of the newly merged Great Northern/Northern Pacific Railroad. Within a decade, their neighborly situation was to prove of enormous benefit to the business dealings of both men.

In those days, transportation around the city was difficult. The cable-driven tramcars laboriously climbed the Selby Avenue hill from the commercial "downtown" up to the residential neighborhoods along Summit Avenue. In Frederick's time the mud streets were covered with cedar blocks of wood that refused to remain in place. Any good rainstorm would wash the blocks out of their holdings and strew them around the roadbeds, making driving carriages hazardous. Frederick and Sarah owned a team of heavy horses that F. E. later said was more suitable for hauling logs than for drawing his father's Kimball Brougham. Nevertheless, the horse-drawn carriage was the family's usual method of transportation. Frederick, however, regularly chose to walk to and from his new office at the German American Bank downtown or to take the tramcar down the hill.

Because Frederick had necessarily worked all his life, he never had time to indulge himself in ordinary sports. On moving to St. Paul, Frederick was introduced to the Town and Country Club by one of his associates, who took him there to play golf. A cartoon of Frederick swinging a golf club as if he were a lumberjack swinging an ax appeared shortly afterward in the *St. Paul Pioneer Press*. It's not clear if it was a comment on his performance on the golf course or on his reputation as a leading lumberman.

Frederick had become a true outdoorsman through his experience with the rigors of Wisconsin winters. Living with the lumberjacks had demanded a certain level of physical stamina. However, his son F. E. later writes, "In the field of sport, Father would have been rated a sub-zero, even in the limited competition of his own day."

Sarah and the daughters may have enjoyed the social whirl in St. Paul, but Frederick had little time for anything outside of his business, save for that one notable golf game. The other exception seemed to be dinner parties at his house for his friends and associates, which he persuaded Sarah to give frequently and where he could continue to discuss the day's business. He mainly focused on the search for the next group of forests that would yield timber for him and his associates. Many conversations, later repeated to F. E. by his father's friends and business associates, indicate an active frame of mind even as Frederick was moving through his seventh decade. His old friend John Hill (not to be confused with James J. Hill) later related one such exchange to F. E. On an occasion when John Hill was having dinner with Sarah and Frederick at their Summit Avenue house, he recalls that he casually suggested to Frederick that a man in his sixties might be expected to take life a bit easier, to slow down somewhat in his work. Frederick replied, "Why John, if I did that I would die."

Another guest, Archibald Stewart of Ontario, Canada, later told a similar story. Frederick was recounting his exploration of the southern timberlands and his reservation about how much personal investment the proposed venture would demand from him. Sarah interjected a teasing comment, "Don't you have money enough?" The reply from her husband came swiftly, "It's not the money. I like to do big business."

FREDERICK INVESTIGATES
OPPORTUNITIES IN THE SOUTH

In searching for new opportunities, Frederick first considered the South. He did not have great experience in that region of the country, although he had been a minor stockholder in the Southern Lumber Company of Louisiana in 1882. But in 1894 Frederick was persuaded to go along on a rail trip organized by E. W. Durant of Stillwater. The Mussers of Iowa, father and son, were interested in exploring options in the South. However, although Frederick seemed to have enjoyed himself on the trip, in the end he was unwilling to commit to any activity there.

There were several reasons for his initial resistance. He had never liked the heat, and he feared malaria. He thought the heat and the fear of illness might make it difficult to transfer managers he trusted from the North to work in any new southern venue. And finally, there was the issue of the quality of timber, which was generally inferior to that of the northern forests. Instead of the much-valued white pine, beech, and red pine, the southern forests contained long-leaved yellow pine, cypress, and other trees. Frederick was accustomed to better quality.

In addition, he had some lingering Civil War resentments to overcome, no doubt remembering the young men he had sworn into the army on his front porch in Coal Valley. They had returned utterly changed by the war, if they returned at all.

During this first southern trip, however, his resistance was challenged by what he saw. In one instance, watching men working hard to process fine white oak timber, he made the remark, "I think I would [sic] better take back my idea of this southern lumber and the people."

Frederick's changing views were illustrated in a story F. E. tells about his father's hands-on experience with workers in his newest venue:

> One Saturday morning as he was there the mill was running with a very short crew . . . The mill was cutting back on an order for small timbers which were literally being dumped out of the back end of the saw floor and which left it in hopeless confusion . . . Father did not like the way it was being done

and . . . took three big negroes with him, and in short time had the timbers properly piled. On going up to the office, he told me and Harvey Clapp that he never saw better workmen—better than the Swedes in Minnesota. When pressed, he finally admitted that he had given each of them a dollar.

By 1896, when Frederick made a second trip to the South, he was growing more amenable to the idea of a southern business strategy. The area was still in a post–Civil War depression, and yellow pine was available for five dollars to eight dollars an acre. At the end of his 1896 trip, Frederick announced that he was willing to invest one million dollars in the South. Unfortunately, none of his colleagues was willing to take the risk with him. Frederick passed on the opportunity when he could not find others to share the risk.

Eventually Frederick did participate in several southern timber investments. The largest was the Southern Lumber Company of Louisiana, later renamed the Southland Lumber Company. Weyerhaeuser and Denkmann were joined by the Laird-Norton group in this investment, which had been preceded by Frederick's smaller 1882 investment with the Lindsay, Richardson, and Ainsley families.

Frederick took a greater interest in the South with this new holding, especially as he had appointed young F. E. to be president of the company. Fred, who had cut his teeth on the lumber business working for Rudi in Cloquet, was delighted to be given this assignment. "I had the thrill of a lifetime," he later wrote, "when Father, returning from Rock Island, told me I had been made president of the Southland Lumber Company and was expected to oversee the building of the mill in the South."

F. E. never spent any considerable time in the South. He was married in 1902 to Harriette Davis and was living on Summit Avenue in St. Paul in 1906, so it appears that his trips to the new region did not involve living there for any significant period, nor did Harriette ever move there. This scenario would be consistent with Frederick's longstanding reservations about moving any of his family to the South. However, F. E. was there long enough to oversee relocation of a mill, completely installed with new machinery, from Wisconsin to a site in Warren, Arkansas. One of the problems the lumbermen faced, particularly in Arkansas, was poor public roads. F. E. quotes a sign some wag tacked to a fence post near Warren:

This road is not passable
Not even jackassable
So you who travel it
Turn and gravel it.

Despite F. E.'s lack of long-term residence in the South, a later assessment by Ralph Hidy, Frank Hill, and Allan Nevins, authors of *Timber and Men,* is quite positive. These scholars give great credit to F. E. for the company's success: "Altogether, with [young] Fred as its chief and members of the Denkmann and Lindsay families as dynamic aides, the Southern Lumber Company of Arkansas became a flourishing organization."

FREDERICK'S INTERESTS MOVE WEST WITH THE RAILROADS

Frederick did not show the same reluctance for large-scale investment opportunities in the western timberlands as he had in the South. A major difference was his developing friendship with his neighbor on Summit Avenue, James J. Hill.

Stories are told of Jim and Mary Hill visiting the Weyerhaeuser couple's home on many an evening. The four of them would sit in the parlor while the gregarious Jim Hill held forth on the marvels of his newly formed merger of Northern Pacific and Great Northern railroads. This grand feat was accomplished in 1893 with the assistance of investment banker J. P. Morgan and the establishment of the Northern Securities Trust. This trust was later challenged by President Teddy Roosevelt at an early stage of his attacks on the big "combinations."

Frederick, who was an early-morning person, would doze off as the long soirees wore on, but Hill, who liked to stay up late and smoke cigars, appeared not to notice. He would continue talking until one of the wives had the good sense to bring the evening to a close. The younger Weyerhaeusers were amused at the pair of men who were becoming friends but appeared to take little notice of each other's habits.

As it turned out, Frederick wasn't asleep all the time during those long social evenings. He was apparently musing on the prospect of tying the western railroads to his search for new forests. At some point he and Jim Hill came to an understanding about their common interests.

Frederick's initial approach to the possibilities of the western timberlands could be described as "careful." In 1885 he had received an overture from Northern Pacific (not yet merged with Hill's Great Northern and still suffering from Jay Cooke's disastrous management) to buy a mill and some timberlands near Tacoma, Washington. Frederick said no. A year later, however, he took an option on eighty thousand acres of Douglas fir near Tacoma with Peter Musser of Iowa. They never exercised it. As Hidy describes the situation, "Weyerhaeuser and his friends gave the west a very gingerly look."

The transcontinental railroad had been completed in 1869, opening the great lands of the West. The rail traffic brought settlers and excitement, and

Frederick saw the country changing. In 1893 Jim Hill made Frederick a cut-rate offer of forty cents per thousand for shipping lumber from the West Coast to St. Paul, and the Alaskan Klondike gold rush in 1897 added urgency to the push westward. Frederick's attention was drawn evermore toward the timber of the western slopes.

Late in 1899, Weyerhaeuser and Denkmann bought half the stock of the Sound Timber Company in the Puget Sound area, and they also took up Hill's offer and began to ship shingles from the West Coast over the Northern Pacific. Hill could afford to offer this low rate in the spring when the railroad needed the freight.

Frederick's blockbuster timber investment in the West was to come in 1900. There is no question that Frederick's many informal conversations late into the night with Jim Hill bore fruit for both men, for Frederick's agreement with Hill established a new era in the lumber history of North America. Frederick and his associates bought nine hundred thousand acres of western timberland from the Northern Pacific Railroad for six dollars an acre. This purchase changed lives and reshaped the world of American timber.

When the agreement between Hill and Weyerhaeuser was finally struck, confirmation came in the form of a coded telegram from Hill to Frederick on December 19, 1899, announcing that the Northern Pacific Railroad accepted the terms the Weyerhaeuser group offered for the major western land acquisition:

> Thwarted (tell) Weyerhaeuser toothed (that) pensiveness (parties) here faction (expect) tripped (to) additionally (accept) humdrum (his) oscillate (offer) caleb (without) (conditions) implorer (if) tower (they) cannot duchy (do) bleeds (better).

> (Note: It's not clear why James J. Hill used code, but it may have been customary at the time to keep business transactions done by telegraph confidential.)

Although direct negotiations between Hill and Weyerhaeuser had preceded the formal event, the agreement to purchase this land was signed by Frederick (on behalf of himself and his partners) and the railroad's land agent, William H. Phipps, on behalf of James J. Hill.

It was going to be difficult to raise the large sum of money from prospective partners for this purchase. Frederick had his work cut out for him. It is a credit to the trust his associates placed in him that Frederick was able to pull the deal together. Five-million-plus dollars was a lot of money in those days. Not only that, but the agreement required that the first three million be paid immediately. (Hill needed the influx of cash to keep his railroad solvent.)

MAKING THE DEAL AND LIVING WITH THE CONSEQUENCES

How did Frederick raise the money? It was indeed a case of rounding up the usual suspects. His longtime associates were aging, but a number of them decided to make this final gamble with him. Weyerhaeuser and Denkmann put in $1.8 million, and the Laird-Norton group from Winona was close behind with $1.2 million. R. L. McCormick, S. T. McKnight, and O. H. Ingram put up $350,000 each, and a number of lesser partners were also corralled. One man recalled later that it took practically all the lumbermen on the Mississippi to raise that much money.

The rationale for the sale of the land from the railroad's perspective was clear. The Northern Pacific Railroad, which by this time was run by Jim Hill much more efficiently than it had been under the schemes of Jay Cooke or even Frederick Billings, had a desperate need for capital. The railroad had been poorly managed for years before Hill was in charge. The railroad was paying eight percent on the bonds it was carrying after its second bankruptcy and reorganization in 1893, when Hill had added the Northern Pacific to the Great Northern. The recently merged railroad needed to exchange some of its land for badly needed cash.

Within a short time it became apparent that this transaction was a very good deal for Frederick and his partners. Watching this purchase, others suddenly decided that they wanted a piece of the western action. Many smaller owners moved in, and land prices soared. Frederick reaped the benefit of being the first to take a major risk in the western timberlands.

Hidy and colleagues assessed the situation this way: "The Weyerhaeuser purchase loosed a flood of speculative activity in the Northwest. Smaller capitalists who trusted Frederick's judgment followed with lesser purchases in the same area. Land that could not be given away was suddenly worth $10 an acre. Within a dozen years the price of timber was as high as it was going to go. But at the time [the deal was made], even the partners were concerned that the purchase was too speculative."

An exchange recorded at an early meeting of the venture's partners in Tacoma illustrated Frederick's personal faith in this land purchase. Some members expressed anxiety about the future, and one suggested the possibility of letting the land go by simply not paying the taxes. Frederick mischievously introduced a motion to allow all the abandoned lands to be deeded to him. His motion ended that particular discussion. If Frederick had that much confidence in this purchase, his associates would go along with him.

Later, the Randolph Hearst publications leveled sharp criticism at the Weyerhaeuser associates' Northern Pacific land purchase. The charges were complex: that the transaction involved a huge amount of land; that the land in question was part of the congressional land grant to the railroads made in Abraham Lincoln's time to encourage building; and that the expectation had been that individuals would buy the land and settle on it. (A number of smaller landholders did buy land, much of it closer to the western coast.) The railroad's immediate need for cash, however, outweighed any other consideration. Hill made a rather convincing argument that to sell off small parcels to individuals over many years with capital only dribbling in would threaten the economic survival of his much-needed transcontinental railroad. The fraudulent behavior of the early owners Jim Fisk and Jay Gould, who took money from Congress to build the railroads and then squandered it, leaving the railroads bankrupt, was not Hill's way.

The Weyerhaeuser partners were right to be concerned about their prospects in this exchange. Logging was still primitive in the western forests. Although the situation was in some way similar to the early days in Wisconsin, the challenges in the West were much more severe.

In the western mountain forests, lumberjacks had oxen drag timber over greased roads to rail lines rather than simply putting the logs in the streams that fed rivers, as they did near the Mississippi. Much of the timberland in the higher mountains was inaccessible, since some places lacked roads for carts. Getting the timber back to the Midwest and the East was another problem. The Panama Canal was still a dream of the future, and the cost of sea shipping was astronomical. Also, the quality of the western forests was thought to be inferior to the timber of the East and Midwest: white fir and hemlock were practically worthless, while Douglas fir was still not widely used. Fires were always a problem in the West, even in later years. Often, when a forest fire began, there would be no way to navigate the mountainous roads to contain it.

But the greatest challenge was this: the area had never been completely "cruised." (In cruising, foresters move through the forest to assess the value of the timber for harvesting.) About three-fourths of the area sold to the Weyerhaeuser associates had been cruised five years earlier, but the report on what the forests held was incomplete. The partners truly did not know exactly what they had purchased in terms of saleable timber.

In light of all this, the issue of naming the new company seemed a minor one. Frederick preferred the title "Universal Timber Company," but at the first board meeting in Tacoma, his associates insisted that the new organization bear the name of the man who brought it into being with his organizational skills. Over Frederick's objections, the name chosen was the Weyerhaeuser Timber Company.

Frederick never had any intention of moving west to manage this new effort. And every indication is that he did not want his sons that far from home, either.

Fortunately, one of Frederick's Minneapolis associates, Sumner T. McKnight, had a solution. He recommended a young man who was then working in the Wisconsin timber operations and in whom he saw a most promising future manager: George S. Long. After Long extricated himself honorably from his contract in Wisconsin, he moved west to become head of the new organization. In so doing, he assumed a key place in the complex timber industry developments that would change history.

We know the story of regional events that followed, much of it the result of the purchase. There was steady growth in the entire region. There was, despite the difficulties just listed, an ongoing boom in the timber industry, and many jobs were created, which, in turn, drew new settlers. Eventually friction erupted between the large and small landholders in the forested areas, and ultimately politicians made an issue of that friction. Long later said, "The job that confronted me for the first ten years was not a lumberman's job, but a diplomat's."

Frederick Weyerhaeuser had organized his associates to make a land purchase that would have an effect on the settlement of the western states and the development of the timber industry for generations to come. As historian Chuck Twining notes, "No one was Weyerhaeuser's equal when it came to seeing far into lumbering's future and they realized they could do no better than attach themselves to Weyerhaeuser's coattails, if given the chance, and hang on."

CHAPTER 14

Family Matters

THE DECADE OF THE 1890s that led up to the acquisition of the Northern Pacific land and the opening of the western timber country found Frederick still vigorous and still, as he had said in response to Sarah's jibe, able and happy to do "big business."

While his enterprises were expanding, his family was also changing with the addition of spouses and grandchildren. Frederick's connection with his sons was strengthened further by their participation in his business efforts: John in Rock Island, then northern Wisconsin; Charlie in Little Falls with Drew Musser; Rudolph in Cloquet; and young Fred in Cloquet, then Arkansas, then St. Paul in his father's office.

WEDDINGS AND NEW PERSONALITIES
EXPAND THE FAMILY

Suddenly there was a flurry of family weddings. John married first, to Nellie Lincoln Anderson on March 26, 1890. The couple had three children, Elizabeth, Frederick King, and John Phillip Jr. They made their home in Rock Island, living in a rented house until Frederick and Sarah moved to St. Paul. From that point, Nellie and John occupied the house on the hill in Rock Island until 1899, when they moved to Lake Nebagamon in northern Wisconsin. Apollonia and her husband, Sam Davis, then moved into the family dwelling and lived there until they died, leaving the large house to Augustana College.

After John's wedding came, in rather quick succession, all three of the daughters' weddings. Apollonia and Sam Davis were married in the old Culbertson house in St. Paul on September 21, 1892, followed three months later by Elise and William Bancroft Hill on December 29, 1892. Sarah must have had her hands full with preparations for these festivities so soon after the move.

Two years later, in 1894, Margaret and James Richard Jewett were married in the Weyerhaeusers' new house, 266 Summit Avenue, which Frederick and Sarah had just purchased from Frederick Driscoll, grandfather to Walter B. Driscoll, who would later marry Rudolph and Louise's only daughter, Margaret. St. Paul was a small town in those years.

The men who married the Weyerhaeuser daughters were varied in their pursuits. For two of them, William Bancroft Hill and Richard Jewett, the business world held no interest professionally. Academic men for their entire careers, they taught and traveled widely. The third, Sam Davis, entered the commercial arena and made his career entirely in Rock Island in the developing energy industry of the time.

William Bancroft Hill possessed many talents. He was a teacher, a philosopher, and the author of many books, primarily on the New Testament and religious topics, although he also wrote a book with the intriguing title *Chimham and his Khan*. He was a man of broad learning with degrees from Harvard and Rutgers and further study at Columbia Law and Union Theological Seminary. Admitted to the bar in Baltimore, he practiced law there for a time. Bancroft Hill's settlement house work in New York City led him to meet Elise, who shared his passion for helping the less fortunate.

Later Bancroft Hill became a lawyer, then a professor of biblical literature at Vassar. Eventually he was made a trustee of widely varied educational institutions: Rutgers College (now University), the American University at Cairo, Fukien University at Foochow (now Fuzhou), China, and the American Indian Institute at Wichita, Kansas. He had an enormous educational influence on Elise and, indirectly, on the education and development of her siblings.

James Richard Jewett pursued different studies. He became a student of Arabic and Syriac, and after he was awarded a bachelor's degree from Harvard, he studied in Syria and Egypt. His PhD in Arabic studies was granted from the University of Strassburg [sic] in 1891. He pursued an academic career, teaching at various colleges and universities, including the University of Minnesota, the University of Chicago, and eventually Harvard University, where he was a professor until his death in 1933. (Frederick made a donation of five thousand dollars to the University of Minnesota to support Richard's teaching there.)

Margaret, always close to her father, lived with her parents on Summit Avenue for several periods of time before and after her marriage. This arrangement was usually occasioned by Richard's academic absences but also by her parents' health. This was especially true as Sarah became increasingly frail. The Jewett couple's time apart yielded many letters that testify to their intense affection for each other as well as to Margaret's great attachment to and concern for her parents. Margaret's letters offer a view into the social life of St. Paul that is bright with candor, detail, and humor. Her descendants still have many of those letters, and those of her parents to her.

A letter from Sarah to Margaret, dated November 8, 1894, describes Frederick's busy schedule and the St. Paul social calendar:

> Mrs. Davis invited Mrs. Musser and myself to luncheon on Thursday, only 6 at table. Madam Davis is visiting here. She had Mrs. Olmstead, Mrs. Chamberlin, Mrs. Musser and myself. It was very informal . . .
>
> Father left Monday evening (for Ottawa) and was home again on Friday morning. That is he went to Ottawa, Canada. He was four nights and two days on the [rail] cars. Poor man, he has very little rest. He left on the one o'clock train [again] the same day he got home.

The following letter from Margaret on January 25, 1894, to Richard (James Richard Jewett) shortly after their engagement, illustrates her concern for her parents' welfare, when they would be alone after the young couple's marriage:

> If only we can eventually come to St. Paul. Darling, if some one else can be with mother, if one of the boys would get married and they would live at home, I wouldn't feel half so anxious and worried about it. My idea is to live at home only as long as father is so actively engaged in his business and is so much away from home. I do love my mother and father so much. I wouldn't for the world give them any pain—My love for you is much deeper but of course it hasn't lessened one bit for my parents and the thought of leaving them makes me feel it so much stronger.

Samuel Sharpe Davis's family came originally from Kentucky. His father was a riverboat captain who settled in Rock Island, and Sam Davis had often traveled with him as a youth. Eventually Sam made his living, as did his brother, in the development of utilities in Rock Island, where he and Apollonia lived most of their married life. He supervised construction of the town's waterworks and then organized the People's Light and Fuel Manufacturing Company, which he ran until he retired. Sam's main professional career was in managing the Rock Island Plow Company, a competitor of the John Deere Company of Moline, Illinois, right next door.

Rudolph was married in 1896 to Louise Lindeke, the daughter of a Summit Avenue neighbor. It was Louise's genteel upbringing that caused Rudolph concern about bringing her, as a new bride, to the rough ambiance of Cloquet, Minnesota. She adapted well to the environment of the North Woods, but as a cosmopolitan she was equally capable of enjoying the Mediterranean sea voyage she took with her father-in-law in 1901.

The final family marriage of the decade was that of Charles to Frances Maud Moon on December 14, 1898. Maud Moon was the daughter of D. H. Moon of Virginia, Minnesota. D. H. organized the Moon and Kerr Lumber Company, in which Weyerhaeuser and Denkmann took a minor position. Frederick was initially interested in the company because it owned a small sawmill in Virginia. The operation was successful until one night a neighboring butcher accidentally started a fire while rendering lard and burned down the structure. Nevertheless, the partnership had served a greater purpose, for it introduced Charles, working in Little Falls, to his future bride, who lived less than one hundred miles to the north.

All of these Weyerhaeuser family celebrations took place during a decade in which Frederick was checking out the possibilities for timber in the South and exploring a western land purchase while working in several trips to his native Germany. Meanwhile, Sarah, with help from her daughters, managed the social aspect of their lives in St. Paul.

FRED HAS ADVENTURES AT YALE

The youngest Weyerhaeuser, not yet ready for marriage and settling down, was having an adventurous college life during these years. "Freddie" was now Fred and a graduate of Phillips Academy Andover in 1892. He followed his older brother Rudolph to Yale in the fall of that year.

Fred participated in many activities at Yale, graduating Phi Beta Kappa in 1896. He was a member of Skull and Bones his senior year, was elected to the *Yale News* board for a year, and was assigned to the *Alumni Weekly* as editor along with another St. Paulite, William Forepaugh. Frederick was "quite shocked" when his youngest son returned home and presented his father with a check for five hundred dollars, his share of the profits from the *Alumni Weekly*. Perhaps Fred could have had a career in journalism if he had not been born into a lumber family.

The youngest son also escaped another sort of career. In his freshman year he was involved in an incident at Yale that caused his father some concern. At the time, it was quite a serious affair for Frederick. Fred's difficulties began on the night of the "Freshmen Games," in which the newcomers to Yale were expected to do something outrageous, ostensibly to make their presence known to the New Haven community. A group of young freshmen chose to disrupt the local opera production on December 10, 1892, at a crucial moment in the staging by releasing from captivity some well-fed pigeons, one of which had a blue ribbon tied around its neck. The freshmen also targeted the actors with peashooters and, one newspaper article reported, some "explosives," which were tossed onto the stage. The students persisted in catcalling and, in general, creating mayhem in Proctor's Opera House.

Fred came late with a friend. They had scarcely taken their seats when a local police sergeant arrested Fred. He went with the officer, unaware of the raucous events that had transpired before his arrival. As he was leaving, one of his classmates cautioned him not to give any names of those who were in the box to the police. Another said he would speedily raise thirty dollars to bail Fred out of jail, but somehow that did not happen. Fred spent the night in jail and returned to his dorm room the following day, unaware that after the curtain was rung down at the opera house his classmates and the "townies" had melded into an unruly mob. They had done some serious damage to local establishments.

Much to his surprise, before breakfast he received a telegram from a former St. Paul man, H. C. Davis, offering to come from New York to get him out of jail. Fred's answering telegram was "Thanks. Do not need help but please don't tell Father."

The young student was therefore astonished to find that his story was headline news across the country and that he, himself, was cited as the leader of a disgraceful piece of "Yale rowdyism." Eventually forty Yale freshmen were charged with disorderly behavior. The assistant city attorney, Mr. Mathewman, said there was no proof that "Mr. Wirehouser" was the student who threw the "torpedo" onto the stage, so Fred was not charged in that event.

Later it became clear that Fred's arrest had been a case of mistaken identity. He had been taken for a fellow classmate named Cox, who had been involved in the earlier mischief in the opera house. They were similar in height, coloring, and dress.

Frederick's response to all this was quick and to the point, and it survives in a telegram he sent that day to his youngest son: "Dear Fred: The newspapers report that you have been arrested on a charge of breach of the peace. Your good mother worries very much over it. Is it true? If so, it hurts. Your father."

It was not until a friend of the family in New York, Tom Cochran, looked into the matter that things settled down. Cochran explained fully the circumstances of the event, and Frederick was persuaded that his youngest son had not disgraced the family.

Margaret wrote several kind letters to her younger brother over the matter. The irrepressible Bancroft Hill wrote to Fred that it was "exceedingly unfortunate that Fred should disgrace the family just a few weeks of his [Bancroft Hill's] marrying into it." Perhaps Bancroft Hill's humor was lost on young Fred at the time.

In order to fully clear himself, Fred would have had to give the names of those who were in the opera box before his arrival and who were responsible. He could not, in terms of the fraternal ethics of the time, do that, so he took the consequences. He thus became the "president" of the Criminal Club of '94, the first in his class to be arrested: a dubious honor, but one that did not prevent him from an otherwise illustrious career at the university.

A member of the orchestra sued Fred, claiming his eye had been injured by one of the peashooters. He had not been injured in the slightest, Fred later contended, but an attorney finally settled with the man for $450, which was collected from all the Yale students who had been in the box when Fred was arrested.

The entire affair, F. E. later relates, "appears to offer the only criminal record of which the family can boast."

FREDERICK AT HOME

Frederick was working hard and often gone from St. Paul on business. Still, he found time to take an interest in his children's well-being. This letter from Frederick to his daughter Margaret on October 14, 1894, is replete with fatherly advice, to the point that he inquires about her bank interest:

> John, Nellie, Lonie and Charles are having quite a gay time. They all went to the Opera last night. Mother [Sarah] went with them. I staid at home factoring my books.
>
> I may go east when we can get our logging contracts completed. I have been spending some time in the woods among the fire killed timber. It's not very bad on the Chippewa River but the damage . . . on the Mississippi River and Mr. Rutledge's near Bayfield is quite larger . . .
>
> How much interest does the savings bank pay you? I just as well can send you more money providing you can get interest on it. I loaned $5,000 to the Northern Grain for you last week for which you will get 6% interest . . . Would it not be better to take your interest from here and Rock Island and put it in the Savings Bank?

He rarely seemed to have time to spend on anything but work or his family and travel, but there is a record of his attending an 1897 Minnesota-Wisconsin football game in St. Paul with his son Charlie. It was Frederick's first football game, and Wisconsin defeated Minnesota 35–0. Frederick told Charlie that he thought of himself as a Wisconsin man and thus enjoyed the game hugely.

While all of this was going on, Frederick and Sarah found time to take several trips abroad, beginning in 1889 with their children. The first vacation took them back to their common birthplace in Germany, Niedersaulheim.

Margaretha Weyerhaeuser,
Frederick's mother, in an
undated photograph

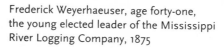

Frederick Weyerhaeuser, age forty-one,
the young elected leader of the Mississippi
River Logging Company, 1875

Sarah Weyerhaeuser, age thirty-six,
mother of seven children, 1875. This
portrait is from about the time of
the affectionate letters between
Sarah in Rock Island and Frederick
in Chippewa Falls.

The Coal Valley home, where Frederick and Sarah spent the first ten years of their married life and where most of their children were born

Weyerhaeuser and Denkmann Mill in Rock Island

Two lumberjacks felling white pine in Wisconsin's Chippewa Valley, where Frederick first built his timber business

Hauling logs in Wisconsin, around 1898

Logging camp cooks had to be ready to feed hungry men. They served a durable meal with lots of baked beans but no fresh vegetables.

Logjam on the St. Croix River, 1886

Typical log raft on the Mississippi. The boat in front, mounted crosswise to the raft, is used to steer left and right, allowing for much larger rafts. The stern boat is traveling through a swinging pontoon bridge in McGregor, Iowa, as did the Weyerhaeuser-Denkmann boats.

An early Rock Island Lumber Company yard in Ponca City, Oklahoma

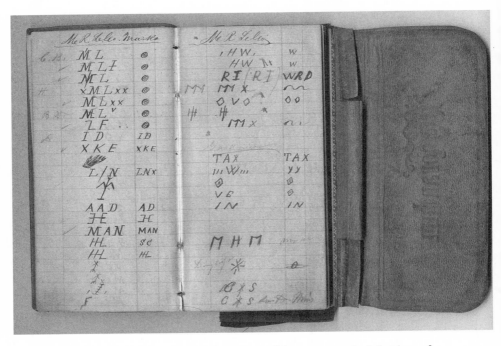

An early F. W. brown leather notebook. Many of the entries on the left side are for Mississippi River Company logging companies.

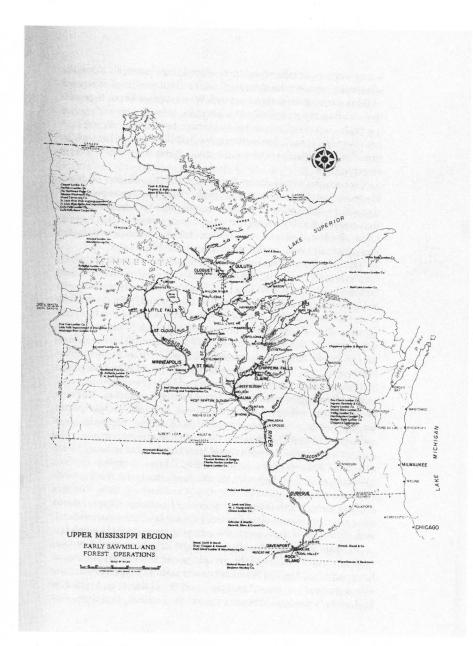

UPPER MISSISSIPPI REGION

EARLY SAWMILL AND
FOREST OPERATIONS

SCALE OF MILES

A map of the Wisconsin and Minnesota areas of timber operation during Frederick's time

The "House on the Hill" in Rock Island, Illinois, where young Fred was born and where all the children were raised to adulthood

The second generation of Weyerhaeusers: from left, John Phillip (seated), Charles (standing), Fred (in front), Margaret, Apollonia (seated), Elise (with parasol), Rudi

The Weyerhaeuser family all grown up, 1890. From left: Margaret, Fred, Rudi, Elise, Frederick, Charles, John, Sarah, and Apollonia.

The house at 266 Summit Avenue, St. Paul, Minnesota, where Frederick and Sarah took up residence in 1893, two years after their move to St. Paul. It became their principal residence until Sarah's death in 1911, after which Frederick wintered in Pasadena.

The newly formed Weyerhaeuser Timber Company directors and stockholders at an annual meeting in Tacoma in 1900. Standing, left to right: Horace Rand, William Carson, W. L. McCormick, H. H. Irvine, C. R. Musser, F. C. A. Denkmann, R. M. Weyerhaeuser; seated, from left: George S. Long Sr., Frederick Weyerhaeuser, F. S. Bell, and P. M. Musser.

Sarah, Elise, and Frederick on the Brule River in Wisconsin, 1903. Frederick donated land on the Brule to the state of Wisconsin three years later.

Frederick with grandchild Virginia, F. E. and Harriette's daughter, in 1905. Virginia was born in 1904 and died young in 1922.

Sarah and Frederick with grandchildren Elizabeth (born 1892) and Frederick King (born 1895), both children of John and Nellie Weyerhaeuser

The Sangerhalle in Niedersaulheim, funded by Frederick's donations of thirty thousand marks

The early interior of the Sangerhalle, set for a banquet. German village choruses still frequently blend choral concerts and good local food.

Frederick with schoolmates outside
the Sangerhalle when it was
opened in 1906

Frederick relaxing on the
Mississippi River

Anton Weyerhaeuser of Niedersaulheim
and his wife, Elisabetha, with, at left,
his son Peter and his wife and children.
Peter became Frederick's most enduring
correspondent from the village. Elisabetha
may have been the childhood sweetheart
Bancroft Hill teased Frederick about in
his anniversary poem.

The formal family portrait in 1907. Standing: F. E., Apollonia, Rudi, Margaret, Charles; seated: Elise, Frederick, Sarah, and John Phillip.

The steamer *F. Weyerhaeuser,* owned by the Denkmann family, brought Frederick and Sarah to Rock Island for their fiftieth anniversary celebration.

Frederick and Sarah Weyerhaeuser's fiftieth wedding anniversary invitation cover, October 11, 1907

Frederick and Sarah in their formal fiftieth-anniversary portrait

Frederick with his son and namesake F. E. and new grandson, also named Frederick

Frederick with grandson Edwin Davis, Edwin's father, Sam, and John Phillip
Weyerhaeuser, youngest son of Nellie and J. P.

Three generations of Weyerhaeusers: this 1907 portrait shows Frederick and Sarah at the center of their children and grandchildren. The baby at far right, F. E.'s young son Fred, held by his mother, Harriette, is still in his baptismal gown, having been baptized that morning by Bancroft Hill. The baby at the center is Sarah-Maud, held by cousin Elizabeth.

Frederick tending oranges on his property in Pasadena, California, in his later years. Around this time, he was mistaken for the gardener by a reporter, which amused him greatly.

Allison W. Laird (of the Winona Laird-Norton family), Frederick, and Peter Musser in Idaho

Archibald Stewart, J. S. Taintor, Frederick, and W. R. Coffin inspecting Anthracite Mine in Alberta, property of Canadian Anthracite Coal Company, Ltd., 1895

This picture of Frederick and Sarah's four sons was taken sometime in the 1920s. From left: Frederick (F. E.), John Phillip (J. P.), Charles, and Rudolph (R. M.). Their father watches over them still.

CHAPTER 15

_____ ❧ _____

Frederick and Sarah
Become World Travelers

E'VEN AS FREDERICK EXPLORED new timber sources, he began another kind
of search: for his own roots. This experience would lead him back to his
childhood village for several visits and into relationships with the companions
of his youth and their children that would last the rest of his life.

THE FIRST EUROPEAN VOYAGE—1889

Frederick and Sarah set sail for Europe from New York on June 12, 1889. They
left on the liner *Brittania*, of the White Star Line, for their first return to Germany since they had emigrated to America decades earlier. Two children
joined their parents straight from school: Rudolph from Yale and Fred fresh
from his first year at Phillips Academy Andover. Apollonia also accompanied
her parents on the voyage. When they arrived they met Charles, Margaret, and
Elise, who had been traveling in Europe since the previous spring. Only the
eldest son, John, stayed behind. It's not quite clear whether he did so to mind
the business or to court Nellie, his soon-to-be wife.

The entire travel project was Mathew Norton's idea. He booked passage
first and then persuaded Frederick to come along and to bring his family. Norton, Frederick's close friend and business partner from Winona, and his wife
Emma, as well as two of their children, Matt and Beulah, made up the party
with Frederick and Sarah. (The other two Norton children, Herbert and Mary,
were already in Europe, having previously joined the young Weyerhaeusers in
their travels.)

After an uneventful voyage across the Atlantic, the family docked in England
and were about to take transport for Liverpool when they unexpectedly encountered their nephew, Edward Denkmann, F. C. A.'s son. He had come from
Paris to welcome his aunt and uncle to England, which his cousin Fred later
indicated was typical of his thoughtful and generous nature.

The group toured the major cities of England before moving on to France. Fred records only one anecdote of this period, and does so with some amusement. The dinner service was particularly slow at the Manor House Hotel in Leamington. While waiting for what seemed an interminable time for their food, Rudolph and Apollonia pecked at the strawberries in front of them. When it came time for dessert, the waiter haughtily informed the company that "the young lady has already eaten it."

Paris was much more inviting, and no doubt the food was better, too. The party arrived in Paris on July 3 and were met by Margaret and Elise, who had secured rooms at 45 rue de Clichy, the pension of one Mdme. Glatz. The family had planned their trip well, for 1889 was the year of the famous Paris International Exhibition. F. E. later shared his diary entry on viewing the newly constructed Eiffel Tower:

> In front [of us] stood the enormous Eiffel Tower whose graceful arches were ablaze with gaslights. On all sides, in the form of pyramids, globes etc. were blazing gas jets whose flickering light fell on splendid lawns, miniatures lakes and beautiful sparkling fountains. Some thousand feet back of the tower, one of its great, fiery arches forming as it were, an enormous frame rose the majestic dome of the main building. It was so encircled by thousands of lights, both inside and out, as to resemble a huge ball of pale yellow flame. On top stood the Angel of Peace whose beauty was grandly shown by light reflected from the towers. A little to the right, yet still within the arch, was the waning moon which much resembled a silver boat riding on billowy clouds.

The amazing event offered many exhibitions from all over the world. Fred later recalled that "the marvelous gardens, the endless treasures of art and architecture, the glories of historic Paris and the glamour of Parisian life left an indelible impression upon the simple folk from the Mississippi River."

The family journeyed from Paris through Switzerland. F. E. had noted in his diary an amusing account of his father and the German language of his childhood. As F. E. said, "In a family record of this kind, it seems entirely proper to include from time to time accounts of rather trivial incidents such as the following, as they often illustrate family traits and the characteristics more clearly than the more important events." He then goes on to describe an exchange between Elise and her father, in which she "innocently suggested to him that, having been in America so long, he might have difficulty in making himself understood in Germany."

Frederick was very upset at this inference. Whereas he readily admitted his difficulty in speaking English well, he was astonished that someone, and a family member at that, would question his ability in his native tongue. This was not the first time Elise, meaning to be helpful, generated a surprising response. But as F. E. noted, "sensitiveness is a family trait."

Frederick, determined to show that he could converse in German, seized the first opportunity. While the family was tramping up a hiking trail, Frederick stopped a passing traveler and asked a few simple questions in German, to which the passerby responded. Frederick then said to him, "My children think I have forgotten how to speak German. Do you understand me?" To this question the hiker responded, "Ja Wohl!" as he hurried on.

This encounter gave Frederick the courage to meet his former boyhood friends at Niedersaulheim several days later. "The family journeyed down [sic] the Rhine to Cologne," F. E. recounts, where Fred and Rudolph had to depart for their duties at school. Frederick and Sarah continued into Germany to reunite with long-lost companions in their hometown. On this first visit, the villagers had little idea of the success and wealth Frederick had achieved. The reception and accompanying festivities were modest but welcoming. A distant relative, Anton Weyerhaeuser, quietly hosted a small party at his home and offered coffee, cakes, and grapes. There Frederick met Anton's son, Peter, who would become his primary connection to the villagers in subsequent years. In later visits a much greater fuss was made over Frederick. But this journey was simply a time for Frederick to take Sarah to see his family home and the house of her birth.

THE SECOND EUROPEAN VOYAGE—1894

The Weyerhaeuser couple's next European trip took place not many years later, in 1894. On the day of their departure, Friday, July 13, Frederick and Sarah were accompanied only by Apollonia and her husband, Sam Davis. The group left St. Paul by train for Montreal in order to avoid Chicago, which was experiencing a great rail strike. They sailed from Montreal on the White Star Line again, this time on a ship named the *Germanic*. As on the previous trip, the party docked at Liverpool. After spending time in London, the group crossed over to Rotterdam and made their way to Cologne, from whence they took a steamer up the Rhine.

They were fortunate to have Sam Davis along with them. He displayed enormous ingenuity when it came to meeting travel challenges. When the Weyerhaeusers wanted to see the highly fortified Ehrenbreitstein Fortress at Koblenz in western Germany, Sam was able to gain the party access by going around the guards—a great feat, for the German army fortifications were draconian. He managed to hire a taxi, circumvent the roadblocks, and convey the family to the top of the mountain, where they could all enjoy the view. His tactics delighted Frederick, who always appreciated a clever plan.

On this second visit, Frederick was eager to see his childhood home, so when their steamer docked in Mainz he hurried on ahead to Niedersaulheim, leaving Sarah and the others to follow a few days later. Frederick spent a week with his childhood friends. Sarah, Apollonia, and Sam joined him for only one day, Tuesday, then returned quickly to Mainz, perhaps finding the small village less exciting than the larger city.

Frederick, on the other hand, was happy just to be among his old friends. He was made welcome in their houses and at their tables, although he reported when he returned to his family that he had trouble sleeping in the German featherbeds. F. E. later wrote that Sarah suspected there had been many parties given for "Unser Fritz" and that the wine had flowed rather freely at these affairs.

Sarah, Apollonia, and Sam finally moved on to Wiesbaden, where Frederick joined them at the end of the week. He admitted he had seen enough of his old friends for a while and was pleased to continue on the itinerary they had originally planned, down the Rhine to Strassburg and then on to Dresden.

Sam and Apollonia had left for Paris at one point, and Frederick and Sarah joined them there a few days later. They all traveled on to London and then sailed from Southampton on September 15. When they arrived home, Sarah and Elise stayed in Poughkeepsie to visit Margaret, while Frederick and John (who had come to New York to meet their ship) hurried back to St. Paul to attend to business.

THE GRAND MEDITERRANEAN VOYAGE—1901

Frederick's most extensive trip was an extended Mediterranean voyage beginning January 31, 1901. This trip, taken without Sarah, lasted until April 8. It was planned because, as Bancroft Hill reported, "Father [Frederick] seemed to need a rest." Sarah said she was a poor sailor, and so she decided to stay home. She may have begun to feel the effects of the Bright's disease which would later be diagnosed. Frederick took Louise, Rudolph's wife, as a companion in Sarah's stead. Elise and Bancroft Hill also accompanied them. (At their own expense, Bancroft Hill notes helpfully.)

The voyage over seems to have been a rough one: "Father miserable," Louise writes in her diary. With stops at Gibraltar, a brief hello to Spain, and then on to Algiers, the busy itinerary kept the little group on the move. Frederick was amused by the sight of two vendors chasing after Mr. Noyes, one of their party (they had made friends of table partners on the way over), calling out "Father, father." Apparently they had heard Bancroft Hill call Frederick "Father" and thought it was an honorific.

Louise noted that Frederick had to be rescued more than once from vendors who were pressing goods upon him. "He might be good at trade," she writes, "but with no acquaintance with the language and no knowledge of what the goods really were worth, he was helpless."

Two days were enough for Genoa, and they moved on to Villefranche-sur-Mer, near Nice, from whence the little party took a drive along the High Corniche to Menton, and a carnival. The ladies of the trip were eager to see the gambling at Monaco, but, except for Mrs. Cooke (the Hawaii Cookes had become friends of the Weyerhaeusers on the long boat journey from America), not one of them could be admitted to the casinos because they wore "travel caps." Mrs. Cooke had the foresight to wear a proper hat. She went in first with the gentlemen of the party, then came out and loaned her hat to another of the women. One by one they each entered the hallowed gambling grounds, wearing Mrs. Cooke's hat.

The acquaintanceship with the Hawaii-based Cookes had additional consequences for Frederick and his family. Bancroft Hill later wrote,

> Mr. Cooke, a leading business man of missionary stock in Hawaii and Father became very intimate. It was from him and what he was doing for his own family that Father gained his idea of forming a family holding company. Mrs. Cooke and Alice were delightful companions and most of our excursions were taken jointly with them.

The boat and party traveled on to Cairo, Egypt, where they met Margaret's husband, Richard Jewett, at the Continental Hotel. Richard was studying in Beirut at this time. He provided knowledgeable guidance for the group's tourist plans. Elise climbed to the top of the Great Pyramid, but Frederick gave up at the halfway point. However, they all rode the camels.

Bancroft Hill relates how Frederick loved to go into the shops and dicker with the merchants for small items—"awful Oriental pieces of embroidery or bits of pottery." One memorable item was a deep red satin table cover, embroidered in gold and silver. None of these artifacts ever was seen after he came home, and his children suspected that Frederick dropped them overboard while on the boat. He had had his fun in the negotiation. Perhaps he also had second thoughts about what Sarah might make of his newly acquired purchases, or it may be that Sarah quietly disposed of them.

Then it was on to Palestine and Jerusalem, where Frederick was appalled by the wretched conditions of the Palestinians under Turkish rule. This stop was followed by a trip to the Dead Sea: "one of the hottest rides I have ever taken . . . As we approached Jericho the temperature reached 100 degrees," wrote Louise. Next was a visit to Constantinople, where the family celebrated three birthdays on the boat with their friends to encompass all the birthdays that had occurred while on the trip. Athens and then Palermo followed by Naples were next on the itinerary. The party's energy was flagging by now, but there was one more port of call at Genoa before sailing home.

The companionship on the boat was recorded as entirely pleasant until a group of the Kaiser's friends arrived for the Constantinople part of the trip. Bancroft Hill remembers the experience:

> I think father enjoyed the trip but found it rather too fatiguing. Everything was novel; much was exciting; and the days on shore were crowded with incidents. Our fellow passengers were pleasant and companionable until we reached Genoa. Then there came on board a group of Germans who were very disagreeable. They were "guests of the Kaiser" who, for some reason, had the right to give a certain number of persons a trip to Constantinople and return on this boat. Being petty officials they were much swelled up by this attention . . . They felt they owned the boat, and were ready to push us aside.

The trip provided the opportunity for Bancroft Hill to probe Frederick's memory, which he found was quite keen when it came to Frederick's young years. His recollection of events in more recent years, however, was problematic: "On the way home I tride [sic] to gather from Father the incidents of his early and later life. He did fairly well in recalling the early part; and I set it down carefully and later wrote it up for the family. When we reached the business years, his interest flagged and his memory was less clear. He said: 'It is all down in the books of the different firms; and you'd better seek it there.'"

Whether this lack of clarity was an indication of advancing age or simply too many complicated business arrangements to remember is unknown. But it appears that memories of his childhood, stimulated by several trips to Niedersaulheim, had pushed that period to the forefront of his thoughts. The book *Pioneer Lumberman*, published by Louise Weyerhaeuser with the help of Bancroft Hill, resulted from these conversations. It is the only surviving set of personal recollections of Frederick's early years.

Frederick had traveled for sixty-eight days on this voyage, the longest continuous time he had ever been away from Sarah. He must have been especially glad to sail into New York Harbor on April 8, 1901.

THE LAST VISIT TO NIEDERSAULHEIM—1906

Sarah accompanied Frederick on his last trip to their childhood birthplace in 1906. Frederick wanted to see the Sangerhalle, the music hall he had funded for the villagers after his visit two years earlier. They embarked on September 4, 1906. Several family members went with them to see the village for the first time. Apollonia and Sam Davis and their son Edwin and Elise and William Bancroft Hill made up the party. Elise wrote to her brother John Phillip on September 12, 1906, describing the family's entrance into Niedersaulheim: "The whole family drove out in a large comfortable surrey . . . all of the Nieder-Saulheim [villagers'] heads . . . sticking out of the windows or the doorways to see the circus, children and geese followed us in the street and the Kaiser himself could not have had a greater innovation."

Apollonia wrote her impression of the visit in her diary:

> The next day we all drove over [from Mainz] in a wagonette—eight with the driver—drawn by two horses. Mother hesitated about getting into the conveyance, as it was uncomfortably high, but she finally decided to do so.
>
> We were taken to the little village church and saw the Weyerhaeuser window which Father had given. We also went to the cemetery where we found many Weyerhaeuser graves . . . We called on a number of Father's boyhood friends, including Mr. Braun's [*sic*], Mr Herzog and Mr. Tobias, each of whom offered us native wines . . . We also visited the Music Hall given by Father to Nieder-Saulheim in 1904 and saw the houses in which Father and Mother were born.

Apollonia also told of the dinner at Anton Weyerhaeuser's house that night. (This Anton is presumed to be another son of Elisabetha and Anton—Peter's brother.) While the guests were at dinner, the barber arrived to shave Anton. Everyone assumed the dinner was finished and rose from the table. However, after the barber was finished and had departed, all were invited back to finish the meal. The startled American family later decided the barber must be such an important person in the village that when he could provide his service, one was compelled to stop everything and accommodate him.

Immediately after the party left the village it was clear that Frederick's blood pressure was up, and the family took him to the Frey-Gilbert Sanitarium at Baden-Baden. The time at the clinic seemed to improve his health, although the best therapy may have been that he amused himself by dickering for oil paintings with some tradesmen in town. When he left the city on October 20, 1906, he had a number of new paintings. He had hoped to go to Rome, but his tenuous health condition argued against further travel. Sarah and his children persuaded him to return to the United States. It was to be his last trip to Europe.

PART SIX

THE FINAL YEARS—
JOYS OF FAMILY, SORROW OF LOSS

SCENE 5

Sarah and Frederick before the anniversary celebration, October 10, 1907

"Setta, you must come now, quickly." Frederick appeared in the doorway of their bedchamber.

"Freiderich, you become so impatient when there is a social occasion." Sarah was engaged in applying several pins to her chignon, to hold the long hair in place through the evening. There would be dancing, of course. And toasts and poems. It would be a long and lovely evening with all of the family present.

"But you must come and see Elizabeth. Our oldest granddaughter has just come downstairs, and she is wearing the gown you wore on our wedding day." Frederick was grinning broadly. "She looks so like you did then."

"That dress!" Sarah laughed. "I didn't even know we still had it. Lonie must have gotten in the attic trunks to find it. It was nothing special you know."

"But it was special. It was not elegant but we had no money. And no other family besides Denkmann and Anna Catherine."

"Yes, and they were kind enough to let us have the ceremony in their parlor." Sarah paused, looking thoughtful. "But she never approved of our marriage. We didn't even have a meal together afterward. It was many years before she could admit our marriage had worked out well."

"If she were here tonight with all the children and grandchildren, she would have to say that we made a good couple. And that it was the right thing to do, for both of us." Frederick looked at his wife of fifty years, her lined face still beautiful.

"You were the best of all my partnerships," he said.

"Freiderich," Sarah smiled, patting his cheek, "that is not the most romantic thing you could say to me tonight."

"But it is the truest," he laughed, offering her his arm to descend the stairs.

Based on Elise's diary notes of the occasion.

CHAPTER 16

Frederick Withstands
Personal Challenges, 1900–1906

N O SOONER HAD THE NEW CENTURY DAWNED than Frederick found himself subjected to a series of curious incidents that tested his mettle and interrupted his peace of mind. Despite all of his business success in the previous decades and the happy festival events of his cherished family, Frederick suffered under a set of personal challenges. He was not immune to surprises or attacks from others, some of which—like the earlier affair in Wisconsin, when he felt his integrity under fire—may have adversely affected his health. But his reactions to these new events in his older years also illustrate the strong character he had developed in his youth, maintained throughout his working life, and carried into his later years.

The stories revolve around a mentally unstable former employee, Teddy Roosevelt, some serious health issues for Frederick, and a muckraking journalist.

BLACK DAN McDONALD

The episode of the disgruntled former employee began in 1900. The man's name was Donald McDonald, but everyone called him Black Dan. He was known to Frederick from his Wisconsin logging days, when Black Dan and his brother John were river drivers (men who rafted logs down the Mississippi) for the Mississippi River Logging Company in the 1870s. Their working relationship seems to have been positive in those early days. Frederick even notes, in one of his letters to Black Dan, that he remembered him as a fine river driver.

In later years, however, Black Dan became something of a mystery to Frederick—and eventually he evolved into a major nuisance, demanding money. Beginning in 1900, and continuing until two years past Frederick's death in 1914, McDonald sent a total of sixteen letters to Frederick or his sons. In addition, McDonald wrote to Sarah, and McDonald's wife to Frederick. The letters all make the same charge: that Frederick personally owed McDonald money from the Smith-Ellison land deal in Wisconsin, which had taken place thirty years earlier.

Black Dan had lived and worked as a driver in Wisconsin, but the initial letter to Frederick in early 1900 was sent from Everett, Washington. Apparently McDonald had read in the newspaper that Frederick was in the West inaugurating his bold, new venture with his partners, and the former river driver decided to confront his former employer on this old, alleged debt connected to the sale of land called "Smith-Ellison." The letter was a complete surprise to Frederick.

Black Dan's initial approach to Frederick may have been generated by the publicity surrounding the Northern Pacific land purchase and the board of directors' decision to name the company after Frederick Weyerhaeuser. McDonald, living in the region, had no doubt seen reports of the Weyerhaeuser Timber Company and decided that Frederick had money to spare.

When Frederick received McDonald's letter, he went to great lengths to ascertain if the claim were real. He immediately wrote to his associates in Wisconsin to get the history of this land deal and McDonald's role in it. The claim, if there had been one, would have been against the Mississippi River Logging Company, not Frederick personally, as the MRLC was purchaser of the Smith-Ellison land. Letters in the file from Artemus Lamb, vice president of the MRLC at this date, Thomas Irvine, secretary, and C. O. Law, an employee, testify to the thoroughness of their inquiry into past documents at Frederick's request. Law did the heavy lifting in researching this matter. His notarized statement specifies not only the Smith-Ellison land transaction but the detail of every interaction Dan McDonald had with MRLC over the years and every payment made to him by the company.

The Mississippi River Logging Company vigorously protested the McDonald claim with careful analysis. The following letter was written on March 22, 1900, by C. O. Law of the MRLC, Chippewa Falls, Wisconsin, addressed to Mr. Thomas Irvine, St. Paul, Minnesota:

> Dear Sir:
>
> At the request of Mr. Weyerhaeuser I enclose a [notarized] statement of the Smith Ellison Land upon which Mr. Donald McDonald here in 1896 claimed he was to have an interest in. I told McDonald at the time just what I have stated in this paper, that he told me he did not want any interest in these lands, and supposed at that time he was convinced, but it seems he still claims an interest.
>
> I have also shown that two years afterwards when he was owing the company [MRLC] and anxious to pay up, that he never mentioned that he had any claim or interest in these lands. However, the cutting of the land and the sale

of the logs shows that there was no profit in the deal, and that is a fact for on 50,000,000 feet of logs which we cut and put in the waters of the Red Cedar we did not any more than come out even and we think we got all for the logs that we could have gotten at the time. It was a hard country to log in and a long, hard and expensive drive, and from what I know of this matter I know that there would not have been any profit in it for Don McDonald provided he had retained his interest, which he did not.

Yours truly, C. O. Law

Nevertheless, the Mississippi River Logging Company ultimately made a payment to Black Dan McDonald of $3,500 on May 19, 1900. The legal document McDonald signed at the time released the company from "all future actions, debts, suits etc." The agreement contained the signatures of Artemus Lamb as well, and a notary public witnessed it. The statement does not provide an exact description of what the payment is for, and the company admitted no earlier wrongdoing.

It may have been a coincidence that the payment and signing of the official, notarized form by McDonald came several days after McDonald had written to Sarah, pressing her to intervene with Frederick on his behalf. On the seventeenth of May, 1900, McDonald wrote,

Dear Lady:

His [Frederick's] excuse he can't find it on the books I paid him $3000 for scale [logging term] . . . then he had me branded as a thief and then his gang kidnapped and through [sic] me in the madhouse . . . he turned me over to Mr. Irvine . . . if there is $8,000 sent to me one month I will call it settled for all time.

Perhaps Frederick wanted to protect his wife from further distress as a result of McDonald's importuning. Or perhaps the MRLC officers decided that some payment would encourage their disgruntled former employee to cease pestering them. That course of action was to prove futile. Black Dan continued harassing Frederick for the next fourteen years, even though he had accepted payment and signed a release in May 1900.

When Frederick was at the Yosemite Hotel in Bullards, Oregon, a year later, McDonald tracked him down and wrote again. McDonald claimed in this letter that he was owed $16,000 for twenty-four years plus seven percent interest and that he had been "wronged and put in the madhouse" by Frederick.

Frederick by now had had enough. When he returned to St. Paul he sent McDonald a stern reply:

Dear Sir:

Your favor of even date at hand. In reply, I will say I cannot loan you $8,000.00 as I haven't the money to spare. I have, for the last two or three years, been sending all my spare money to Washington, but I will make you this proposition: You claim the Mississippi River Logging Co., or I, owe you $16,000.00 on the Smith Allison [*sic*] deal. You claim we made a $40,000 profit. Now, I will permit you to hire any book-keeper you wish; I will pay him a reasonable compensation for doing the work and will give him the Mississippi River Logging Company's books to figure them all over and where he can show that we owe you one dollar, I will agree to pay you two, but for you to simply say that we made $40,000.00 out of that deal and you not knowing anything about it, I do not think it is fair treatment toward us . . .

I am sorry to see you grow old and poor, but the Lord knows it is not my fault. I always treated you as a friend until you commenced setting up claims against me which I think are not fair . . . I will say this: as long as you worked for us you did your duty to the fullest extent . . . I am ready and willing to investigate matters and . . . if there is anything coming to you I will be very glad to pay.

Yours most truly,

F. Weyerhaeuser

Frederick had C. O. Law investigate McDonald's commitment to a "madhouse." Law reported to Thomas Irvine that the county records showed that James Cheaters was the person who made the petition for McDonald's commitment. The commitment papers reference testimony about Black Dan's heavy drinking, his purchase of pistols, and his habit of threatening people in his hometown with guns, people he claimed owed him money or had cheated him.

McDonald's letters continued even after Frederick's death, when he wrote to John (J. P.) Weyerhaeuser. On the last letter someone wrote simply, "File this with the others." No payments were made to McDonald after the 1900 settlement with MRLC.

In spite of the somewhat scattered and deranged nature of McDonald's communications, Frederick never patronized him. Perhaps he was motivated by recollections of earlier years and the work McDonald had done on the river for MRLC. But eventually, even Frederick's patience had given out.

TEDDY ROOSEVELT'S INVITATION

While Frederick was wintering with family members in San Antonio in 1903, a letter arrived from Theodore Roosevelt, president of the United States. Roosevelt had become interested in conservation of U.S. forests and had established the post of chief forester with the appointment of Gifford Pinchot, who had taken his forestry training in France, focusing primarily on German forest conservation practices. Congressman John F. Lacey had mentioned to the president that Frederick Weyerhaeuser "was starting to come around, that he was becoming a forest advocate of sorts, that he was an untapped potential arborist."

This information intrigued Roosevelt, and he sent the following letter to Frederick on March 5, 1903:

> My Dear Mr. Weyerhaeuser:
> Could you not come down here sometime next week so I could see you with Mr. Gifford Pinchot? I should like to talk over some forestry matters with a practical lumberman. I earnestly desire that the movement for the preservation of the forests should come from the lumbermen themselves. With regards,
> Theodore Roosevelt

Some back-and-forth exchanges followed. Sam Davis apparently wired to the president that Frederick was ill and could not travel, but the secretary of the Weyerhaeuser Timber Company, R. L. McCormick, was in Charleston, South Carolina, and could represent Frederick in any Washington meeting.

Roosevelt's office contacted McCormick, who then wired Frederick to ask what instructions he should follow. The president had asked that young Fred (F. E.) come with McCormick. Unfortunately, neither McCormick nor Fred went to meet the president. If such a meeting had taken place, perhaps Roosevelt's attitude toward the lumber industry might have been modified, and he would not have made his aggressive attacks on the industry's leaders shortly after this time, creating an irreversible animosity between his administration and leading lumbermen. That, at least, was F. E.'s opinion in later years.

Roosevelt's public attack on leaders of the lumber industry took place at the American Forest Congress, held on January 3–4, 1905, in Washington, DC. Invitations came from Chief Forester Pinchot, who let it be widely known that they were issued at the behest of the president. Frederick was invited, but Fred informed Pinchot that his father never made public speeches and, besides, he had been ill and was still too fragile to travel. He would not be coming.

Pinchot then invited Fred himself to prepare and read a paper; Fred accepted. Fred had known Pinchot through their Yale connection (both were Skull and Bones), and at the time of this forest congress Pinchot invited Fred to stay at his own home in Washington. At Pinchot's suggestion, Fred shortened his paper. Pinchot also asked Fred to review the speech Pinchot had prepared for the president to deliver. Fred was quite satisfied with Pinchot's draft of the president's proposed remarks and felt that the lumbermen would be accepting of its contents.

Pinchot's forest conservation ideas had come from his intensive European education in these matters. However, he seemed to believe that ideas that worked in Europe could be put into practice in the United States, whereas the lumbermen, according to F. E.'s later account, saw that there were vast differences in the two environments. For example, because the forests in Europe were so much smaller at that time, one standing tree in Germany had the value of a thousand feet of finished lumber in the United States.

Fred had used his father's influence to encourage other lumber leaders to attend this important first conference to discuss the future of forestry. Most of the country's prominent timber owners and lumbermen were present, and they were invited to sit on the stage to hear the president's address. The opera house where the American Forest Congress meeting was held was packed.

In the event, Roosevelt did not perform as either Fred or Pinchot had expected. He hurried onto the stage at the congress, acknowledged the applause that followed him, and then turned to face the assembled leaders of the lumber industry arrayed before him. (F. E. later recalled that the president was grinning. No doubt he was enjoying the moment of surprise.) Entirely ignoring the speech Pinchot had prepared for him, he proceeded to give the lumbermen a severe "tongue-lashing." With intemperate language, he called the assembled leaders "skinners of the soil" and "despoilers of the national heritage." The lumbermen, who had come in good faith to learn something about future forestry practices, left the meeting disgusted. The next morning, however, Roosevelt was undoubtedly pleased by the reception the press gave his performance. The media's consensus was that the president was the savior of the American forests.

Excerpts from F. E.'s letter to his son C. Davis Weyerhaeuser written February 25, 1932, while Davis was at Yale, regarding Teddy Roosevelt and the American Forest Congress episode:

Dear Davis:

While your recent letter in some particulars amuses me, the request that I write you about Roosevelt's forest conservation policies disturbs me, in that it threatens to postpone a much needed game of golf . . .

Your Mr. Darling's [evidently a professor at Yale] charges make me think of Mother's enthusiasm about hearing Mr. Einstein talk Saturday evening on International Relations . . . I have repeatedly cautioned you to take with a grain of salt the statements of your college instructors especially when they talk on a subject outside their own field of research. One is not necessarily an authority on religion because he happens to be an eminent sociologist or physicist.

Not very long after I left college, [Chief] Forester [Gifford] Pinchot held his first important Conservation Congress in Washington. At that time Forester Pinchot's Conservation Program covered only timber resources; later he expanded the idea politically to include everything from Alaskan coal to Bowery babies. Pinchot requested my father to address this Congress. As he was ill at the time I wrote Pinchot that he could not do so. Pinchot then asked me to read a paper. In my youthful enthusiasm I agreed to, and making rather free use of my father's name and influence, at Pinchot's request, I urged many prominent lumber manufacturers and timber owners of the country to accept an invitation to attend . . . I never think of my temerity in addressing this Congress without a laugh.

Roosevelt, barely recognizing the audience, almost immediately turned on the group of 100 or more well known lumbermen seated on the stage, shook his fist, his teeth gleamed, he called them skinners of the soil and shouted many other insulting and characteristic Rooseveltian phrases . . .

Incidentally, I received the abuse of my friends whom I had urged to come . . . They went there earnestly desiring to learn something about forestry and returned home disgusted with Roosevelt.

In an account of these events written years later, F. E. admitted not liking Roosevelt, whom he also fairly called "the greatest personality of his generation." (He believed that the president's grandstanding had imposed a heavy cost on both the conservation effort and the lumber industry—not to mention contributing to his own embarrassment at having lured his father's associates to the congress where they were publicly harangued.) He wrote,

It is probable that the real cause of forestry in this country was delayed not less than fifteen years because of this one speech . . . Pinchot went about the country proclaiming that in twenty-five years the forests of the country would be exhausted . . . The great era of speculative buying of timber-lands followed lasting until the beginning of the Great War. The Administration's ill advised attacks on the lumber industry brought many unhappy results and to a considerable extent are responsible for many of the industry's troubles today, especially those that grew out of excessive private ownership of lands.

Efforts that might have been made in common between the conservationist Roosevelt and his forestry administration and the lumbermen were no longer possible at that time. The spectacle had severed any possibilities for cooperation. F. E. wished that things had turned out differently.

FREDERICK'S HEALTH AFFLICTIONS

What, exactly, were the health problems that prevented Frederick from coming to Washington to meet with President Roosevelt? F. E. recalls that in the winter of 1902–3 Frederick was in a "nervous" condition, undoubtedly suffering from insomnia and perhaps high blood pressure. He had recently undergone extensive dental work, which may have contributed to his problems.

Sam Davis and Apollonia had gone to San Antonio, Texas, taking with them Margaret and Richard's son, Fritz, along with their own son, Edwin. The Davis couple persuaded Sarah and Frederick, along with the boy's parents, to join them in the more agreeable Texas winter weather. However, on this trip, F. E. later wrote, "[Frederick] was giving unmistakable indications of an impending nervous breakdown."

There may have been some contributing factors to the stress Frederick felt at this time. Some of the Denkmann cousins had made an unfortunate investment in a sawmill property and timberlands near Hammond, Louisiana. There was some confusion or misunderstanding about the ownership, in which Frederick had a significant interest. This matter, and others, seemed to weigh more heavily on him through the following winter than was normal, for according to diaries kept by F. E.'s wife, Harriette, Frederick expressed great distress in his conversations with her. He did not, however, tell her what troubled him.

Then, on the morning of April 17, 1904, when he was seventy years old, Frederick awoke to an unpleasant surprise: some serious difficulty in speaking. He also had trouble dressing but managed to finish the task and walked to church as usual. The walk was downhill, to the Presbyterian church located "downtown" in St. Paul. Frederick must have appeared pale; after the service some friends insisted that he ride back home in their carriage. When Sarah saw him, she wanted to call the doctor, but Frederick refused. That afternoon a friend, George F. Lindsay, stopped by for a visit and, seeing Frederick's condition, knew instantly what had transpired. He called Dr. William Davis, who came immediately. Frederick had clearly suffered a stroke.

Family members later could not fix the date for this event, but Frederick himself had written in his diary an entry that identified it as April 17: "I took sick with a stroke of A—." His inveterate habit of recording detail was still operating.

In the course of the following weeks Frederick began to show improvement, although his speech was never again as clear as it had been. His handwriting also changed. A letter fragment started to his son John, dated April 22, 1904, was all the more poignant for the brevity and shaky scrawl in which it was written: "Dear John. Come home." On the same sheet Frederick had also written several times, "Dear Margaret." Apparently the letters were never sent. Gradually, the handwriting in his letters returned to something close to its previous elegant form.

Frederick continued to struggle with ill health for the next several years. His own fragile health could have been additionally compromised by worry over his eldest son's situation. John's wife Nellie had died in 1900, leaving him with three young children. A year and a half later John married Nellie's closest friend, Anna Mary Holbrook. She was possessed of a "fine mentality and quite unusual executive ability." Leaving her job in Chicago, she devoted herself to raising John's children. However, in 1906 a large tumor was discovered in Anna Mary that required surgical removal. Although she came through this surgery and began to improve, the effect of another trauma caused John to develop a serious nervous disorder, an affliction more severe than his father had experienced a few years earlier in San Antonio.

At this time Frederick and Sarah were about to embark on their final trip to Germany. He must have worried about John's condition when they left on August 3, 1906, after visiting Anna in the hospital in Chicago. It was no surprise that Sarah and Frederick returned home earlier than planned, after Frederick's short stay in the clinic at Baden-Baden.

Frederick appeared to recover from these events, but it took some time. A semblance of his health returned along with the clarity of his handwriting. But the stroke and depression left their mark on him. Some of his former vigor was dissipated, and he began to turn over many of his day-to-day business responsibilities to his sons. He continued to take an interest in what was happening and went to the office regularly, but he now seemed willing to relinquish, gradually, his strong leadership role.

"Richer than Rockefeller"

Less than a year later another event that must have affected Frederick's well-being took place. At the turn of the century a brand of journalism arose in the United States that came to be known as "muckraking." The original purpose of this type of reporting was to expose corruption. But the approach ranged from Lincoln Steffens's reporting on corruption in politics in St. Louis and Minneapolis to highly sensational personal attacks on public figures. The latter describes the article about Frederick Weyerhaeuser published in *Cosmopolitan Magazine* in January 1907. The piece was written in what today would be termed a tabloid style and was intended to boost magazine sales. The public was hungry for startling opinion and flamboyant charges. Like Teddy Roosevelt's dramatic address at the American Forest Congress, the *Cosmopolitan Magazine* article met both criteria.

Charles P. Norcross was writing for *Cosmopolitan Magazine* in 1907. He came to St. Paul for an interview with Frederick's neighbor James J. Hill. The journalist was interested in Hill because of the Northern Pacific Railroad sale of land to Frederick and his partners. Norcross thought that Hill himself was the buyer behind Frederick. When Norcross found out the land sale was exactly as it had seemed on the surface, he had to create another story. He then turned his attention to Hill's partner in the land deal—Frederick.

But how to make the quiet, retiring lumber businessman interesting to the public? The journalist hit upon a novel approach: tie Frederick's lifework to "a national crime." Under the title "Weyerhaeuser—Richer Than John D. Rockefeller," the preface to the article set the stage for the opinion behind it.

> That a comparatively obscure man possessing properties worth billions of dollars should be living among us, silent, unobserved and unexploited, is in itself an astonishing fact. That this excessively modest, not to say secretive, character, despite his widespread dealings has managed to keep out of the lime-light of publicity is well-nigh a miracle. But the Cosmopolitan has uncovered him and, through its investigator Mr. Charles P. Norcross, gives to the world in the following article a complete exposition of this remarkable person, the story of his slow but certain accumulation of a gigantic fortune, and the national crime which made the Weyerhaeuser billions possible.

The article goes on to describe Frederick as

> Timber king and recluse . . . lord of millions of far-flung timber lands . . . Weyerhaeuser's wealth and opportunity grew out of a national crime. One of the most wanton wrongs ever committed in this country has been the spendthrift waste of forests. It was only recently that the nation awoke to the vandalism that has been going on unhindered for years and began establishing forest reserves . . . Weyerhaeuser, born in a land where forestry is an exact science, realized that the methods in vogue, if left unchecked, would in time exhaust even the prodigal wealth of the land and bring on a timber famine that would cause forest lands to appreciate in value. Fifty years ago he sought out timberland and secured the best of timber properties.

Norcross had reduced Frederick's decades of tramping forests, fostering partnerships, and building a lumber business to a conspiratorial land grab whose purpose was to acquire timberlands before conservation took over the country.

The article was based on misunderstandings of major proportions about how the timber business worked and how Frederick had organized his various partnerships for investing. Norcross knew little about the lumber industry and seems to have confused dollars with board feet of lumber, turning billions of feet of timber into billions of dollars. F. E. wrote later, "Not a single statement discrediting to Father in the entire article had one iota of truth. It is an amazing and brazen fabrication of lies and gross exaggerations." Nevertheless, this article and the disagreeable publicity that followed caused the Weyerhaeuser family an immense amount of annoyance and left the impression that it was tremendously wealthy.

The allegations that Frederick would have had a grasp of German forest conservation practices when he was a farm boy in Niedersaulheim were unreasonable and unfounded. Frederick's understanding of emerging forestry practices in the United States was grossly misrepresented to make it appear that his entire career was an effort to forestall conservation efforts. Yet once the article with its inaccuracies and misrepresentations was written, published, and read, the appalling picture of Frederick as the perpetrator of a "national crime" took hold in the public mind.

Frederick, F. E. later reported, "gave little attention to the article. He was rather amused than offended. It never occurred to him the American people would accept such drivel."

But politicians read magazines. Frederick was eventually summoned to Washington to explain his alleged nefarious activities to Congress. He went with one of his longtime partners, William Irvine, and gave the information that was required. The Moline daily newspaper headlines were inflammatory, but the investigation came to nothing. A series of antitrust actions began at this time, and although the impact on the lumber industry was not positive, the suits generally petered out or were dismissed. As F. E. noted later, his father's multiple, unique partnerships with various men for specific timber deals did not meet the criteria of Teddy Roosevelt's targets, the huge conglomerates that Roosevelt labeled "combinations."

Sensational headlines on Frederick's 1911 testimony before Congress on the alleged "Lumber Trusts":

Moline Evening Mail, June 8, 1911, regarding interest in Frederick's congressional subpoena:

> No Immunity for F. Weyerhaeuser
> Subpoena for Secretary of Big Lumber Operator, but Not for Him
> Wants Private Papers of Lumber King: Absolute Secrecy Commanded
> Uncle Sam is pressing along the trail of Lumber-man Frederick

Weyerhaeuser, the most influentialy [sic] character in the lumber world of this country.

> It was disclosed yesterday that while the federal grand jury lumber trust investigation under direction of Judge Landis does not intend to overlook smaller game that may be routed from cover, sharp eyes are peering ahead in the expectation of sigh[t]ing the giant of the forest.

Further sensational headlines the following day, in various type sizes:

Lumber Trust Faces Facts Before Jury

Government Agents Have Mass of Evidence Against Weyerhauser Combines

Witnesses So Numerous Courtroom Too Small

Investigation Will be Complete as the Dealings of the Giant Combination

Chicago, Ill: June 9, 1911 That agents from the department of justice had made a complete secret investigation into the dealings of the lumber trust and knew exactly where to place their hands on the evidence they desire to submit to the secret federal grand jury was made manifest today. The jury appeared before Federal Judge Landis and asked for large quarters, declaring they had already secured such a mass of documentary evidence they could no longer work in the room furnished in the federal building.

Most of these documents are said to have been secured by means of subpoenas from the office of Frederick Weyerhauser the lumber king. Judge Landis at once adjourned his court to the quarters of Judge Kohlsaat and turned over his large court room to the grand jury.

(Note: No legal actions ever resulted from this highly publicized investigation.)

Another of the so-called muckrakers, Lincoln Steffens, had a markedly different experience with the "lumber king." In *The Autobiography of Lincoln Steffens*, Steffens writes that his editor at McClure's sent him to St. Paul to interview Frederick, who was reportedly wealthy and a recluse. He gave the following account in his memoir:

I went to St. Paul, found Weyerhaeuser's modest, orderly office, and learned from his clerks that he always refused to be interviewed. They told me a little about him, how precise he was, how quiet, methodical, prompt. "Gets down here at the office every day at exactly 7:30." I think that was the minute; maybe it was 7:15. Anyway I was there five minutes before the hour named the next morning, and when the round, gray, smiling German arrived I asked him for an interview.

"I am never interviewed," he said. "I don't care for write-ups." He was about to go through the swinging gate.

"I don't propose to write you up," I said. "I want to write you down."

He stopped, looked. "Come in," he invited, holding the gate open . . .

I told him I had learned that he had started with nothing and acquired great wealth and half the forests of America. "What did it cost you?" I asked.

He started to shake his head, as if to say, "Nothing," but he was staring at me and his intelligent, wide-open eyes saw something of my meaning. His smile vanished. His face grew serious. "You mean . . . ?"

Steffens claims to have spent several hours with Frederick and to have promised not to write an article in return for some candid conversation on the topic of Frederick's wealth. He asked, "What did it cost you?" Steffens said Frederick told him how he got the timber, how he used power in politics and made campaign contributions during the Wisconsin river battles. Steffens implies Frederick confided in him. At the end of their conversation, Steffens asked how wealthy Frederick actually was. Frederick called the bank to inquire. The man at the bank could not tell him.

> "He doesn't know either, can't say offhand."
>
> "It doesn't matter now, does it?" I said.
>
> "No, that isn't the point. We've got the cost; the profits don't matter."
>
> This he said absentmindedly, and absentmindedly he saw me to the door. I went away and back to Chicago, like Weyerhäuser absentmindedly, thinking how much better a man can be than he thinks he is.

Steffens never published any article about Frederick Weyerhaeuser.

During these years, Sarah's health worsened. Frederick, as he explained in letters to his friends in Niedersaulheim, wanted to do what he could to alleviate her difficulties. Because she found the Minnesota winters burdensome, he purchased a house in Pasadena, California. At one point, after the unwelcome notoriety caused by the *Cosmopolitan Magazine* article, the press had difficulty locating Frederick for comments. International headlines blared that Frederick Weyerhaeuser, the lumber king, was missing. However, as he telegraphed with typical brevity in response to an anxious telegram from his distant cousins in Germany, he "never was lost."

On the matter of Frederick being "Richer Than Rockefeller" and the episode of alleged "lostness," the irrepressible Bancroft Hill had his own amused response from Poughkeepsie on March 12, 1907.

> Dear Father:
>
> I see you are again making trouble. After having become the richest man in the world—greatly to the mortification of Rockefeller and the despair of Harriman—now you have gone and lost yourself in California, and have got all the poor, overworked employees of the Southern Pacific hunting for you. Really, you ought to be ashamed of yourself at your time of life—to keep the public mind so stirred up.
>
> I have had short distance and long distance telephones asking me if I could throw any light upon the matter. I told them it was just what I expected—that you had most mysteriously appeared as richer than Rockefeller and I expected

that at any time you would just as mysteriously disappear; that both stories came from the same source and there was as much truth in the one as in the other. Evidently the Hearst reporter has got Weyerhaeuser on the brain and whenever he takes a drink too much he sees visions of the billionaire.

The whole affair is annoying; but it can't be cured so we might as well endure it cheerfully. Elise gets impatient sometimes and thinks something ought to be done by way of denial in the papers; but I tell her that the least said the sooner the whole matter will be forgotten. It is one of the penalties we have to take along with increase of riches.

W. B. Hill

FREDERICK SEES DANGERS TO
FORESTS AND THE FUTURE TIMBER SUPPLY

Part of Frederick's legacy was the evolution of his thinking on the future of forests. In the early part of his life, he was not concerned with supply. As he said himself, when he saw the forests of Wisconsin he felt as though he had seen a secret treasure. After forty years of working in the logging and lumber industry, however, his views had modified somewhat. In 1908 he still saw a nearly inexhaustible supply of timber in the nation. "There is very much more timber than folks have an idea of and it will last longer," he said at that time. But by then he also saw certain threats to a future supply of lumber, due to multiple circumstances. Some of these were man-made and could be alleviated by laws, like the system of timberland taxation, and some were less easily controlled, like the threat of forest fires.

We know of his views because Frederick was called to testify before a committee of the Sixtieth Congress of the United States in 1908. The committee was concerned about the future of the nation's wood supply, so they held hearings in Wisconsin and Minnesota from September through December. It was particularly appropriate to have the hearings in Wisconsin because severe fires had recently raged through that state's forests, leaving devastation and destroying tens of thousands of acres of trees.

The "Pulp and Paper Investigation Hearings" panel interviewed Frederick on Monday, October 26, 1908, at ten o'clock AM. The purpose was to find out his thoughts on the future of forests and timber.

The chairman, James R. Mann, congressman from Illinois, asked Frederick for his views on "the present and future of pulp paper, including in its relations the situation concerning the forests and the future supply . . . We have been told by a great many people both in the East and in the West that there was no man in the country whose judgment would be worth more than yours, and we would like to hear your impressions of the subject."

Frederick, with characteristic modesty, demurred that he "did not know more about the timber country than those men that travel around there," but the chairman pressed him further for his thoughts. He complied by offering a series of comments about the future that appear, in retrospect, to be remarkably modern. They included thoughts on the preservation of forests for generations to come.

His statements about timber and the future supply of lumber had repercussions in subsequent years, particularly in actions by government or legislative bodies to protect forests. While there is not an exact cause and effect between his statements and these developments, his foresight and advice to Congress remain part of his legacy.

Frederick's key points to the congressmen were these:

> The major problem causing timber loss is forest fire and laws should be created to enforce that those in the forests take care not to create man-made fires through carelessness.
>
> Taxes have an enormous impact on the timber output. Lumbermen have to pay taxes annually on their full crop of standing timber, yet it takes two hundred years to raise a good pine tree. Even if the trees are cut early, the Lumberman pays taxes fifty or sixty times for the pine tree he eventually cuts down.
>
> The state should buy some land and try to raise forests for the future, such as is the practice in Europe.
>
> We will not conserve until the value of a tree is recognized, and that will be when it is scarce.
>
> We should be thinking about what comes after us and our children and grandchildren.

In retrospect, it's amazing how forward-looking Frederick was on these issues. Many changes in the areas he cited subsequently came to pass. For example, state help for private associations to combat fires occurred in the West within a few years. Other changes, such as the Weyerhaeuser Company tree farm (reforestation) program, came decades later but continue down to the present. The seeds were sown when Frederick raised these issues.

CHAPTER 17

"Unser Fritz"
Takes Care of the Villagers

As FREDERICK ENTERED HIS FINAL YEARS, even as he continued his business explorations and dealt with health issues, a new interest claimed his attention: his increasingly close connection to the village of his birth and childhood. His visits in 1889, 1894, and 1906 resulted in many gifts to the village and a connection of kinship with his birthplace.

In 2009, the family was told of a cache of letters in possession of Georg Weyerhaeuser, one of the villagers in modern-day Saulheim (the Nieder, or lower, and Ober, or upper, parts had long since merged). These letters from Frederick to his distant cousins tell this story more eloquently than any summary. The letters from Frederick, written in the German of the time, were over one hundred years old and had been kept by the descendents of Peter Weyerhaeuser, the son of Anton Weyerhaeuser, who entertained Frederick and Sarah on their first visit. Peter became Frederick's chief correspondent in the village. Frederick wrote warmly to the villagers, although occasionally his patience was tried with their constant requests.

The surviving correspondence began in 1903, some years after the initial reunions had taken place and three years before Frederick's final visit to Niedersaulheim in 1906. The letters continued until a few months before his death in 1914.

THE FIRST GIFT—THE SANGERHALLE

After Frederick had made several visits to the village, a group of men gathered the courage to write to their distant American cousin. The men—Messrs. Oehler, Peter Weyerhaeuser, Dechent, and Koehler—wished Frederick good health. Then they presented a proposal to him. In those days every German village had a men's choral group, a tradition many towns continue to modern times. But the village chorus of Niedersaulheim had no adequate place for its

178

rehearsals and performances. Would Frederick donate funds to help build a hall for that purpose?

This request was made a few years after the Northern Pacific Railroad land purchase and the establishment of the Weyerhaeuser Timber Company. The news of Frederick's good fortune may have reached the German cousins, generating hope for some contribution.

Frederick wrote back on October 31, 1903. After thanking the villagers for their kind words and wishing them all good health in return, he makes the following pledge:

> I am quite satisfied with the use and the purpose of the choir's building. If the costs for the building and property are 20,000 marks, I will give you 10,000 marks . . . Later I may be able to do more. This year we are building a big library in my old hometown of Rock Island. My contribution there is substantial. When I'm finished there, I can probably help you more.

Only a month later, on December 1, 1903, Frederick writes again with many good wishes and encloses the promised ten thousand marks.

But Frederick did not confine his generosity to the Sangerhalle. Early the following year he wrote to Elisabetha Weyerhaeuser, Anton's wife and Peter's mother. Frederick thanks Elisabetha for the report she sent on buying the "churchbells" that Frederick had funded. It is clear from this letter that Anton, host to Frederick and Sarah in their first visit, has died in the interim. Frederick also makes a reference to another Peter Weyerhaeuser, from Stadecken, who had written to Frederick asking for funds because his father had recently died. Frederick asks Elisabetha if she knows anything of the family's circumstances. (This Peter is not to be confused with Anton and Elisabetha's son Peter Weyerhaeuser, from Niedersaulheim.)

On September 14, 1904, Frederick writes again to the village men, thanking them for their invitation to come for the "consecration" of the Sangerhalle, as their guest. He says he will not be able to join them but sends them every good thought. This correspondence was around the time of Frederick's stroke, and he was unable to travel.

On September 20, 1904, he follows that letter with another:

> Dear Sirs:
>
> Peter Weyerhaeuser, Jean Oehler and Jacob Dechent:
>
> On September 14 I wrote you to let me know how much debt the society still has before the building is completely paid for.
>
> But the consecration is coming much too fast and I think it would be much nicer and better if you didn't have any debts then.

So with this letter I am sending you the second 10,000 marks in order to
settle everything.

Have a wonderful and happy time at the consecration.

With best regards,

Your friend,

Fr. Weyerhaeuser

After Frederick had paid the entire cost of the hall in time for its 1905 consecration, he was clearly anxious to see the results. The following year he felt
well enough to travel to Germany one more time.

NOT EVERYONE IN THE VILLAGE
WAS HAPPY WITH FREDERICK'S GIFT

When Frederick came to see the Sangerhalle, the villagers created a festive
occasion for their benefactor. However, as an illustration of the ancient maxim
that no good deed goes unpunished, Frederick was to discover that the construction of the music hall, while a wonderful event for the chorus and the village audience, was making a small contingent of the town's innkeepers very
unhappy.

During the celebration at the Sangerhalle, someone handed Frederick several letters. He did not have time to read them until the next day, when he
was in Mainz. Much to his surprise and chagrin the letter writers harangued
him for making the Sangerhalle a reality with his donation. One letter even
demanded that he rescind his gift, which would not, incidentally, have done
away with the sturdy wood and stone Sangerhalle.

According to the first letter, Frederick was responsible for the Sangerhalle's
construction and, thus, he had taken away work from honest villagers. It was
signed, simply, "The innkeepers." Dated September 5, 1906, the note begins in
a strong tone:

Dear Mr. Weyerhaeuser: I'm sure it was your intention to donate your place
of birth something good. Instead of that, you had a choral society's hall built
which isn't of use to anybody, but which on the other hand ruins our innkeepers. Either you are glad about taking away our work from us or the society is
betraying you because the hall is no club hall but a public inn in which again
next Sunday and Monday at our parish fair there will be public dance music. Mr.
Georg Sander and Philipp Niebergall have had to give up because of that.

If it was not your intention to beggar the local innkeepers and through this
to attract the terrible curse of our grandchildren and great grandchildren to you,
then please kindly interdict the society the public dance mused by otherwise

taking back your donation . . . We wish you all the best until our certainly justi-
fied wish has been complied with . . . Yours faithful, The innkeepers.

The second note, also hand delivered at the festivities and dated September
5, 1906, is more temperate but still injured in tone:

> Concerning the choral Society Hall here:
>
> The signatories take the liberty of introducing the following to Mr. Fritz
> Weyerhaeuser:
>
> At the beginning of the year 1904 in Nieder-Saulheim the happy lore was
> heard that the choral society Liederkranz was going to build a singing hall for
> the purpose of cultivating singing, whereby a question was asked: How, where
> from and from which means can the choral society's project be realized. The
> choral society Liederkranz has not in a very short time found the man in your
> highly adored person who had the means to have built such an adornment for
> our village . . .
>
> From this time on, more and more a small hatred against the choral society
> has been felt from the side of the other inhabitants, business people, mainly
> innkeepers. The reason for this discord, this hatred can be trace[d] back to the
> choral society's hall, in which . . . the Liederkranz performed a dance entertain-
> ment at last year's parish fair in the hall and thus badly affected the owners of
> dance halls and the other innkeepers and wine restaurants/bars.
>
> The choral society's hall today is [not] only a "house" . . . in which singing
> shall be cultivated; no, it has turned out to be a big restaurant as something
> that brings decay and strife to our community. It won't be a lot of joy and delight
> for you adored sir to be received in your home town where you were born, com-
> ing back . . . It was a pleasure for us to hear that you had come back to your
> home town, in order to bring more light into this situation. May you please work
> towards ending this action and activity as soon as possible. Signed: All the
> innkeepers of Nieder-Saulheim.

Neither flustered nor defensive, Frederick sent these letters to Peter Weyerhaeuser, Frederick's contact for funding the Sangerhalle, with a brief note:

> Dear Friend Peter:
>
> I received part of the enclosed and the letter yesterday in the choral society's
> halle, but I didn't read it before I arrived here in Mainz. I'm sorry there are some
> people in Nieder-Saulheim who have such feelings against the choral society.
> It was not my intention to cause conflict or envy in the community of Nieder-
> Saulheim. I would like to be friends with all of them.

I'll close now, thanking you and your dear mother and all your loved ones with all my heart for the friendly reception and the warm welcome.

Your friend, Fr. Weyerhaeuser

No more is heard from the innkeepers. The Sangerhalle still stands and is constantly in use for choral presentations. It continues to serve beer and schnitzel, but so do many of the other village restaurants.

LETTERS AND GIFTS CONTINUE

Frederick's last visit in 1906 must have been pleasant, notwithstanding complaints from the innkeepers. He writes from the Hotel Regina in Baden-Baden to thank Elisabetha Weyerhaeuser for her hospitality. His daughter Elise also writes to express her thanks and sends gifts for the village children: dolls for the girls and knives for the boys. She tells Elisabetha the gifts are from herself and her sister "Lonie." One of the dolls survives, having been stored in a Saulheim attic along with Frederick's letters.

Several more letters are exchanged before Frederick and Sarah leave Germany in the next few weeks. At one point, also from Baden-Baden, Frederick writes to thank Peter Weyerhaeuser for a gift of some grapes and sends his regards to Peter's mother. Following this 1906 visit, Frederick continued a frequent and affectionate individual correspondence with Anton's wife, Elisabetha, and with Peter, her son.

In his letter of October 11, 1906, Frederick responded to Peter's explanation of the cranky villagers who objected to the Sangerhalle:

> Your explanation in the Cologne letter is almost as I had imagined. A lot of people can't see anything good (however good the intentions) if it isn't for their own advantage (selfishness). We hope that the choral society's hall will bring the people in Nieder-Saulheim blessing and no curse.

When Frederick returned home, he sent a further contribution of ten thousand marks on December 13, 1906, with the wish that it would be used to pay off the remaining debts of the choral society's hall. (This makes a total of thirty thousand marks Frederick provided for the hall, for which the initial estimate was twenty thousand marks.) In the letter accompanying the donation, Frederick said, "I hope you will get the money in time to be free of debt on the first day of the New Year. I wish for the society to stay out of debt for the future. I'll close now, sending best wishes to you, your loved ones, your dear mother and all friends, Merry Christmas to you all."

THE RELATIONSHIP WITH THE VILLAGERS CONTINUES

On January 29, 1907, Frederick wrote to Peter to acknowledge pictures sent and to reiterate his hopes that now that all the society's debts were paid, it would stay out of debt. On March 23, 1907, Frederick wrote to his friends in the village in response to a wire they had sent. The national news service had reported that Frederick had been lost in California, alarming his German correspondents, who sent a telegram expressing their fears. Along with this letter he sent another eighteen hundred marks for a new piano in response to a request by Elisabetha.

From this point on it becomes clear that the German residents of Niedersaulheim began to depend on Frederick for frequent contributions to all kinds of things in the village, including donations to individuals. There is a pattern to the succeeding letters. For his part, Frederick continued to share with the villagers news about his life, as in this letter, written from St. Paul, Minnesota, October 5, 1907:

> I wanted to answer the letters right after my return, but I can't find them. Since I became the richest man in the world [a reference to the *Cosmopolitan* article] I have received a lot of letters from all over the world and in a lot of different languages. But I don't see most of them, many get burned. [Frederick then describes his fiftieth wedding anniversary celebration surrounded by family and concludes] But do not believe what the newspapers write about me. I am by far not the richest man in the world, but I think I am the happiest.

When Frederick wrote on October 16, 1908, to Anton Weyerhaeuser (Peter's brother) inquiring after everyone, he received a letter back and a new request for money. Frederick sent, as requested, four hundred marks for August Koch's blind mother along with two hundred more for the choral society. On January 20, 1909, he wrote again, enclosing "the demanded 5,000 marks" for the good of the inhabitants of Nieder-Saulheim. Frederick expresses the wish that the funds are used for the good of all, especially the youngest members of the community.

On August 4, 1910, Frederick responds to Peter and Vicar Uhls's letter asking for funds for the "Sick Nursing Society." On October 18 of that year Frederick (probably in a vain attempt to institute some kind of discipline for all these requests) is now paying the villagers interest on money he has set aside for their purposes, which at this time amounts to four hundred marks.

Frederick's letters to the villagers are about much more than the funds he continues to give. His reports contain the news of his life and, often, of his feelings. He talks about how business is going and reports on the great western forest fire of 1910 that destroyed millions of dollars in timber. In December of that year he notes, for the first time, a personal sadness: Sarah's illness. She seemed to be getting better, though, he reports with hope. As he advanced in age, Frederick was willing to open his heart to these distant kinsmen in the village of his birth.

FREDERICK'S PATIENCE IS TRIED

On March 5, 1911, Frederick received an unctuous letter that provoked a tart response. The letter was from Georg Philipp Kappesser of Partenheim, Rheinhesse. It referred to "Sincerely beloved Uncle Weyerhaeuser" and was an appeal for twenty-five hundred marks to counterbalance the adversity that had struck Georg's household: three cows dead in one year and a sick wife, noted in that order.

Frederick was seriously annoyed. He responded by writing to Peter Weyerhaeuser, sending along Georg's letter. He begins by saying,

> I am writing to tell you that I won't be sending any more money to Nieder-Saulheim after the 10,000 marks have been paid for the Sick-Nursing Society. You make it public right away when I promise you something long before it has been paid. That brings me many letters coming from people who think they should have it because they are my relatives.

He then relents and says,

> Enclosed I am sending you the [Georg Kappesser] letter. I wish you would find out whether it is true that my young friend has had so great losses in cattle as he is writing to me. If it is true, I shall help him.

Frederick wrote this letter from Pasadena. He tells of his own misfortunes: "I am here 2400 miles from my hometown with a sick wife and have had great losses in the past year. I hope that this year, if it is God's wish, it will be better."

Frederick conveyed his decision to focus his giving on needs closer to home in a rather forlorn letter of May 30, 1911, like the others, written in German. Of course, he enclosed a contribution of ten thousand marks while doing so.

> You cannot set your hope on me any more or expect anything. Now I want to help my poor friends and relatives here . . . I will soon be seventy-seven years old and working is not as easy as it used to be when I was young. I have bought a home for my wife in Passadena [sic], California, she cannot stand the cold climate in Minnesota.

This letter apparently did nothing to stop the flow of appeals for personal contributions: Frederick received requests in November 1911 from various other German villages and even one from a German immigrant who wrote from Chicago asking for help.

The affectionate, almost familial letters between Frederick and the younger Peter Weyerhaeuser continued for the next several years, with the last surviving one written by Frederick little more than a year before his death. Frederick decries the incompetence of the Sangerhalle builders but ends on an affectionate note.

Pasadena, California, February 24, 1913
Dearest Friend Peter Weyerhaeuser!
Nieder-Saulheim
I have received your highly valued letter of December 15th. With all my heart I thank you, your dear mother and family for the good luck wishes and blessings for Christmas and the New Year.

May God keep all of you in good health for the next year and give you heaven's greatest blessing. That is my wish. On December 26 we left our home in St. Paul and arrived here on December 30. The winter has been quite cold for southern California so far. Here you don't see ice or snow except for on the high mountains, but this winter there was half an inch of ice in the streets and oranges and lemons have suffered greet [sic] damage. All our southern fruits, our roses and other flowers have perished by the cold.

Not long ago I received a letter from Mr. Oehler together with a newspaper where dry rot is being described in detail. Mr. Oehler claims that as it is not the choral society's fault it must be my fault. Did the society think I would come to Nieder-Saulheim every spring and would open the air vents, windows and doors under the society's building or didn't you put any air vents, air windows or air doors in the foundation? In no case can it be my fault. If it is not my fault, it must be the society's fault. If you convince me that it is my fault then I will pay for the damage soon.

If it is to learn the hard way (damage and experience) [sic]. I am totally convinced that the dry rot is nothing but dry rotting which can only develop if you don't let any fresh air under the building. It struck me that you had to have experts come in to tell you that it was dry rot. When I was still living in Nieder-Saulheim every little boy knew that late in the year you had to stop up the cellar windows or air vents with straw so that the potatoes and apples don't perish by the cold and in spring you had to open the air vents again or take out the straw from the air vents.

No, I am certainly of the opinion that it was nothing but negligence by the society that it has suffered such great damage . . . In 8 or 10 years the dry rot will be there again under the same circumstances. It will do the same damage if the society is so negligent and doesn't let any air under the building. The society would say the same again, Fr. Weyerhaeuser can well do it, probably [*sic*] W. won't be here then.

Enclosed I am sending you the newspaper which Mr. Oehler has sent me. From it you can see how little it costs to prevent dry rot and prevent it from doing damage. Please be so kind and write me what Mr. Oehler has to say. Best wishes to you and all your loved ones.

Your friend, Fr. Weyerhaeuser.

P.S. Is my friend Ludwig Schuhmacher still alive?

It was Frederick's last communication with the villagers who had become, over the years, almost a part of his own extended family.

CHAPTER 18

The Joys of Family,
1907–14

THE YEARS IN WHICH FREDERICK was writing to his friends in Niedersaulheim were also the years in which he was turning more toward family
at home. His children were all married and having their own offspring. And
with most of them living in or near St. Paul, Frederick and Sarah saw a lot of
these young families. Surprisingly, the man who had spent his life on rivers
and rails and in forests and business meetings grew to enjoy the simple plea-
sures of children. Perhaps he treasured playing with the little ones because he
had had so little leisure time when his own children were young.

FREDERICK TURNS TOWARD HIS FAMILY

F. E. remembers his father showing great affection to the younger children
in the family. "In his association with his grandchildren Father was especially happy . . . He greatly enjoyed playing simple little German games with
them."

Young Fritz Jewett, son of Margaret and Richard, the Arabic professor,
was the only grandchild who spoke fluent German. (Richard, a "Rhode Island
Yankee," as F. E. notes, was the only adult member of the family who could
speak correct German, much to Frederick's dismay.) Frederick and little Fritz
had a game they played in German that involved guessing how many fists were
placed on his head while his eyes were covered. The boy's uncle F. E. recounts
how Frederick affectionately teased his grandson about his handwriting: was
he trying to make chicken tracks in the snow? Frederick's own handwriting was
the large, cursive style taught at the time and easily readable today.

Perhaps the German language was a special link between Frederick and
young Fritz that led the grandfather to write the following letter of advice to
him and his cousin Ed Davis in 1909. The letter survives in Frederick's original
handwriting.

Dear Fritz,

Your grandma and I were so glad to get yours and Edwin's letter day before yesterday. We are happy to know that you are learning your lessons, going to church and Sunday School. Also that you are happy in your new home.

I trust you will try and get a good education as long as you are young. You can easily see how hard it is to try and get an education when you're old, on the poor letters I am writing you. I did not go to school much (even in Germany when I was young to the English school I never went). When you come home I will tell you the reasons why I neglected my opportunity. Very poor writing, poor spelling, no grammar whatever. Boys are you not ashamed of your grandpa. How much boys do you think I would give now, if I only went to school 6 months, when I came to this country and learned a little? . . . Now, boys, is the time of your life. Make good use of it now.

I should like to live long enough to see you good and well educated men, but please and never forget it is better to be good than even educated. I feel sure I will not be disappointed in you boys.

Grandmother and I will pray every day that the good Lord may keep you and bless you. With much love for all of you from Grandma and Grandpa Weyerhaeuser.

Frederick took great pleasure in creating riddles for his grandchildren, such as, "If two were three, what would five be?" or "If a hen and a half lays an egg and a half in a day and a half, how many eggs will ten hens lay in ten days?"

These games eventually infected the entire family. J. P.'s wife, Nellie, wrote the following to Frederick in an admirable effort at one-upmanship: "If a hen and a half lays an egg and a half in a day and a half, in a barn and a half, a mile and a half from a town and a half . . . how many eggs would the hens lay in ten days and in ten towns?" This riddle was later found on a slip of paper in Frederick's effects. Perhaps he had kept it all those years, enjoying her elaboration of his game.

In his exchanges with the grandchildren, Frederick's wit was also apparent. When Ed Davis, Lonie and Sam's son, was in Europe in 1905 with Frederick, his father had promised to buy him a gun if he would learn five hundred German words. Young Ed was working hard at the task, which amused Frederick. But, ever the negotiator and dealmaker, Frederick had a question for the boy: "Have you all the conditions and provisos in your agreement with your father?"

Young Ed said he thought he did.

"Has your father agreed to give you some cartridges?"

"No, I forgot about that," said young Ed and promptly went to find his father to amend the agreement.

When Ed returned to his grandfather and announced he had obtained promise of the cartridges and all was now in place, Frederick had one more question for him: "But Edwin, has your father agreed to let you shoot the gun?"

In a letter describing an early encounter with Frederick, William Carson of Burlington, Iowa, described how Frederick's "eyes commenced to dance when he was amused." From the tales of Frederick's dealings with his grandchildren, one imagines that the old man's eyes danced often.

Frederick was gentle with all children in his later years and treated them with attention and respect. William Irvine recalls a story when he and his wife were guests in Sarah and Frederick's home, accompanied by their young daughter. Frederick was amusing her by showing her the house. They came to the spacious dining room.

"Here we shall have dinner pretty soon." Frederick said.

"Yes," the little girl responded, "but I can't have dinner here for there is no high chair."

"Well, let us see what we can find," said Mr. Weyerhaeuser and hand in hand with the little girl he climbed to the top of the house and in the lumber room in the attic found a high chair and brought it down to the dining room, greatly to the joy of the little girl. Only a few weeks ago I hear[d] that little girl—now a woman with a little girl of her own—proudly relate this incident.

In the years leading up to the grand celebration of Sarah and Frederick's fiftieth wedding anniversary in 1907, Frederick had more time to enjoy his grandchildren because he had shifted much of his business responsibility to his sons. In 1904, as Frederick was recovering from his illness, his doctors ordered him to free himself from his business worries so as to conserve his strength for his recovery. Frederick took this advice to heart and immediately delegated greater responsibility to his sons. He divested himself of much of his property, creating holding companies instead. F. E. notes that his father asked nothing in return; nevertheless, his children voted him a continuing salary from the companies he had built and which they now controlled.

The Fiftieth Wedding Anniversary

The Mississippi River winds slowly down from Minnesota through Rock Island, Illinois, and Davenport, Iowa, and if the sun shines brightly and a soft breeze blows, a sparkle plays across the water. In October an artist's palette of red, brown, and yellow spreads over the gentle hills bordering the river.

Frederick and Sarah's gaze met just such a scene as they journeyed down the Mississippi in early October 1907. A festive week lay ahead, for they were going to celebrate their fiftieth wedding anniversary with the entire family. They would hold the party in the house where they had spent so many of their early and happiest years, the house on the hill.

Apollonia and Sam had spent the previous year working hard on preparations for the celebration, including adding extra sleeping rooms to the large house. However, Apollonia reported later to her brother Fred that she didn't want too many changes; family members should feel at home.

A letter from Lonie later in life to her brother F. E. describes their parents' departure from the St. Paul home: "Just what happened the day the family left St. Paul, you doubtless know better than I do. Mrs. Lindeke and others decorated the new limousine with the old white satin slippers, white ribbon, etc. Father and mother knew nothing of the new car until it arrived at the door to take them to the boat. When they drove away neighbors threw rice at them, making them appear like a real bride and groom."

Sarah and Frederick stopped to visit friends in Winona, Minnesota; La Crosse, Wisconsin; and Clinton, Iowa, on their journey to Rock Island. The steamer on which they made their trip was named *Weyerhaeuser,* and it had a venerable history as one of the early steamboats on the Mississippi. The Denkmann family owned the steamer and gladly loaned it for this occasion. Twelve other family members were on board with the happy couple.

Apollonia (Lonie) wrote a detailed report of the events of the next few days, based on her diaries and memories, and sent these to her brother Fred nearly thirty years later. Because she was the hostess she probably remembered well how she managed the complex sleeping arrangements. All twenty-six members of the family slept in the house on the hill, along with three maids and a nurse for Rudolph's daughter, Peggy, who was recovering from a bout of typhoid fever. It was, in every sense of the phrase, a true family reunion.

The day after arrival was the actual day of the anniversary celebration, but it began with a focus on youth, not age. Fred's young son, also named Frederick, was baptized by Bancroft Hill that morning, and an early lunch followed. Then preparations for the dinner began. Lonie mentioned in her letter to Fred years later that her preparations included making a place in the laundry room to sterilize and prepare baby food, as the group included several tiny children of the third generation.

The main event was a celebratory dinner the night of October 11. Tables were spread throughout the house, and gold and white decorations appeared everywhere. What did Frederick and Sarah feel when they sat at dinner, in the beautiful artisan-carved cherrywood dining room that Frederick had joked about when he got the cuckoo clock? Or as they looked into the parlor where the two long tables had allowed Frederick to work after dinner while his children did their school lessons? Memories must have crowded in on them. Perhaps they shared their thoughts with one another, or perhaps they were struck silent in the face of the happy evidence of their long family life together. Many friends from everywhere sent flowers, more than they could take care of in the house. A reception began at four o'clock in the afternoon, and Sarah was "resplendent" in her black chantilly lace dress, her face "radiant," reported Lonie. Frederick had on his "conventional dress suit" and looked equally happy. Elizabeth, J. P.'s daughter and, at fifteen, the oldest of the grandchildren, wore Sarah's wedding dress. Elizabeth looked fetching in the blue plaid outfit with a very full skirt that her grandmother had worn fifty years earlier. All of the matrons in the family, except for Sarah, wore their own wedding dresses for the occasion.

The celebration went on into the night, with dinner following the reception. The dinner was elaborate, and the program gives an unusual order: five poems were interspersed throughout the evening from reception through dinner. Only the Virginia reel put a stop to the family members' literary efforts. Outstanding rhymes by Bancroft Hill and first cousin Apollonia Denkmann were among the offerings. Apollonia Denkmann had been at Wellesley with Elise and Margaret. Like Bancroft Hill, she had a gift for rhyme as well as wit, and she later covered herself in glory with her contributions to the thirtieth-year anniversary publication of her Wellesley class.

Bancroft Hill's Verse:

On the occasion of the Fiftieth Wedding Anniversary celebration.

> Now we've gathered together this glorious day
> And we have Lonie's good dinner packed snugly away,
> I will sing you a song in rather rough verse:—
> The sentiment is fine and the rhymes might be worse.
> In Niedersaulheim, that village of peace,
> Surrounded by vineyards and crowded with geese,
> There the pigs, cows and horses live close by the door,
> And for each window-pane there is one child or more,—
> A baby was born and was given the name
> Of Frederick, after a king of much fame,
> And received just the training a lumberman should,
> By cutting his teeth on a chunk of pine wood.
> When he grew somewhat older a name he made
> As a wonderful fellow to dicker and trade;
> He managed the farm from his father's death,

And on Sunday cast eyes at Elisabeth;*
And once in awhile, when the weather was fine,
He travelled as far as to Mainz on the Rhine,—
A city so ancient, so great and so fair,
'Twas the dream of his boyhood to have a house there.
Now, when sixteen [sic] years had slipped quickly away,
With his mother and sisters he sought U.S.A.;
The voyage was long, for the ship it was slow,
But he never was seasick (at least he says so);
And somewhere near Erie he learned to make beer,—
His wages were princely,—fifty dollars per year!
"But the business" he said, "puts its boss in a fix,—
If he drinks much of the stuff, his profits are nix;
And if he refuses, his patrons will think
The beer, in his judgment, is not fit to drink."
So he packed in a satchel, his best Sunday breeches,
And pushed farther West in search of new riches;
And striking the river at the town of Rock Island,
"From all I can see," said he, "This town should be my land;
For, where everything is new and a little bit raw still,
There is fortune and fame to be found in a sawmill;
I used to build castles of air in the Rhineland,
But here I'll do better by buying up pine land."
When a man thus starts in for the work of his life
The thing he needs most is a capable wife,
To love and console when he meets with a loss,
And straighten him out when he's cranky and cross;
He needs cash and credit and all men's good wishes,
But he must have a helpmate to wash up the dishes;
And when in his shirt-sleeves he wrestles for riches,
His partner must put a neat patch on his breeches.
"Since I must have a wife," so Frederick planned,
"I will choose me the best to be found in the land,
At Erie I picked out a maiden most rare,
With round, rosy cheeks and brown, wavy hair,
With a heart true as gold, but a will of her own;—
If she'll only live with me, I'll not live alone.
Her name is Elisabeth, but since there's another,*
I will just call her Sarah, and avoid any bother.
So Frederick dressed up in a stunning white vest,

And went to see Sarah to push his request;
And just what he said he has never revealed;
But somehow or other the compact was sealed,
And before a good parson a few words were said
By which the fair Sarah became Mrs. Fred;
And in a small house, which to them seemed a beauty,
They started to share in life's joy and its duty.
Since that little event there have passed fifty years:
How important it was now most plainly appears.
If instead of a "yes" had sweet Sarah said "Nay,"
Then where, tell me where, would you folks be today?
Or if Frederick had never gained grit to propose,
Who would now be my wife, do you really suppose?
There are problems prodigious in mystery hid;
But we're all of us glad that they did as they did.
Then here's love and best wishes to Sarah and Fred!
Would you think it is now fifty years since they wed?
It is true that his hair has got past the divide,
But she is as young and as fair as a bride.
Let us now drink their health—since my song it is sung—
Long may they both live and forever stay young.
And in what shall we drink it? We cannot in wine,
For they never had met when they both left the Rhine.
And since as a brewer his way was not clear,
It would not be fitting to drink it in beer.
There's a beverage better to show our good will—
Let us drink it in water—that brings logs to the mill.

* Bancroft Hill was known to tease Frederick about the rumor of his youthful attraction to a girl in the Niedersaulheim village, also named Elisabetha. She may have been the elder Anton Weyerhaeuser's wife (and therefore Peter's mother). The identical names of the women may be an explanation for Frederick's calling his wife Sarah from the beginning, even though her full name was Elisabetha Sarah.

Much to the delight of those present, the food was outstanding. Lonie had engaged the cooks more than a year ahead of time to be certain that all would go well in the gastronomical department. A series of hors d'oeuvres began the affair, including jumbo shrimp cocktail and crab-stuffed mushroom caps. Dinner itself included "forest" salad with candied walnuts, beef filet with wine and wild mushrooms, scarlet snapper with citrus cream dill sauce, potatoes mélange, and Mediterranean medley vegetables. Dessert, for those who could still indulge, was berry torte with ice-cream log. The dessert plates of shining gold had the names of the ten grandchildren on the back, and each eventually received his or her plate. They have been handed down in the family from parents to children.

This lovely fête must have brought back bittersweet memories for Sarah. Her sister, Anna Catherine Bloedel Denkmann, with whom Sarah was living at the time of her marriage, disapproved of the union and "did not offer even so much as a cup of coffee on the day of the wedding." Here, fifty years of faithful and companionable marriage later, a large and extended family, including many of the Denkmanns, had gathered to provide the festive air that was so lacking on her marriage day. Sadly, F. C. A. had died in 1905, and Anna Catherine had died in January of the Weyerhaeuser fiftieth-anniversary year.

The day after the gala dinner, a visit was organized to the Coal Valley area where Frederick and Sarah had spent the first twelve years of their family life. Harriette Weyerhaeuser, F. E.'s wife, wrote in her diary entry for that day that Frederick was "particularly full of fun" on the outing. He recalled that he had bought his house there for $151 at the Mead, Smith and Marsh auction. The first wagon he had purchased for the Coal Valley yard was still standing, and he inspected it with delight.

The following day, October 14, the steamer *Weyerhaeuser* left Rock Island at 1:15 PM with Sarah and Frederick, together with fourteen family members and several nurses. The boat arrived at St. Paul shortly before noon Thursday, October 17.

This entire affair was the culmination, for Frederick, of his long and happy family life. He wrote to his friends in Germany shortly after the celebration, in a letter dated October 15, 1907, apparently composed on his journey home: "I and Mrs. Weyerhaeuser went to our old home in Rock Island with our children and grandchildren, where we celebrated our golden wedding anniversary on the 11 of this month . . . All I can say about it is that we had a lovely and enjoyable time among friends and family. We want to thank God for his mercy and goodness that he gave us so many happy days and for his richest blessing which became new with us every morning."

CHAPTER 19

The Final Years—
The Sorrows of Loss

WHILE FREDERICK HAD RECOVERED FROM some of his health setbacks, Sarah's health seemed increasingly precarious. She was diagnosed in mid-decade as having Bright's disease, a chronic kidney malady. Fortunately, daughter Margaret could spend some of her days at 266 Summit Avenue while Richard was abroad teaching. She was a support to her mother while her father continued his travels.

The family was spreading out, and when Margaret was not there, her parents were coping alone. In 1906 Charlie wrote to Margaret from the Pine Tree Lumber Company in Little Falls, "John is in Boise, Idaho, Rudolph in Chicago, Fred in Gulfport, Mississippi and Father in Europe." In 1907 Sarah wrote to Margaret that she was glad her youngest son, Fred, was coming home soon.

Sarah was beginning to experience daily fatigue with her illness. In March 1908 she and Frederick were visiting Apollonia and Sam Davis in Rock Island. Apollonia wrote to Margaret of her concern, "Mother has been working so hard [volunteering] on the YWCA building and she needs a rest and change . . . Mother and I have had long walks every day. She thinks she feels better when she exercises. I mean to get some sea salt tomorrow and try her on salt baths for awhile."

Soon Sarah wrote to Margaret that she and Frederick would be returning to St. Paul from Rock Island instead of making the trip to Chicago as they had earlier planned. In February 1909 Sarah wrote to Margaret, "Your father wishes me to give another dinner party next week. He does not realize how much work it is to get up a nice dinner! I cannot do it next week."

In the late autumn of 1911, Frederick and Sarah did not make their journey to Pasadena as they had in the previous few years. Sarah was finally succumbing to her illness and was not well enough to travel. Frederick had gone to the West Coast in July of that year, probably on business, but he hurried home when he learned that Sarah was failing. It was clear that her end was approaching.

The three daughters were with their mother and father in Sarah's final days, as were the sons, and again it is Margaret's letters to Richard, preserved in the Greer family home in Woods Hole, that tell the poignant story. On November 21, 1911, she writes, "This is Father's 77th birthday and it looks as if we are going to have a pleasant day. Yesterday afternoon mother seemed better and we were encouraged again but this morning she is not so strong."

Frederick was stricken with sorrow over Sarah's suffering. Margaret wrote again to Richard on November 23: "It breaks father all up to go into mother's room—[Sarah] told Lonie how much father cries—and of course it is awfully hard . . . I doubt if father will want to go to California—If he should and will want me to go with him, I want to do as much for him as I should for mother . . . Father is three-quarters used up and nearly sick."

The next day she wrote again: "Poor father is so broken up all day that I am fearing it will make him sick. He sleeps very little and can't think of much else—fortunately he goes down to the office so he is out of the house for a part of the day."

Elise wrote much the same in her diary, as this entry on November 27:

> Mother so low I telegraphed Bancroft to come with Elizabeth. Spent some time rubbing Mother but no recognition from her.
>
> Heartbreaking to see Father crying all the time. He held her hand and said: "Setta! Danke an Christus!—Verlasse dich auf Christus." Once she seemed to hear. He said: "Sarah I wish I could go with you!" She said: "Where am I going" He said: "To Heaven." But his voice was so broken I think she did not understand. She so quickly dropped asleep.

And a later entry on Wednesday, November 29, announced the end: "At 7 o'clock this morning—just as Father kissed her, Mother's spirit left the poor sick body. There was no struggle—Just one last short breath. John called us girls, who were sleeping in the 3rd story room. We hurried down. The body was still warm as we kissed her. John and Charles had been up all night. Fred and Rudi slept in the billiard room We were all soon there. She looked sweet."

Frederick had lost his life partner and great love. He was bereft. As his youngest son, Fred, later wrote after Sarah's funeral, "As one would have expected, Father bore his loss with true Christian fortitude. However, when he came back from Rock Island after the funeral those who went with him to his home say they saw in his walk and in his carriage something that had not been evident before. His feeling of loss and of loneliness weighed heavily upon him.

He began to spend more time in meditation and in reading the Bible but he seldom spoke of Mother. Tears came to his eyes when he did."

During this difficult time, Frederick grew much closer to the head of his Presbyterian church, the House of Hope. There were two Presbyterian churches quite close together in the downtown area of St. Paul, and Dr. Howard Swearingen, pastor of House of Hope and consoler of the family upon Sarah's death, thought that his church might be better placed in a location farther from his competitor's church. Frederick agreed with him and promised to donate the cost of the parish house and chapel for the new church in memory of Sarah.

Ground was broken for the House of Hope Presbyterian Church on Summit Avenue in November 1912, just a year after Sarah's death. Frederick turned the dirt for the buildings he had promised, to be dedicated to the memory of his beloved wife, Elisabetha Sarah Bloedel Weyerhaeuser. To the present day the name of her building remains the Elizabeth Chapel. Frederick's close association with Swearingen also led to his interest in the newly formed Macalester College in St. Paul. At Swearingen's request, Frederick became a trustee of the college in the last three years of his life.

In December 1912 Frederick wrote to his young friend Peter Weyerhaeuser in Niedersaulheim of his great loss. The letter (translated from the German) is the poignant statement of a man who has suffered irreparably from the loss of his partner.

December 11, 1912

Dear Friend Peter Weyerhaeuser:

A short time ago I received your letter of November 12th with the lovely photos of your two daughters. I thank you and your young ladies cordially. Enclosed you will find the 100 marks, with them I want you to buy the girls a Christmas present. It is nice that they remember me (think of me). You have long since informed me of receiving the 10,000 marks. I think I didn't answer your letter. Last winter I was in Pasadena with my wife and some of my children. I came back in May, finding much work to do and in July I went back to the west. My wife did not go with me, the weather was too hot. I came back as fast as I could, my wife fell ill and was ill for almost four months and died on November 29th. We buried her in Rock Island, Illinois, on December 17th where her mother, father and my mother lie buried. It is a hard blow to me and my children. They all loved their mother very much. My heart is bleeding. I loved her very much. Last year I bought her a new home in Pasadena. She furnished it partly herself, everything new. She enjoyed it very much. She leaves me with four sons and 3 daughters—all seven have families and are good children. They are well. I have nothing to complain about apart from being lonely.

Wherever I look, the loving mother is missing. May God be kind to her soul and have mercy with me.

After Sarah's death, Frederick spent his winters in Pasadena. Margaret, Richard, and their son, Fritz, were with Frederick much of the time. His company also included his youngest (and perhaps favorite) sister, Eliza, who, with her husband, Hugh Caughey, had moved from Rock Island to make a new home in Pasadena.

Frederick established a considerable orange grove on his property and took pride in pruning the trees himself. One family story has a reporter pulling up in front of the house and mistaking Frederick, in his working clothes, for the gardener. Frederick, always as comfortable in the logging camps in Wisconsin as he was in the boardrooms of his companies, was greatly amused.

Frederick's own death came quite suddenly. On March 24, 1914, he went for a car ride in the afternoon, and when he returned he seemed chilled from the sudden drop of temperature, as often happens in California's shifting March weather. In the night he was taken quite ill and tried unsuccessfully to wake Richard. Later Louise heard him, and in a few minutes all were up and trying to help. Doctors were called immediately. Margaret, John (J. P.), and his wife and son had gone for an overnight trip, but they returned as soon as they received the telephone call. Frederick was diagnosed with pneumonia.

A day or two later, he seemed to rally. Harriette's diary records how the party arrived from St. Paul during this time to breakfast with Frederick. He was talking much of the time, although given oxygen constantly, and Harriette was startled to see how frail he was. Still, he asked for her to return to his room when she left for a brief period so he could ask about her children; he especially wanted to know if her baby, Davis, was talking yet.

Perhaps because of his deep faith, bred in him as a young Lutheran and later continued in the Presbyterian tradition, Frederick was not afraid of death. Harriette recorded this exchange with Frederick in those last days: "He spoke of death and said that he was sorry I felt as I did about it, that he would be [only] in the next room. I replied: 'Yes, Father Wey, but the door will be closed; I can't see and talk with you.' Whereupon he said 'It will be only for a minute and we will be together again.'"

After luncheon that day, they felt he was failing, but he rallied and joked with them when they gathered again. He said at one point, "Mother is there—waiting for me," and later, "If this is dying, it is easier than being born." The end came a few days later, on Saturday, April 4, 1914. He just stopped breathing, Harriette later reported. All of his children were with him.

On Sunday, Bancroft Hill led memorial services in the parlor. The family took Frederick's body by train to Rock Island, to be buried alongside Sarah. They arrived on Thursday, April 8. On April 9 services were held, with Dr. Swearingen traveling from St. Paul to speak about the Christian side of Frederick's character and Dr. Marquis, the pastor from the little church in Rock Island to whom Frederick had been so generous, giving the scripture verses.

F. E. beautifully described his father's resting place:

Flowing past the city of Rock Island, from east to west, the Mississippi immediately makes a great sweep southward. At the lower end of this bend in the river was the site of the original Weyerhaeuser and Denkmann Sawmill. The bluffs which form the sides of the Mississippi River gorge gradually grow less impressive as one travels southward from Beef Slough. At Rock Island they appear as hills of moderate height. On the lower slope of one of these wooded hills, two or three miles south of town on the road to Milan, lies Chippianock [sic], "The City of the Dead." The outlook [for the cemetery] is westward across the quietly flowing "Father of Waters." Here, side by side, at the foot of a lone burr oak tree, are Mother's and Father's graves.

Frederick had come home to rest at last.

PART SEVEN

FREDERICK'S LEGACIES

The Weyerhaeuser Timber Company board meeting, June 18, 1914

"This is a great loss."

"Now that he's gone, we need to reorganize."

"At least, we need to reconsider how we'll manage without the strong leadership."

"George Long is doing a good job. Frederick always did know how to tap talent."

"But he's not quite the chief. Frederick always knew the right direction. It was uncanny. And we listened."

"Most of the time, anyway. But now we're on our own. It may be different."

"We'll have to organize some committees to see how these partnerships can work together in the future."

"Or not."

"Gentlemen." The temporary board chairman was pounding the gavel. "We must have order. We will dispense with the reading of the minutes of the last meeting.

"This is a sad day for all of us, with the passing of Frederick Weyerhaeuser two months ago in Pasadena. Thank you all for making time to come to this quickly convened meeting. We are in a time of great change with the death of the man who brought most of us together in the first place.

"We have a formal resolution that we will now read, and it will be recorded in the minutes for today."

This company has been builded upon the personal courage and foresight of Frederick Weyerhaeuser; they were its foundation stones; and the superstructure was put together largely out of the trust his friends reposed in him. The great railroad holding had been long seeking a purchaser and was open to anyone whose faith and whose funds were equal to the opportunity. Mr. Weyerhaeuser believed the property worth what it could be bought for and invited many who shared with him the risks and labors and also the successes of other ventures to join with him. Possibly none of them would otherwise have interested themselves in it or any portion of it and so this enterprise must be said to bear his spirit and personality as well as his name . . .

Resolved: that in the death of Mr. Frederick Weyerhaeuser, founder and president of the Weyerhaeuser Timber Company at Pasadena, California, April 4, 1914, there came to this corporation an irreparable loss, inevitable in the course of nature, but grievous beyond words to all of us; that we here inadequately record our gratitude and admiration for the creator and guiding spirit of this business, whose great qualities of mind and character made him the most eminent of lumbermen, and our love and esteem for the self-sinking friend and high minded gentleman with whom to have been associated has been a great privilege and an enduring inspiration.

Based on an actual resolution from the company's board meeting on June 18, 1914, two months after Frederick's death.

CHAPTER 20

_◦❧◦_

Frederick's Many Legacies

So ended the life of Frederick Weyerhaeuser. He was an immigrant, forester, business leader, family man, and world traveler. He evolved through many changes in his life and could be said to have piled up many achievements. His involvement in the lumber industry greatly facilitated the country's movement westward. At the same time, he and his associates were responsible for altering the forest landscape of much of the United States. He influenced the rapid growth of logging and distribution of lumber, first in the area of the Mississippi River and then in the South, and finally—with the massive Northern Pacific land deal—opened the forests of the West. What did all this mean for future generations?

CONSERVATION AND PRESERVATION

Part of Frederick's legacy was his view, shared with the congressional committee in 1908, on how a good supply of timber might be secured for the future. While he voiced the opinion that "there was very much more timber than folks have an idea of, and it will last longer," he also saw a need for preservation.

Frederick promoted the theory, startling to hear from a lumberman at the time, that forest preservation was the responsibility of the states or of private enterprise with state assistance. In outlining his ideas for state protection of the forests, Frederick noted both that the state had responsibility for preventing fires, at the very least by making laws that promote safety, and that states should preserve areas of forest or take some responsibility to foster wise use of timber, as was the practice at that time in Europe.

The source of these ideas in the United States, a version of which President Theodore Roosevelt was already promoting through his federal efforts, could be traced back some forty-plus years to the publication of George Perkins Marsh's book *Man and Nature*. Perkins wrote the book while in Italy, where he saw everywhere the results of the role of humans in environmental degradations.

Since the publication of that book in 1864, the U.S. populace had become increasingly aware of the need to care for and protect nature, specifically the American forests. In 1891 the so-called Creative Act, also called the Forest Reserve Act, had begun to slow the transfer of land from public to private usage, a practice that had been in effect since the early influx of immigrants. Through this act, the government began to acknowledge its responsibility for preserving some of the forests for the general public. The Organic Act, passed in 1897, replaced and expanded on the earlier Creative Act by outlining a government mandate to "preserve and protect the forests," "secure favorable conditions of water flows," and "furnish a continuous supply of timber for the Citizens of the United States."

Frederick's testimony before the Pulp and Paper Investigation U.S. Congress Select House Committee Hearings, April 29–May 9, 1908:

CHAIRMAN: CONGRESSMAN JAMES R. MANN (ILLINOIS): We are a committee appointed by the House of Representatives for the purpose of investigating in regard to the present and future of pulp paper, including in its relations the situation concerning the forests and the future supply of pulp wood. We have been told by a great many people both in the East and the West that probably there was no man in the country whose judgment would be worth more than yours, and we would like to hear your impressions as to the subject.

MR. WEYERHAEUSER: I do not know any more about the timber country than those men that travel around there.

THE CHAIRMAN: You speak with modesty, but we would like to have your impressions, as far as you can give them, for the benefit of the present and succeeding generations, of the forestry conditions.

MR. WEYERHAEUSER: Pulp wood I could not tell you much about because I never looked after that much of any. There is lots of pulp wood . . . Timber has increased wonderfully and keeps increasing as it gets valuable. You make it valuable and it will last a long while, but make it cheap and we will get through with it sooner . . . Every time you cut a tree down there is a tree less.

I can tell you this. There is very much more timber than folks have an idea of and it will last longer. When I commenced lumbering fifty-two years ago I went up on the Black River, a stream that flows into the Mississippi River at La Crosse [Wisconsin]. I was manufacturing at La Crosse. Some men who were in the business for years asked me where I expected to get my supply. I told them I expected to get it on the Black River. They said no, the Black

River is *ausgespielt,* played out. We were taking about 40 million feet a year
on the Black River, and then increased it to 200 million feet a year. That was
fifty-two years ago . . . We are getting logs out of the Black River yet.

THE CHAIRMAN: What we want to do, if possible—and I do not know that it is
possible—is to find some plan that we can recommend that will provide
timber for the future.

MR. WEYERHAEUSER: The main thing is to make laws to prevent the fires. I have
been reading about California and Washington. We suffered very little there,
and see how timber has been burned this last year in Wisconsin and
Minnesota and within the last eight weeks . . .

THE CHAIRMAN: We went through in Wisconsin over a hundred miles of burned
forest.

MR. WEYERHAEUSER: You have an idea then, what it means when a forest is on
fire. The only way to prevent it is to cut all the dead trees down. It is the
standing tree that scatters fire. It gets on fire on top and the wind blows it 5
or 6 miles. After the trees are cut down and they are lying on the ground they
make some fire, but not much. If the trees are standing they scatter fire
everywhere. Then make a law that each one shall burn his rubbish before it
gets dry . . . If one does it and the other does not, it doesn't do much good.

THE CHAIRMAN: Do you think it is possible for the owners to protect the forests
from fire without the aid of the State of Government?

MR. WEYERHAEUSER: The state ought to help and ought to make laws for it.
We would have raised some timber or tried to raise it, but a man can not do
it on account of the taxes. It takes two hundred years to raise a good pine
tree. You can raise a white pine tree in eighty years that is merchantable,
but full grown it takes about two hundred years. The way they are taxing us
[lumberman] we cannot do it. We have to pay taxes every year on our full
crop. We pay taxes on our land and then pay for the standing timber, and
you cannot pay that more than fifty or sixty times during your lifetime,
can you?

The taxes are governed largely by local people. We had school districts
where there were but two scholars, but we had to build a schoolhouse and
keep the school up for two children. We could have sent them to Chicago
and boarded them at the best hotel for the same money.

THE CHAIRMAN: If some satisfactory law could be passed in reference to taxes
and in reference to fire protection, do you think that the owners of a good
deal of this forest land that is not valuable for farming would endeavor to
reforest it?

MR. WEYERHAEUSER: Yes. We have been giving some land away to the State of
Wisconsin and to other States . . . In place of giving it away, we would try to

see if we could not raise trees as well as the State, if we could. [Now] we give
it for park purposes.

THE CHAIRMAN: That means to raise forests?

MR. WEYERHAEUSER: Yes; That is what we give it to them for, for park purposes.
If they do not use it for that, it comes back to us.

THE CHAIRMAN: You have seen a large share of the forests disappear since
you came on the face of the earth . . . What will they do for timber after
awhile?

MR. WEYERHAEUSER: Have you ever seen that when one thing disappears
something else is substituted? I have traveled through Germany and France
and some of those countries and when I looked out of the car window I have
thought I was up in Chippewa in the pines. They have been raising it there.
The government contends that when you cut a tree down you should plant
another tree. A forester comes around and tells you how to cut the tree, and
what kind of logs to make out of it and you take it to a sawmill and get it
sawed there and they know how.

THE CHAIRMAN: You have doubtless thought the matter over a good many
times in a way. What has your opinion been as to the future of the forests of
this country?

MR. WEYERHAEUSER: I think we ought to protect the forests. We ought to save
the timber. There is no question about it. But a thing is never saved until it
has a good value.

[The chairman and Frederick then have an extended exchange on what types of
trees grow in what kind of soil. Frederick makes the point that as timber
becomes increasingly scarce, other materials like iron and concrete will
replace it. The following exchange occurred before the end of Frederick's
appearance.]

THE CHAIRMAN: The raising of timber for the future is necessary, not merely for
the man who raises it but for the people generally.

MR. WEYERHAEUSER: Yes, there are not a great many who care for the people
who are to come afterwards. Some do. As a general thing, the farmer won't
care much about what comes after him . . . Let the government buy the land
at $2.50 an acre and the State should buy some and try and raise forests. In
nearly all the old countries the forest is owned by the Government. That goes
back many hundreds of years.

(Note: The term *conservation* was just coming into common usage at this time.
Conservation implies balancing economic needs and natural resources.
Preservation would be the more common term Frederick and his associates
might have used, implying the preservation of forests.)

Frederick's advice to Congress that the government ought to play a role in forest preservation was a reflection of current developing views, but it carried the added weight of recommendation from a leading lumberman. Frederick testified on his own donation of land in the Brule River area in northern Wisconsin to the state "for park purposes." Although he did not mention it in his congressional testimony, his positive intercession in the sale of land to the state of Minnesota also resulted in the completion of the planned Itasca State Park. These two land donations gave a great boost to those states' fledgling state park programs.

The Brule River Donation

Frederick was responsible for a donation of 4,320 acres of land on the Brule River in Wisconsin, which he gave to the state in 1906 with the stipulation that it be conserved as a state forest. His donation was made in a contentious political environment, and a complex story surrounds the gift. This is how events unfolded.

The Nebagamon Lumber Company operated a sawmill in Douglas County, Wisconsin, for nine years beginning in 1898. (Nebagamon grew out of earlier partnerships between Frederick and Ed Rutledge, one of his closest friends.) Toward the end of that period, the timber available for logging in northern Wisconsin had become scarce. The company made more than $3.5 million in profits in those nine years and employed many area residents. When the mill closed February 23, 1907, the economic effects were felt throughout the county and region. Many believed that agriculture was the best substitute for residents to earn a livelihood now that the logging operations had ceased. Leaders looked around for other developments that could create economic stability in the region as well, such as shipping.

Between 1890 and 1900, 162 farms had been established on lands that previously had been logged, and the number of farms rose after logging operations ceased altogether. However, this land was not well suited for farming. By the late 1920s more than 4,600 small farms in northern Wisconsin had failed in one generation.

Other economic developments were pursued. In 1903 the prospect of a power dam across the Brule River was proposed. Also under consideration was a canal project from Lake Superior to the Mississippi River that would have demanded numerous locks and dams on the Brule and the St. Croix. Such developments would have altered the ecological integrity of the river, ruined trout fishing along the upper river, and brought increased settlement and industry into the area. A conflict ensued between residents who wanted the dam and the new industry it would bring and those who represented the burgeoning conservation movement and sought to preserve the river's pristine nature.

Joseph Cullon positions this scenario as a disagreement with overtones of class conflict in his unpublished paper "Landscapes of Labor and Leisure: Common Rights, Private Property and Class Relations Along the Bois Brule River." Cullon draws a clear division between local residents who wanted the dam to spark industry in the area and wealthy summer residents from urban areas who desired to preserve nature for their own benefit. However, the situation could also be construed as a fight between the dam builder, Alvin A. Muck, with his business allies in the legislature and the residents along the river who valued its natural beauty. In the bigger picture, it was an early model of the ongoing struggle between those who favored the new conservation movement and those whose priorities were for development at any cost.

Frederick's help was sought, according to Cullon, by Edward Saunders, president of Northwestern Fuel Company, at a St. Paul Summit Avenue dinner party. He suggested that a gift of the Nebagamon Lumber Company lands along the Brule should be made to the state of Wisconsin to create a state park and that the condition of the gift should be a ban on all future dam developments in the area.

The struggle over the river's future finally concluded in the legislature in 1906, and the proponents of conservation won. There would be no dam on the Brule River. In the same year the state accepted Frederick's land gift with its attendant condition to preserve the environment.

Although Cullon finds class conflict in this situation, a far different picture emerges from the description of events published by the Sigurd Olson Environmental Institute of Northland College in Ashland, Wisconsin. This report describes the Brule River donation as a part of a larger effort initiated by the state of Wisconsin to conserve its forestlands. In 1897 the state's Second Forest Inquiry Commission called for the immediate creation of a system of state forests. In 1903 the state established a Department of Forestry and appointed E. M. Griffith as its superintendent. Griffith began to acquire land that would be protected as forestland.

While Cullon reports that Frederick's help with the land gift was solicited at a dinner party, in fact young Fred Weyerhaeuser (F. E.) had gone to Yale with the new state forester of Wisconsin (just as he had formed a relationship through the Skull and Bones Society of Yale with Gifford Pinchot, a forester of even larger responsibilities). Fred and Griffith had sailed together during their college years on Long Island Sound. The Sigurd Olson report describes how the youngest Weyerhaeuser son's relationship with his college friend, not a casual conversation at a dinner party, facilitated Frederick's land donation.

The Itasca State Park Intercession

The second major piece of public generosity in land was not exactly a donation by Frederick but a negotiation that favored the state in putting together the final piece of what was to become Itasca State Park at the headwaters of the Mississippi.

Pine Tree Lumber Company of Little Falls, managed by Charles Weyerhaeuser and Drew Musser, owned 3,191 acres of timberland in north-central Minnesota. This land, which had already been logged, fell inside the boundaries of the new Itasca State Park organized in the early 1890s. Weyerhaeuser interests had acquired these acres from the Northern Pacific Railroad some years earlier.

In 1893 the state's park commissioner, J. V. Brower, produced a report for the governor, William Merriam, on the progress of buying this land for the state. Evidently negotiations with Charles and Drew were going nowhere (described by Brower as "slow and unsatisfactory"), so in 1892 a committee of the Minnesota Historical Society (including former governor Alexander Ramsey) met with Frederick himself to see if they could move things along.

At the end of the meeting Brower noted with satisfaction that "lands will soon be placed at the disposal of the state by formal contract at a reasonable price by a favorable recommendation of Mr. Frederick Weyerhaeuser." Brower goes on to inform Governor Merriam, "As these lands are closely surrounded by other land within the control of the state, their value for park purposes can hardly be overestimated."

The satisfactory land-transfer negotiations with Frederick stand in contrast to efforts with other lumbermen of the time. T. B. Walker and John S. Pillsbury also owned land within the new Itasca Park boundaries, but Brower felt the price they insisted upon for their stumpage was far outside what should be paid. He was much happier with the arrangement Frederick proposed.

Fire and Loss

Frederick's warnings in his congressional testimony on the dangers of forest fires were to prove all too accurate. Fire plagued the burgeoning forest industry for years, often caused by the loggers' own carelessness in their lack of campsite management. A major fire had occurred in Wisconsin just prior to the committee hearings, prompting the congressmen to journey to view the damage for themselves.

Fire was an even greater problem on the West Coast after the 1900 purchase of the Northern Pacific lands opened up timber development there. George Weyerhaeuser, later president of the Weyerhaeuser Company, said that when he was a young boy he could smell burning wood from forest fires all the way into Tacoma. Well into the latter decades of the twentieth century, the problem remained. Once fire started in the Cascades it was impossible to control because of the forests' density, lack of water, and difficult road navigation, especially in winter.

In Frederick's time wildfires were the chief culprit in the loss of standing timber, consuming between twenty and forty million acres annually. As early as 1908, timber owners in Idaho and Washington banded together to prevent forest fires. These groups worked closely with state associations dedicated to the same cause. Eventually the federal government joined them in helping after the federal Weeks Act was passed in 1911.

The main purpose of the Weeks Act was to enable a network of protected forestland in the eastern part of the United States, essentially recovering this land from private ownership, thus facilitating the growth of protected forestland in the East. But the act also authorized the federal government to begin to assist in the prevention and containment of forest fires that ravaged the nation's timberlands.

Frederick may have been one of the first of many experienced lumbermen to call the dangers of forest fire to the attention of congressmen.

TAXES AND TIMBER

In his testimony, Frederick cited two major problems with taxation of timberlands: that taxes were leveled locally, thus creating some inequities between fair taxation and local needs, and that timberland was taxed on the value of standing trees annually, creating an incentive for owners to engage in rapid liquidation.

With regard to the problem of local taxation, Frederick cited the example of a local government in Wisconsin leveling taxes on timbermen for building a school when there were only two students in the county. He observed dryly that the two young pupils could have been sent to Chicago, boarded at the best hotel, and educated for less than the taxation on timber involved in building a new school for them.

Revisions in the practices of standing timber taxation took some time to come about. It was not until 1929 that the Oregon Forest Yield Tax Law was passed. This law stated that timber would be taxed only when it was cut, not annually on its full value, encouraging the growth of trees to maturity and reducing the (negative) incentive to clear the land as soon as possible. Other states eventually followed Oregon's lead.

THE ECONOMICS OF TREES

Frederick's idea that trees will be preserved only when they have become valuable was right in concept, although he could not know in 1908 how complex economics and environmental awareness would influence the next century and a half of American forests. The value of timber in the United States increased five times during the 1800s, and that trend continued through the twentieth century. There were two direct results of that development: first, it made more sense to use timber wisely, and, second, it made less sense to waste the resource.

As noted earlier, Frederick thought that the state should raise or protect forests, as was the practice in Europe; indeed, Teddy Roosevelt was already at work on that project. But some years later, in 1941, it would be the Weyerhaeuser Timber Company itself, not the state or federal government, that began the nation's first large-tree farming enterprise.

In 1933 Phil Weyerhaeuser, son of J. P. and grandson of Frederick, came from Idaho to Tacoma. He had been at the Potlatch Corporation but now was assigned to run the Weyerhaeuser Timber Company as executive vice president. Although he did not have the title of president until 1947, he had the responsibilities. Phil founded the first "tree farm" to reestablish the forest, a pioneering effort by a major lumber company.

Phil's son George took over the office of the presidency in 1966. Waiting for him was a key report by Gilbert Baker that outlined a plan for the Weyerhaeuser Timber Company to develop its own crops, a high-yield forestry through intensive management. George adopted this plan and began to implement it in earnest. The program's aim was to double the volume of wood obtainable from managed acres of forest, beginning with the harvest year of 2012. The "tree farms" were coming of age.

Weyerhaeuser was responsible for replanting 10.2 percent of the total acreage regenerated with seedlings in the United States in 1973—yet its own land represented but one percent of the nation's commercial forestland at that time. More needed to be done. And more was done between George Weyerhaeuser's arrival on the scene and his retirement. By the year 2012 the Weyerhaeuser Company managed 6.4 million acres of commercial forestland worldwide. The average age of the timber it harvested in 2011 was fifty-one years. Today, the company owns 5.7 million acres and leases 0.7 million acres with additional long-term leases in Canada.

George Weyerhaeuser, who retired as president of the company on April 21, 1988, and as CEO on July 31, 1991, remained as chairman until April 1999. He was the leader in creating and nurturing the Weyerhaeuser tree farm program into its present form. In 2012 the Weyerhaeuser Company, through a program of intensive management and continuous improvement, grew all of its own timber, meeting the lumber needs for each of the regions in which it operates.

Frederick Weyerhaeuser was wise when he offered his opinion that forests must be conserved. His descendents have implemented his ideas in ways he could not have imagined.

FREDERICK'S CHARITABLE GIFTS
DURING HIS LIFETIME

Edward Nelson Saunders, reported to be instrumental in persuading Frederick to make the Brule River donation of land, commented on Frederick's gift. When Saunders encouraged Joe Lucius, a prominent citizen of northern Wisconsin, to present the gift to the legislature, he quipped, "It's the only thing Frederick has ever given away in his life." Saunders knew Frederick as an intelligent and focused businessman, so it is no wonder that he felt free to make his joke. As a businessman, Frederick did not make a habit of giving things away. But as a person, the case was quite the opposite.

Frederick gave many gifts in his lifetime. Unlike Andrew Carnegie, his largesse was not strewn across the country in libraries. His gifts were smaller, given when his heart was touched by a cause, such as the needs of his childhood village Saulheim or the little Lutheran church in Rock Island. But these gifts expressed, perhaps better than any larger material legacy, who Frederick was.

Frederick's gifts to his distant cousins in Niedersaulheim were only a small part of donations he made during his lifetime. The practice of generosity began in his early days in Coal Valley, where he participated with vigor in community life through various volunteer commitments. He joined the Masons and attended church regularly. He even became a Knight Templar, at that time an honorary post within the Masons. Later he was postmaster and as such was responsible for getting checks to the families of men fighting in the Civil War.

The Rock Island Library would not have been built without Frederick's initial pledge, but in the event, his son F. E. recounts, things did not turn out quite as Frederick had expected. In 1900 the library board of Rock Island acquired the land behind the original Denkmann home and made known their intention to build a library there. Frederick went to the library board with an offer to give ten thousand dollars outright and to lend another fifty thousand for as long as was needed to build the library. He intended to donate all the money eventually, but he initially held back the full amount for two reasons: he did not want the newspaper publicity associated with a large, single gift in the community, and he wanted to inspire careful spending on the board's part. Thus he framed his offer in this manner. His true intentions were to be made known later.

However, while he was on his Mediterranean trip of 1901, the industrious library board went to work and raised many small donations from the community, including twenty-five hundred dollars from Frederick's brother-in-law,

F. C. A. Denkmann. On returning home, Frederick was disappointed to learn that he was not to make a gift of the entire building himself.

F. E. thought the gifts that made Frederick the happiest were those he made to the German Lutheran church in Rock Island, headed by Dr. Marquis, for the congregation was known to be so poor as to not be able to contribute individually much beyond the "widow's mite."

The most substantial gift of building was the large contribution in St. Paul to Dr. Howard Swearingen's new Presbyterian church on Summit Avenue. The parish house and the beautiful chapel, called the Elizabeth Chapel after Sarah, were Frederick's own contribution. Although Frederick turned over the first shovel of dirt for the buildings, they were not completed until six months after his death. They remain a grand tribute to Frederick's personal and Christian commitment and to the affection he bore Elisabetha Sarah, his wife.

Many small gifts were solicited of and given by the family over the years, although daughter Margaret became quite frustrated with the constant barrage of requests wherever the family appeared in public in St. Paul. Perhaps she had the right idea when she wrote to her husband, Richard, in 1904,

> I have been on the war-path lately—It seems that a person cannot be generous or liberal but that they are constantly begged or imposed upon . . . The Young Woman's Friendly Association wanted mother to give as well . . . [as other family members]. This morning Mrs. Davis attacked father in church and wanted another $ for the same charity. Two men were here Thursday to see father . . . They are from Rockford and are begging for a church that was burned. Well, father hadn't returned so they said they would see him tomorrow . . . This all happened this past week and when they began again this morning in Church it made me X [cross][.]
>
> I really am as generous and kind hearted as are most people, but when I feel a good horse is being driven to death—it puts me on the war-path . . . Father laughs at it all. I believe it would be a good plan not to give to anybody who asks, but find out where it is needed and then give.

Whatever Margaret's views, the legacy of giving that Frederick left continues today in the family's various charitable works. That philosophy is summed up by Nancy Weyerhaeuser, chair of the Weyerhaeuser Family Foundation from 1984 to 1995, who wrote in the family foundation's history,

> This family has a deep sense of being privileged and wanting to give back to society because of this. Frederick was a man with spirit and soul. He felt humble

about his origins and was humble about his successes. Although he didn't artic-
ulate it clearly [in words] he always felt that giving back was important.

FREDERICK'S LEGACY—FAMILY

Of the many anecdotes concerning Frederick and his children, one stands
out. On one of his return visits to Rock Island, Frederick stopped at a pharm-
acy owned by Dr. Bengston. The two old friends ruminated on life, F. E. later
recorded based on a news report written by George Carlock.

> Dr. Bengston said, "With what ease, seemingly, so great a success has been
> achieved by your life and during all the years since our arrival together in Rock
> Island . . ."
>
> But Frederick replied "Doctor, I am not dead yet! A man's success cannot be
> determined while he lives. At least not until the lives of his children have been
> lived also, and it can be seen how they had conducted not only their own lives
> but directed the lives of their children. No man is successful whose family is
> a failure . . . the mere acquisition of wealth is not success . . . Should I leave
> a fortune to my children, it depends on how they use it . . . to make the world
> better and uplift themselves and their children, then the world shall be better
> able to judge what my success has been."

Frederick's favorite poem was Sarah Doudney's *The Water Wheel*, published
in 1864. He would give prizes to his grandchildren if they could recite this
poem from memory. The text embodies the virtues he held for most of his life
and which came from his early Lutheran formation in Germany. The poem
cautions the reader to make the most of time, which does not come again.

Listen to the water mill
Through the live-long day;
How the clanking of the wheels
Wears the hours away!
Languidly the autumn wind
Stirs the greenwood leaves;
From the fields the reapers sing,
Binding up the sheaves;
And a proverb haunts my mind,
As a spell is cast:
"The mill will never grind
With the water that has passed."
Take the lesson to thyself,

Loving heart and true;
Golden years are floating by
Youth is passing too;
Learn to make the most of life,
Lose no happy day;
Time will never bring thee back
Chances swept away.
Leave no tender word unsaid,
Love while life shall last,—
"The mill will never grind
With the water that has passed."
Work while yet the daylight shines,
Man of strength and will;
Never does the streamlet glide
Useless by the mill.
Wait not till tomorrow's sun
Beams upon the way;
All that thou canst call thine own
Lies in thy today.
Power, intellect and health
May not, cannot last;
"The mill will never grind
With the water that has passed."
Oh, the wasted hours of life
That have drifted by;
Oh, the good we might have done,
Lost without a sigh;
Love that we might once have saved
By a single word;
Thoughts conceived, but never penned
Perishing unheard.
Take the proverb to thine heart,
Take, oh hold it fast!
"The mill will never grind
With the water that has passed."

Frederick left many legacies that survive in his family, but none as powerful as the demonstration of the virtues he valued and lived in his work. The family has stayed connected through seven generations. The liaison formed initially because the sons and even the grandsons found work in one of Frederick's many timber interests. But in the third generation, family leaders thought that a business connection was not enough. They established the Weyerhaeuser Foundation (later called the Weyerhaeuser Family Foundation to distinguish it from the Weyerhaeuser Company's contributions program) to connect the family while giving money to worthy causes. The foundation board draws from every branch of the family, including spouses, and is funded in part by family members' donations. The individual family branches, those lines of descendents from the original seven children, have also started many charitable foundations. Some of these—because of marriages—do not bear the Weyerhaeuser name.

In 1995 the foundation board established the Communities and Forests Initiative (a program focus area), which has funded many organizations working in the conservation and preservation areas. This program focused on fostering sustainability and community-based forestry projects, especially emphasizing the intersection of social, economic, and ecological needs. The Weyerhaeuser Family Foundation has provided seed money for new efforts and brought environmental groups and grantees together to share ideas with each other and with other funders. The foundation later also focused on the needs of very young children, providing grants for a decade of small, innovative children's programs across the country. In 2005 a fifty-year history of the Weyerhaeuser Family Foundation was written to inform all family members of this resource and opportunity for participation.

Most tellingly, Frederick's care for family is still bearing fruit. The entire family, now numbering in the hundreds, with all of the small children, gathers every other year somewhere in the country for a family reunion.

CHAPTER 21

Remembering Frederick

F REDERICK WEYERHAEUSER WAS A COMPLEX MAN. Innovative and industrious in work, devoted to his family but also treasuring the experience of
tramping the North Woods for months at a time, occasionally losing his temper, modest in his public and private demeanor, and highly sensitive to his own
honor, he was always his own man.

After Frederick's death, many of his partners and associates and people who
had known him in varied situations sent letters describing their view to his
youngest son, F. E. Excerpts from three such letters make a final testimony to
Frederick's memory.

This letter from E. J. Palmer, general manager of Victoria Lumber and Manufacturing Company, Ltd., of Chemainus, British Columbia, to James Richard
Jewett, husband of Margaret Weyerhaeuser, was dated May 5, 1914:

> I consider Mr. Weyerhaeuser one of the most wonderful characters I have
> ever seen, and in passing away he left a heritage of which his children should
> be proud, not for the amount of money he may have left, but that he was a
> man as gentle and sympathetic as a woman, and while firm when necessity
> demanded, always just. I do not think there is a man living who can say he ever
> broke his word, and I remember him saying to me: "The way to make a contract
> is always to have in mind to do better than you agree to do, and you will have no
> lawsuits . . ."
>
> Early in the '80's, when they were building the Hayward [Wisconsin] Mill
> and I was running the train, he was on his way to Hayward, and there was
> also on the train an immigrant woman with several children and innumera-
> ble packages. At Stillwater Junction, [when] a crowd of drunken woodsmen
> boarded the train going north, the woman was trying to occupy one seat with
> her children. Mr. Weyerhaeuser gave up his seat, turned over two seats and got

the little family settled. I found him standing in the second class car amongst a crowd of drunken lumber-jacks.

An instance of his control of men, and securing loyalty at all times, was illustrated to me a short time after this, by a man who has charge of responsible work. He had made a mistake in his calculations when he met Mr. Weyerhaeuser. He started to explain, or rather make excuses, for conditions as they were. As he expressed: "[Frederick] stopped and looked at me, said nothing till I finally involuntarily burst forth and gave him the truth, that it was a misjudgment and miscalculation, fully expecting to be severely censured and discharged. Instead of that he put his hand on my shoulders, smiled and said: 'It will never occur again.'"

These remarks by William Irvine, general manager of the Chippewa Lumber and Boom Company, were delivered at a large dinner given by the Weyerhaeuser Sales Company for its employees at the Minnesota Club on February 25, 1925.

Frederick Weyerhaeuser was gifted with wonderful vision and he had the courage of his convictions; he was also a good judge of human nature and was a genius for organization. It is a well known fact that bitter enemies among his business associates would stand shoulder to shoulder behind Frederick Weyerhaeuser in support of his plans for the common good . . . A more kindly, charitable man never lived than Frederick Weyerhaeuser. He was my employer for thirty-three years and I can truthfully say without fear of successful contradiction that he was the best lumberman and the fairest, squarest man I have ever known.

E. T. Buxton, formerly a lumberman of Superior, Wisconsin, wrote his recollections to George Long in a letter dated August 1925.

Dear George:
Your good letter was received. Answer has been delayed because I found [the assignment] most difficult. During a long life in which it has been my good fortune to meet many of the leaders in the business, political, religious life of our country, and to know some of them quite well, yet among them all the mind and character of Frederick Weyerhaeuser Sr. stand out so clear, fine and strong that better command of English than is at my control is needed to express my thought without becoming effusive.

Not being associated with Mr. Weyerhaeuser in business and not living in the same community, my acquaintance with him was not intimate. Interviews with him were so interesting and stimulating that I sought them as frequently as possible and prolonged them whenever I could.

His judgment of men while always charitable and kindly was almost uncanny. His comments on present conditions and judgment as to the future course of events was wonderful.

Never wasting words, there was such a reserve of power, mental and spiritual, that impressed and stimulated one and after each meeting my regard and esteem strengthened.

I have written several letters and destroyed them. This character needs a Boswell or a Walter Scott to begin to do it justice.

Sincerely yours, E. T. Buxton

P.S. He possessed such a chastity of honor as to feel a stain like a wound.

Frederick Weyerhaeuser obituary—*The American Lumberman:*

The Weyerhaeuser Syndicate is a term familiar to the public but it is little understood and generally misunderstood. It was not an organization, formal or informal, but merely the voluntary cooperation of a considerable number of men of means and independent position who had confidence in Mr. Weyerhaeuser's business abilities and were ready to cooperate with him in enterprises which he would recommend. A few of them might be in comparatively small enterprises, a larger number in greater ones and all might be invited to join in some great concern like the Weyerhaeuser Timber Company. They accepted his invitation of mutual cooperation or not as they chose. This broad yet loose cooperation among so many partners accounts for the fact that Mr. Weyerhaeuser was never in stock control of what were recognized as Weyerhaeuser institutions, but usually had a rather small minority interest . . .

So far as the most intimate acquaintances could determine, Mr. Weyerhaeuser never consciously wronged an individual, or that aggregate of individuals called the people. He not merely avoided any violation of the law in his great business transactions, but he scrupulously observed what he felt to be its spirit as well as its letter . . .

His kindly integrity extended not only to individuals with whom he came in contact (a common enough virtue) but it had a broad civic scope as well . . . always mindful of his humble beginnings, he acutely sympathized with those in trouble or in need . . . he was not only just, but kind.

Although Frederick Weyerhaeuser left his mark on the world of both timber and men, his greatest achievement was to be remembered by many who crossed his path in life as a genuine, kind, and just man.

How This Book
Came to Be Written

F. T. (Ted) Weyerhaeuser

Several years ago at a Forest History Society meeting, Rick Weyerhaeuser and George Weyerhaeuser Sr. discussed the fact that while much had been written on Frederick Weyerhaeuser's career as a businessman, nothing of any substance had been written about Frederick as a person. He was a unique individual for his time. A man of strong moral character, he also possessed outstanding leadership and organizational skills.

A great deal of time was spent trying to locate a biographer who would be interested in undertaking this project. The principal problem was that there did not appear to be sufficient information available that had not already been published. We then had several strokes of good fortune that enabled us to proceed. First, Judy Healey, who was a consultant to our family foundation for many years and the author of its history as well as several historical novels, expressed interest and excitement in taking on the project. We entered into a contract with Judy to write the manuscript.

When the family offices were moved from the First National Bank Building to what is now the Wells Fargo Tower in St. Paul, Minnesota, the family found a large amount of original material in the basement vaults. These documents included important personal information about Frederick. There were many letters that he and Sarah had written to one another as well as innumerable letters written in old German, which had to be translated into modern German and then into English. A treasure trove of letters also came to our attention courtesy of one of the villagers in Saulheim, Germany, who had a long connection to our family members. Further queries uncovered many other letters, written by Frederick, Sarah, and their children, in the Greer family's attic. Through all these resources, Judy found more than enough material for her work. This book is the result of that effort.

I wish to thank George Weyerhaeuser Sr., Rick Weyerhaeuser, Lucy Jones, Tom Rasmussen, and Elise Donohue for reading several drafts of the work and making helpful comments. I also want to thank Cathy Morley and Julia Heidmann for help in book design and family genealogy. Many thanks to the Rock Island Company for sponsoring the research effort. And finally, we all owe a great deal of thanks to Judy for her extended effort and commitment to this project. We hope that you enjoyed reading this personal account of Frederick's life.

Author's Note and Acknowledgments

Biography is a challenge for any writer. Stepchild of history, first cousin to fiction, it has elements of both but is neither. It draws from history, for we need the facts, dates, and context within which to set the story, but it also draws from fiction, because we need imagination to make the story live.

When I began this biography, I did not have any opinion on Frederick Weyerhaeuser as a man. What I discovered in the process of reading many of his letters, the letters of others about him, and family members' diaries of the time was the unexpected gift of getting to know a complex, gifted, and interesting character. I also was introduced to the intimate life of one of the fascinating immigrants of the nineteenth century who helped shape America. He accomplished this feat in fifty-plus years of business activity, transferring standing timber from forests to homes, churches, railroad ties, and steamboats and, in the process, building America.

To get to know my subject, I went first to the Weyerhaeuser family archives in St. Paul, where I discovered Frederick's small, leather-bound notebooks. These wonderful items, about the size of today's bank checkbooks, were filled with Frederick's notes to himself, various markings to distinguish his logs from those of others, and private thoughts. He carried these with him from his early days in the forest, and in them we discover a young man immersed in his work and—like Thomas Jefferson—a careful recorder of accounts, both what he owed and what others owed him. It was on these details that he built his life.

I read the memories of his early days in Germany, as he told them in later life to his son-in-law William Bancroft Hill, and then I read many letters he wrote to his wife, children, grandchildren, and colleagues. We are lucky to have access to an extensive account of his life and work compiled by his youngest son, Fred, known later as F. E. This account—*A Record of the Life and Business Activities of Frederick Weyerhaeuser, 1834–1914*—written twenty years after his father's death, held further diary entries by family members and many personal anecdotes. These were drawn from letters filled with stories from men who had known or worked with Frederick Weyerhaeuser. This record has been an invaluable resource.

Letters and diaries from Frederick's time were also found in numerous sources around the country, some in office archives and some in boxes in family members' attics. Letters from Frederick written 110 years ago, in his handwriting, surfaced from a distant relative in his native village of Niedersaulheim. These were translated into modern German and then into English. These letters reveal Frederick at his most personal, most generous, and, at times, most human self, and they are the source of an entire chapter in this book.

Much has already been written about the history of timber and lumber in the United States. This fact, coupled with the availability of so much unpublished, private material giving us insight into character and setting, drove my decision to write the story of this man in as personal a way as possible. What was he like to do business with? How did he get along with his associates? What was he like in his family? What was his relationship with his sons when they followed him into his business?

The tale of how Frederick built his business reveals an intriguing character. Surviving letters, documents, and personal anecdotes sketch the life of a young immigrant who started out as a part-time lumber salesman on the Mississippi and matured into a businessman who eventually organized one of the largest timberland purchases in U.S. history. His method of working was not typical of the successful (and unsuccessful) financiers and industrialists of his time. Rather than consolidate resources like John D. Rockefeller or sell millions of dollars in bonds like the early railroad financiers, he approached his goals more modestly. By organizing small partnerships for many efforts, Frederick developed a network of investors who trusted him and who eventually joined him in the Northern Pacific land purchase of 1900, opening the western timberlands and thus the entire West Coast to development. Evidence in the form of letters from many of these partners testifies to Frederick's character in business far more than any statements made about him from later writers could do.

Frederick was complex, as are all interesting men and women, because he wasn't perfect. He occasionally showed his temper, and not all his business partners got along with him all of the time. He had and recorded some severe episodes of torment over what he felt were misunderstandings by his colleagues about his ethics. Frederick suffered through a bitter public attack from one of the era's toughest muckrakers but impressed another so thoroughly in a personal interview that the journalist never wrote the planned article about him.

Frederick was tough and honest in business, but he was often tender with his wife and children and kind to many semi-strangers, like the residents of his birth village of Niedersaulheim. The anecdotes retold in this story that illustrate all of these characteristics make this immigrant's life compelling far beyond his impact on the forests in which he spent much of his time.

Although I decided to focus on Frederick's personal life, I could not avoid writing about Frederick's business life—it was all consuming for many years—so there is overlap in time between chapters as I weave a description of his logging business and his developing public leadership with a picture of his family's changes during the same time period.

In order to bring the reader closer to the person behind the public man, I have briefly dramatized scenes from parts of Frederick's life. These serve as introductions to sections of the text and are based on actual information derived from sources of the times: letters, diary entries, and conversations reported by others. I hope these bridge the gap for the reader between what we can document and what we only imagine.

I am grateful to the Weyerhaeuser family for opening their personal and family archives to me, funding the research, finding translators for the German letters, and generally supporting the project. Several family members also read drafts and corrected my misunderstandings of the timber, logging, and lumber history and business with kindness and courtesy. Most of all I am grateful that the family never attempted to direct the writing of this story. Special thanks goes to Ted Weyerhaeuser, F. E.'s grandson, without whom this project would never have begun, nor moved to completion.

Frederick Weyerhaeuser's personal life experience—immigration and hard work, success and obstacles, confidence and self doubt—transcends time. His nineteenth-century life stands as a compelling story, for his day and ours.

ACKNOWLEDGMENTS

Many people helped make this book possible. First thanks go to Ted Weyerhaeuser and the six members of the family reading committee. Ted was the inspiration behind this biography, and he marshaled resources to fund the research. He also read endless versions of the manuscript as it evolved and demonstrated amazing patience, even with early drafts. Without that patience and good-natured support, this project would not have come to completion.

I want to thank the valuable members of the family reading committee, who provided many comments and made this history far more accurate than it might have been: George Weyerhaeuser Sr., retired president of the Weyerhaeuser Company, for information and guidance on the evolving nature of the company's managed tree-planting program and for calling my attention early on to the enormous hazards of fire in the West; also for clarifying the differences among the terms *timber*, *logs*, and *lumber*, rather fundamental knowledge I was lacking. Thanks to Lucy Jones and Elise Donohue for their intrepid efforts to get the Germen letters between Frederick and his Niedersaulheim cousins translated, and to Elise for help on German phrases and Lucy for help on one of the Rock Island historical safaris; to Rick Weyerhaeuser for his contribution of vast knowledge about the forestry and environmental fields and for pointing me to research in these areas; to Tom Rasmussen for constant close readings and catching many errors in drafts, especially of the historical-family kind, and for unearthing Frederick's 1908 testimony to Congress; and to Cathy Morley for helping us with design and book production advice and for her invaluable assistance with the wonderful archival pictures which bring the story to life. I am especially grateful that the family readers never asked me to delete or change any of the material in the book. They only, and graciously, pointed out errors of fact.

Thanks also to the following helpers along the way, who welcomed me into their archives and attics to search for material: Megan Moholt of the Weyerhaeuser Company Archives in Tacoma, Washington; Chalan Colby at the Laird Norton Archives in Seattle, Washington, which still preserves bound "letterbooks" of longhand copies of letters between Frederick Weyerhaeuser and Mathew Norton written in the late 1850s; Nathan E. Bender and Julie Monroe at the University of Idaho Special Collections Library, depository of many of the Jewett family papers; Sarah Dent and the Greer family for allowing me access to the boxes of letters kept in the attic of their summer home on Cape Cod; Bobbi Jackson, director of the Rock Island County Historical Society, who was extremely helpful to me on several visits and answered all my follow-up requests; David Mitchell, local Rock Island, Illinois, historian and keeper of lore; and Walt Bennick of the Winona County Historical Society, for help in ascertaining which building was the Huff House hotel, where the meeting of the MRLC leaders elected Frederick president.

Early readers Elaine Tyler May and Annette Atkins deserve special thanks for critical comments. I am indebted to my editors and readers, each of whom provided invaluable advice as the manuscript was developing: Joseph Foote, Dee Ready, and Mary Ann Nord. Finally, my gratitude goes to director Pamela McClanahan and editor in chief Ann Regan of the Minnesota Historical Society Press. Ann's editing skills were especially helpful in finalizing the book. Shannon Pennefeather, who did the final editing round, was skilled, patient, and outstanding in her competence. Without the comments and suggestions of these experienced helpers the manuscript would have suffered immeasurably. Any awkwardness in expression or mistake in fact remains my responsibility.

Frederick Weyerhaeuser's story is more than a Horatio Alger tale. He was a large man for his time in his public achievements, but also a man whose memory is honored by the testimony of his friends, colleagues, and family. Perhaps his greatest achievement is that his family continues; most of his descendents still gather regularly for reunion, nearly one hundred years after his death.

Notes

A Note on Names

Frederick and Sarah's children came to play a key role in both the family and the family's business. This text refers to them by childhood family names early on and by adult names or initials later.

Frederick	always called Frederick in this text
Sarah	baptized Elisabetha Bloedel—Frederick always called her Sarah
John Phillip	John, later J. P.
Elise	Lizzie, later Elise
Margaret	Maggie, later Margaret
Apollonia	Lonie, later Apol (by her brothers) or Apollonia
Charles	Charlie, later Charles
Rudolph	Rudi, later Rudolph or R. M.
Frederick Edward	Freddie, later Fred or F. E.

A Note on Spelling

Saulheim, Germany, was divided into two parts during Frederick's childhood there: Ober, or upper, and Nieder, or lower. This text uses the modern spelling of Niedersaulheim throughout but in quoting letters keeps the spelling of Frederick's day, which is Nieder-Saulheim.

A Note on Translation

The letters from Frederick to the villagers of Niedersaulheim, long in the possession of Georg Koch, a Saulheim resident with lengthy family connections to the Weyerhaeuser clan, were recently translated. Karl Heinz Appenheimer, longtime friend of the family, managed the translations, a two-part process: the letters were translated from the old German handwriting into modern German by Katharine Annaheim (Saulheim resident), and then Barbara Berghofer (also a Saulheim resident) translated them into contemporary English.

A NOTE ON RESOURCES

Much of the material for this biography has been drawn from private resources, the most significant being F. E.'s *A Record of the Life and Business Activities of Frederick Weyerhaeuser, 1834–1914,* which was privately published; a copy is in the family archives in St. Paul, Minnesota. This compilation of letters from his father's colleagues and business associates as well as friends includes also letters from other Weyerhaeuser children and diary entries they made at the time of events. Where not otherwise cited, family anecdotes are drawn from this work.

NOTES BY CHAPTER

WESTWARD HO!

The *Times Concise Atlas of World History* (London: Times Publishing Company, 1991) is the source for the summary of westward growth.

The Henry Lewis quote is from a 1996 local historical-geographical study of the Rock Island–Mississippi area by Roald Tweet, *The Quad Cities: An American Mosaic.* Tweet was an English professor at Augustana College in Rock Island, Illinois; Augustana is now in possession of Frederick and Sarah Weyerhaeuser's family home. Although Tweet's PhD from the University of Chicago is in English and he taught English for many years, he has authored a number of works of local history in the Rock Island area and has particular expertise in Mississippi River history.

Land and Immigrants

Several of the quotations in this section are from *Bartlett's Familiar Quotations,* a collection of sayings. The famous "manifest destiny" quote came from John Lewis O'Sullivan, who wrote it in the 1845 version of *United States Magazine and Democratic Review;* the Horace Greeley quote is from *The Life of Horace Greeley* by James Parton in 1854.

Mathew Josephson's *The Robber Barons* contributed the description by English traveler William Priest (24) and the quotation from Mark Twain (23). Gertrude Stein's quote is from the *Geographical History of America* (New York: Random House, 1936).

Forests and Farmers

Much of the material in this section is taken from the 1963 work by Ralph Hidy, Frank Ernest Hill, and Allan Nevins entitled *Timber and Men* and a monograph by Rick Weyerhaeuser and colleagues Al Sample and James Giltmeir entitled "Forest Management and Policy in the U.S.: An Historical Perspective." A fine explanation of the Indian uses of land before the arrival of European settlers can be found in the article "North American Forests in the Age of Man" by Whit Bronaugh in *American Forests Magazine* (Summer 2012). Frederick Weyerhaeuser's testimony before the Congressional Committee on the Future of Pulp and Paper was given in Wisconsin in 1908; details referenced here can be found on pages 2495–96. Further excerpts from this testimony are cited at length later in this work.

The U.S. Army, Rivers, and Settlements and *Settlers and Natives*

Most of the history in this section comes from Tweet's *Quad Cities.* Tweet is particularly detailed in his description of the harassment of and war on the Sauk Indians and its brutal and unhappy end. The information on the U.S.–Dakota War is drawn from the Minnesota Historical Society's brief history of this affair, *The U.S. Dakota War of 1862*, published on the 150th anniversary of the conflict (http://www.usdakotawar.org/). The story of natives appearing at the back doors of settlers' cottages comes from Fred Kohlmeyer's account of the Laird-Norton lumbermen in Winona, Minnesota, entitled *Timber Roots*. Many other anecdotes of those early settler days on the Mississippi are retold in that book.

Railroads and Lumber

The most riveting account of the early railroad magnates' shenanigans is to be found in Josephson's *The Robber Barons*, from whence comes the term now in common usage. Frederick Weyerhaeuser is not mentioned in the book, probably because he did his business in an entirely different way, without congressional financing, creating giant combinations, or issuing fraudulent stock as did Fisk, Gould, and the others. Some interesting information may also be found in the book on James J. Hill's second son, entitled *The Dutiful Son: Louis W. Hill, Life in the Shadow of the Empire Builder, James J. Hill* (St. Paul, MN: Ramsey County Historical Society, 2010). Edmund Morris opens his *Theodore Rex* with a scene of the Northern Securities Trust formation by James J. Hill and J. P. Morgan. Although Frederick's business organization was much more decentralized, the development of railroads eventually intertwined with his interests and culminated in the western land purchase in 1900.

Forests and Conservation

The conservation movement in the United States got under way just about the time Frederick's lumber business began to thrive, but it was not widely known or supported until closer to the end of the century. A good account of this development can be found in Char Miller's biography *Gifford Pinchot and the Making of Modern Environmentalism*. Douglas Brinkley in *The Wilderness Warrior* relates the story of Roosevelt inviting Frederick to Washington, which is borne out by a longer account to be found in F. E.'s *A Record of the Life and Business Activities of Frederick Weyerhaeuser*.

Chapter 1: An Early Death Changes a Family

Most of the material in this chapter comes from *Pioneer Lumberman*, a book compiled and privately published by Louise Lindeke Weyerhaeuser, wife to Rudi Weyerhaeuser and daughter-in-law to Frederick and Sarah. In 1901 Frederick took a voyage with Louise, his daughter Elise, and her husband, Bancroft Hill. During long days on board the ship, Frederick related much of his childhood experience to Bancroft Hill, and the younger man later wrote it down. Louise compiled these memories into the volume. Although in his sixties at the time, Frederick's memory for details of his childhood in Saulheim, Germany, seemed quite clear.

The quote from Elise is from a short essay in the family's archives. The affectionate letter from Frederick to his daughter Margaret Weyerhaeuser Jewett is part of a collection of private letters in a family home in Woods Hole, Massachusetts. Margaret's granddaughter, also named Margaret Weyerhaeuser Jewett, married William Greer. The Greer family has kept original letters that stretch over a century. These letters, still legible, were a great source of information on Frederick and Sarah's Summit Avenue, St. Paul, years, when Margaret spent a good deal of time with her parents while her husband, Richard, was abroad.

CHAPTER 2: COMING TO AMERICA AND MOVING WEST

Nearly all of this biographical material, including the details of the voyage, is drawn from Frederick's recollections re-told in *Pioneer Lumberman*.

CHAPTER 3: SEIZE THE DAY

Frederick's physical description is drawn from Hidy, *Timber and Men* (6–7). *Pioneer Lumberman* is also the source for the description of Frederick's early days in Rock Island, while much of the Denkmann story is drawn from John Hauberg's book *Weyerhaeuser and Denkmann: Ninety-five Years of Manufacture and Distribution of Lumber* (22ff).

CHAPTER 4: THE FAMILY PROSPERS IN COAL VALLEY

Many of the stories from these years come from F. E.'s memories as related in his compilation of letters and stories titled *A Record of the Life and Business Activities of Frederick Weyerhaeuser, 1834–1914*, hereafter called simply the *Record*. The tale of Frederick and the bee stings is recounted in *Timber and Men*, and Andrew Bloedel's amusing recollections are from the Hauberg book (45). Robert Lee's later description of the young Weyerhaeuser couple at home in Coal Valley comes from an article in the *Chicago Sunday Tribune* (October 29, 1907) written by George Weymouth. The story was reprinted in *Worker's Magazine*, and a copy is in the Rock Island County Historical Society newspaper files in Moline, Illinois. Frederick's comment on happiness was made to John Hill, who later shared it with F. E. (49).

CHAPTER 5: AN ENTREPRENEUR'S ADVENTURES

Some of the material in this chapter comes from *Pioneer Lumberman* and stems from Bancroft Hill's reporting of conversations with his father-in-law on their Mediterranean voyage in 1901. F. E. recounts the story of the Beulah Church (29), and *Timber and Men* related Frederick's reputation for honesty (7). The story of the rogue rafter who finally ruined Mead, Smith and Marsh was told by Frederick himself to Bancroft Hill, as was the description of his early partnership with Denkmann, although F. E. also retells that story, and some of it appears in the Hauberg book as well.

CHAPTER 6: THE FIRST PARTNERSHIP YEARS DURING A CRUEL WAR

The account of the early partnership years may be found in *Pioneer Lumberman* from Frederick's memory, in F. E.'s recounting, and in Hauberg's description. The undertaking's risky nature is outlined in Hauberg (52). Anthony Koch's memory of the ending of his father's part in the Weyerhaeuser-Denkmann partnership is found in F. E.'s *Record* (88) and highlights Frederick's stern expectations for the business but also illustrates the more forgiving family dynamics. Though Michael Koch left the firm, the families continued to interact as before.

Philip Bloedel's characterization of the two partners is in F. E's *Record* (86), as are the stories of F. C. A. Denkmann's all-too-human responses to the issue of Frederick Weyerhaeuser's fame.

Timber and Men (31ff) has a good description of the timber and logging part of the Weyerhaeuser-Denkmann partnership's early forays into Wisconsin forests.

The *Rock Island Daily Union* quote referencing the "Republican platform" comes courtesy of the Rock Island County Historical Society files, as do most of the other quotations from period newspapers. Here may be a good place to insert a note on the Rock Island area's newspapers in Frederick's time. Bobbi Jackson of the Rock Island County Historical Society writes the following information in response to a question on newspaper names; there seemed to be a plethora of them.

> The reader should keep in mind that Rock Island and Moline are towns in Illinois with shared borders.
>
> The Moline newspaper was known as the *Moline Republican* between 1862–1867, when it went out of business. The *Moline Review* was started in 1870 with the "dead" *Moline Republican*'s printing press. The *Moline Review* and the *Dispatch* were separate papers until 1880, when the *Review*'s membership and ownership was merged with the *Dispatch*. After the merger, the weekly paper was published as the *Review-Dispatch* and the daily was published as the *Dispatch*. The *Dispatch* started in 1878.
>
> The Rock Island paper has an even more interesting history. It was begun as the *Rock Island Republican*, was purchased by Col. J. B. Danforth in 1855 and in 1858 he changed the name to the *Rock Island Argus*, since he was a member of the Democratic Party, not the Republican. The name *Rock Island Argus* continues to the present day.

The story of the Civil War and its effects on Rock Island retold here comes partly from F. E.'s account and, again, from Tweet's work on local history. The detailed records of the initial partnership agreement are from Hauberg's book, while the comment on Frederick's early lack of accounting expertise is F. E.'s opinion.

Page 66, Scene 3: The quote at the end of the scene is from *Pioneer Lumberman*, from Frederick's recollections as told to Bancroft Hill.

Chapter 7: Frederick Likes the Forest Life

The quote from fur trader Joseph Bailly is taken from *North Woods River: The St. Croix River in Upper Midwest History* by Eileen McMahon and Theodore J. Karmanaski (76), illustrating some of the fur traders' attitudes toward the natives even as they were dealing with them and marrying into the tribes. Other accounts, such as Tweet in *Quad Cities* and Kohlmeyer in *Timber Roots*, describe a range of relationships between the settlers and the native tribes in the developing Midwest of the nineteenth century.

Much of this chapter's logging information is drawn from Hidy's *Timber and Men*, perhaps the most complete single resource describing the early days of this industry in the Midwest. There is also great detail in the McMahon and Karmanaski book, the source of the story on the lumberjacks' reading aloud the novel *Jane Eyre*. (The original story appeared in the *Wisconsin Magazine of History* 2 [1927]: 148–49.)

Frederick's amusing response to the loggers' snoring is from Kohlmeyer's *Frederick Weyerhaeuser: A Pen Portrait* (7).

The description of Frederick tramping the forests and his comment to Captain Van Sant that he "love[d] the woods life" is from *Timber and Men* (31–32).

The information on the Mississippi's largest raft is from an article in the *Rock Island Dispatch and Argus* (February 12, 1995). Details about the operation of Beef Slough can be found in several resources, the most reliable being the private monograph written by Mathew Norton in 1915; a copy of this resource may be found in the Weyerhaeuser family archives in St. Paul. Kohlmeyer's *Timber Roots* also has a complete description of events surrounding Beef Slough, as does Hidy in *Timber and Men*.

Frederick's small brown leather notebooks also rest in the family archives in St. Paul. They attest to Frederick's early forest years and his system of keeping track of everything from logs to supplies and negotiations.

The value of white pine at the time was undisputed. A good description appears in a short work by Carl Otto Rosendahl, *Trees and Shrubs of the Upper Midwest*. Kohlmeyer's *Timber Roots* is the source for information on scalers and rules for measuring the logs (154–55) and for the sassy poem on sorting logs (219).

Chapter 8: The Wisconsin Logging Feuds Breed Bitterness

A Clash of Logging Interests

Timber and Men is a good source of information on the Beef Slough conflict overall, but the most detailed telling is to be had from Norton's 1915 monograph on the subject. His view is particularly valuable as he was a principal in the affair and saw events from the inside. The Laird-Norton group was involved in every aspect of Wisconsin logging, as was Frederick, from the beginning. Reference to the violence and the McDonald brothers is in *Timber and Men* (47); Dan McDonald appears later in this story.

Rivers and Logjams Make Things Worse

The comment about Frederick "looking for his logs" by Thaddeus Pond to William Irvine is reported in *Timber and Men* (24). William Irvine later became one of Frederick Weyerhaeuser's most trusted associates, and many of the more personal anecdotes in this story are attributable to him.

The Mississippi River Logging Company Organizes

From Norton's monograph comes the quote on the MRLC organization's brotherly nature (46) and his assessment of Frederick's leadership in not abandoning the Beef Slough (14). *Timber and Men* (44) provides insight into the growing animosity between the Wisconsin lumbermen and the Mississippi "newcomers." The description of the comical events of the MRLC meeting when members turned to Frederick for leadership is taken from the meeting minutes and related by Kohlmeyer in *Timber Roots*.

Ten Years of Wrangling on the Rivers of Wisconsin

The Little Falls dam that figures prominently in Wisconsin logging history is not to be confused with Little Falls, Minnesota, where Frederick later had logging operations in partnership with the Mussers of Iowa. Kohlmeyer's *Timber Roots* is the source for much of the story of the conflict over logs and steamboats on the river, including the quotation from Judge Romanzo Bonn (102).

CHAPTER 9: FREDERICK EMERGES AS FIRST AMONG EQUALS

A River on the Rampage and Lost Logs

The on-the-spot description of the disastrous 1880 river situation is from the *Rock Island Argus* (May 6, 1880). Kohlmeyer also provides dramatic renditions of the scene (99ff).

Frederick's Leadership Creates a New Coalition

Timber and Men (73) notes that the Chippewa Lumber and Boom Company was the one major player omitted from the meeting of all Wisconsin and Mississippi owners after the disastrous flood. Apparently members of the company had crossed Frederick once too often, though he merely said they had "kept aloof."

Again, Norton's account of the reconciliation and Frederick's leadership in log trading following the flood is the best and most detailed of these events. Even Charles Twining, in *Downriver*, the story of O. H. Ingram, admits that all the area loggers understood they had come to a place where cooperation was necessary (206).

Frederick, First Among Equals with Strong Personalities

The Mathew Norton quote referencing Sauntry and the Whitney possibilities is taken from a "pressbook" of letters written in the second part of the nineteenth century. A Chicago firm offered the service of "pressing" copies of these letters, written on onion-skin paper in longhand script that is still quite readable, into bound hardcover books for preservation. These books are in the Laird-Norton offices in Seattle, Washington. Most of these letters to Frederick are from Norton, but a few come from his cousin and business partner, William Laird.

The two incidents taking place in the Wylie House in Fifield, Wisconsin, are described by George Lindsay, a young colleague of Frederick's. Lindsay wrote these accounts in later life to F. E., and they are quoted in the *Record* (314). As Lindsay noted, he was only twenty-five at the time.

F. E. recalls O. H. Ingram's lack of appreciation for what Frederick accomplished after the 1880 flood (216). Twining's admission that not only Frederick but most of the lumbermen on the Mississippi and in Wisconsin at the time were strong person-alities is from *Downriver* (214–15).

Frederick's wry comment on his own lack of speechmaking abilities comes from F. E. (31). Frederick appeared to see both his weaknesses and his skills quite clearly.

Frederick's Reaction When His Honor Is Questioned

Twining's *Downriver* (214–25) contains one account of the situation that disturbed Frederick so much in the 1885 sequence of events, but F. E.'s notes on Frederick's feelings are borne out by Frederick's private diaries in the small, leather-bound note-books he always carried. William Carson's letter can be found in F. E.'s account (778).

CHAPTER 10: MEANWHILE, SARAH KEEPS THE HOME FIRES BURNING

The description of the move to Rock Island and the houses the Weyerhaeusers occu-pied can be found in several places but was originally given by Frederick to Bancroft

Hill and related in *Pioneer Lumberman.* Other early events in Coal Valley are found in Hauberg's book, although he seems to be off by a year in terms of the move, reporting it in 1870 while both Frederick and F. E. state the year was 1869, with the Caugheys following in 1870.

As noted, Augustana College now owns the "House on the Hill." The first floor is mostly intact and sometimes a venue for small ceremonial dinners. The college is only too happy to allow tours and to provide information about current usage. The upper floors have been converted into sleeping quarters for college students, and the resulting changes are quite startling. However, the front room where Frederick and his family spent long winter evenings and the beautiful, carved dining area are preserved in total, even including the beautiful Art Deco stained-glass panel over the fireplace.

Elise's diary entry on Sarah's character was written much later in life and is cited in F. E.'s *Record* (787). Sarah's confidence in Frederick's judgment as related by young John to his father comes from family letters quoted in the *Record* (72).

Many letters between Frederick and Sarah rested in the vaults of the family archives in St. Paul but had not been noticed until the family office was moved and the archives opened a decade ago. Then the letters, written in German, came to light. When the family became interested in telling Frederick's story, contacts in Saulheim, Germany, identified translators. Some of those letters, illustrating the relationship between husband and wife through long winter separations, are included in this work.

CHAPTER 11: THE CHILDREN GROW UP IN THE "HOUSE ON THE HILL"

The Young Weyerhaeusers Get an Education and Find Work to Do

The letters quoted from young John Weyerhaeuser (later known as J. P.) are contained in full in F. E.'s *Record* (105–6). John Hauberg (63) described his mother-in-law Anna Catherine Denkmann's partiality to her nephew John and her scolding of Frederick for his stern treatment of his eldest son.

The young Weyerhaeusers' education at the local schools comes from the *Record* (80), in a section that also contains F. E.'s recollections of his parents' silver wedding anniversary party.

Margaret Weyerhaeuser Jewett's family home at Woods Hole, Massachusetts, contains boxes of letters among family members spanning a century. Along with the letters are souvenirs from her time at Wellesley College, including the Wellesley fifty-year reunion booklet that printed Margaret's poem.

Frederick and His Children

The excerpts from Frederick's letters to his young children are taken from F. E.'s *Record* (68–84). Many of the letters are still in the family archives in the original versions as well.

The Young Weyerhaeusers, Grown Up, Travel Abroad

Maggie's letter home is part of the Greer family collection at Woods Hole, and Charlie's letter of brotherly advice to young Fred is quoted in full in the *Record,* as are the letters that illustrate John's advances in spelling and writing in his middle school years and his increasing interest in his father's business (64–75).

Page 123, Scene 4: The imaginary scene here is based on F. E.'s recollection of a conversation with his father as a young lumberman in Cloquet (640) and also his remembrance of walking to the office in the National German American Bank in downtown St. Paul with his aging father.

CHAPTER 12: MINNESOTA'S FORESTS CALL

The Need for New Forests

Much of the information on forests and population growth during this time comes from Hidy, *Timber and Men* (104–5).

Pine Tree Lumber Company, Little Falls

The anecdote about the exchange between A. C. Akeley and Frederick comes from *Timber and Men* (110), and the story of Frederick's rueful comment in later years about his partners' refusal to take mineral rights in land offered by Charles Davis of Michigan is reported by F. E. (461).

The St. Louis County/Knife Falls Ventures

The history of the Knife Falls/Cloquet lumber development is related in *Timber and Men* (116ff). Rudi's comment about his father's admonishment to "keep out of politics" is quoted in Hidy, et al., as well (119)—interesting advice when one reflects on the conflict Michael Koch found himself in when he worked with Weyerhaeuser and Denkmann early on. Perhaps Frederick learned from that experience that even in the city council a dual position of businessman and political office holder may pose problems.

Archibald Stewart's recollection about Frederick's view of how he was willing to treat his sons and "stand" for their mistakes if need be may be found in F. E.'s *Record* (428), as is F. E.'s conversation with his father on not taking "back-up" with him when he made his first land purchase. Frederick's response to his young son illustrates this philosophy. As noted at the end of Scene 4 (page 123), F. E.'s recollection of walking to work with his father in St. Paul is found in the *Record* (640).

CHAPTER 13: THE FAMILY MOVES TO ST. PAUL, AND FREDERICK TURNS WESTWARD

Starting a New Life in Another River Town

The description of Jim Hill and Frederick Weyerhaeuser as "neighbors" was literally true at the end of the nineteenth century when Frederick and Sarah purchased their home. Whether the two men met earlier when Frederick and Sarah had relocated to St. Paul or only connected once the Weyerhaeuser couple had moved into the house at 266 Summit is unknown, but they subsequently became fast friends who did business together. Today, a grand house—built by Louis W. Hill, Jim's "dutiful" son and business successor—stands between the two buildings. During recent decades the James J. Hill house belonged to the Catholic Archdiocese of Minneapolis and St. Paul, and offices with temporary walls were strewn throughout. Today it is owned and managed by the Minnesota Historical Society, and the restored large rooms are frequently used for community social events and public tours on the building's history. The Louis Hill and Frederick Weyerhaeuser houses are privately owned, but the former is sometimes opened to the public for charitable events.

Frederick's quotes cited in this section are from F. E.'s *Record*, taken from letters written to F. E. by the men who knew Frederick. John Hill's letter can be found on pages 435–38 and Archibald Stewart's anecdote on page 426.

Frederick Investigates Opportunities in the South

The gradual modification of Frederick's views on the habits of southern workers can be found in detail in F. E.'s recollections (530–38). Frederick's announcement after his 1886 trip that he was willing to invest nearly one million dollars in the South is referenced in *Timber and Men* (209). For once, however, his many partners declined the opportunity to invest with him, and he let that moment pass. Young Fred's excitement at being named president of Southland Lumber Company is noted in *Timber and Men* (210).

Frederick's Interests Move West with the Railroads

The merger of the Great Northern and Northern Pacific railroads was significant in its time. For a dramatic rendering of the creation of the Northern Securities Trust by Hill and J. P. Morgan, read the opening chapters of Edmund Morris's book *Theodore Rex*.

An excellent and detailed description of the early railroad booms and busts in financing may be found in Mathew Josephson's *The Robber Barons*. Supplementary information is also available in the less objective *Railroads and Clearcuts* by Derrick Jensen and George Draffan, which tries to make a case of collusion between railroads and the timber industry in the early days. Page twelve of that work describes the Jay Cooke railroad years.

The "gingerly look" commentary on Frederick and his associates' initial consideration of the western timber possibilities is from *Timber and Men* (112). The coded telegram Jim Hill's representative sent to Frederick is taken directly from Twining's book *George S. Long: Timber Statesman* (4).

Making the Deal and Living with the Consequences

The quote on the speculative nature of Frederick's purchase comes from Hidy, *Timber and Men* (214), and some detail was taken from F. E.'s recollections. The results of this purchase were both positive and negative depending on the position of any given commentator. The most negative view came from the Hearst publications, particularly an article by Charles Norcross which is directly dealt with in subsequent chapters of this book. Hidy, et al., have a slightly different perspective (302ff).

Twining's book on George Long (5–13) provides the remaining material in this chapter, including the final quote.

Chapter 14: Family Matters

Bancroft Hill, Elise's husband, had many talents and interests, but his career was spent primarily in the academic world. Richard Jewett was equally interesting. His father, James, had been a ship captain, and surviving letters to his wife, Harriet, profess undying love. Sadly, the captain died at sea, near Hawaii, while Richard was still very young. Richard went on to complete his education in Arabic studies and to progress into the higher levels of academia.

The Greer family letters held on Cape Cod are an amazing compilation of stories of family interactions against the backdrop of world affairs. Among the letters is one from the University of Minnesota president agreeing that a donation from Frederick of five thousand dollars would support the academic appointment of Richard Jewett to the university, although an indefinite term could not be guaranteed. One might conclude from this scenario that Frederick and Sarah were anxious for Margaret to remain with them on Summit Avenue when Richard returned from his studies abroad.

The letters from Sarah to Margaret and from Margaret to Richard are all taken from this collection, stored in boxes at Woods Hole, Massachusetts.

Chapter 15: Frederick and Sarah Become World Travelers

F. E. kept a diary in his younger years, and much of the recollection of the family's trip in 1889 is related in the *Record*, drawn from his writing at the time of the experience (7–8). Frederick and Sarah's second European voyage, with Apollonia and her husband, Sam Davis, is also described in the *Record* (393ff).

The third voyage, in 1901, on which Sarah was notably absent, was the occasion for Frederick's reminiscences to Bancroft Hill, later published by Louise (Rudi's wife) as *Pioneer Lumberman*. Louise also had recollections of the trip, which she shared with F. E., her brother-in-law, when he was compiling his *Record*. Her depiction of Frederick's naiveté in the face of vendors they encountered is shared there (404), along with other memories, including the stories of the Hawaii Cooke family (of Cooke's tour fame), the shared hat at the Monte Carlo casino, and the "disagreeable Germans."

The party of Frederick's final European voyage in 1906 comprised Frederick and Sarah, Apollonia and Sam Davis and their son Edwin, and Elise and the intrepid Bancroft Hill. Some of the recollections are from letters (for example, Elise's letter to her brother John Phillip describes their entry into the Saulheim village as a grand "circus"), while Apollonia's memories are drawn from her diary of the time and later shared with F. E. (415). She is the source of the story of the dinner at Anton Weyerhaeuser's house interrupted by the arrival of the barber and resumed upon his departure.

In 1958 Edwin (Ed) Davis visited Saulheim again. Karl Heinz Appenheimer, a Saulheim resident, recently shared pictures with some visiting members of the Weyerhaeuser family, including one showing Ed and his wife, Kay Davis, along with F. K. (J. P.'s son), his wife, Vivian, and their daughters Vivian and Lynn. One wonders how Ed felt a generation after his childhood visit, inspecting the Sangerhalle his grandfather had gifted to the village.

Page 161, Scene 5: This imaginary scene is based on Elise's in-depth reporting of the family celebration of Frederick and Sarah's fiftieth anniversary in 1907 as retold by F. E.

CHAPTER 16: FREDERICK WITHSTANDS PERSONAL CHALLENGES

Black Dan McDonald

All of the correspondence between Frederick and Black Dan McDonald is contained in a file in the family archives. Apparently it had been cataloged but no one had been curious enough to look into it since the letters were written. The description of events is included because it gives a perspective on Frederick's behavior, especially in the face of a second accusation that he was "not fair." (The first, by Mr. W. R. Young of Iowa, caused him great anguish, as described in Chapter 9.) Frederick directed his people to thoroughly research the transaction McDonald cited and even found out who had been behind McDonald's commitment order in Wisconsin.

Although Black Dan became a persistent scold to Frederick, F. E. records that Captain Henry, who was privy to these events, later said that Frederick often visited Black Dan's brother, who was in a St. Paul hospital for many months.

Teddy Roosevelt's Invitation

Frederick's interaction with President Roosevelt was nonexistent. When Roosevelt invited Frederick to meet with him in Washington, DC, F. E. responded for him. Frederick was in San Antonio with Sam and Apollonia Davis that winter, and F. E told the president that his father was too ill to come to Washington. It's not clear why a representative was not sent in his stead, as records maintain that such a proposal was discussed.

F. E.'s account of the American Forest Congress in 1905 was transmitted to his son, C. Davis, when Dave, as he was called, was a student at Yale. The letter remains in the files and is included in F. E.'s *Record* (413–14). Teddy Roosevelt's behavior at that congress might have been modified if he had met with Frederick two years earlier.

The best account of the life and work of Gifford Pinchot remains Char Miller's *Gifford Pinchot and the Making of Modern Environmentalism*.

Frederick's Health Afflictions

The accounts of Frederick's periods of ill health are described in the *Record*, as is the note from his diary of April 17 indicating that he understood he had had a stroke. When F. E. wrote (408) that Frederick was giving every sign of "an impending nervous breakdown," he was using the language of the time to describe what was probably high blood pressure and depression. Frederick's stroke occurred shortly after he had returned from San Antonio.

"Richer than Rockefeller"

The Charles Norcross article that appeared in *Cosmopolitan Magazine* in January 1907 accusing Frederick of "a national crime" seems to have been more upsetting to members of the family than to Frederick himself. F. E.'s response to the article (505–6) is shared in the *Record*. Bancroft Hill's rather lighthearted comments are also included in this chapter.

The excerpts from *The Autobiography of Lincoln Steffens* are found on pages 365–68.

The sensational headlines from the *Moline Evening Mail* are included to illustrate the somewhat overheated treatment that Frederick's business affairs merited from the press as late as 1911. The term "Giant Combination" apparently refers to the Weyerhaeuser Timber Company, which had many original investors but functioned as one entity.

Frederick Sees Dangers to Forests and the Future Timber Supply

Frederick's testimony on the future availability of timber in the United States took place on Monday, October 26, 1908, and was held most appropriately in Wisconsin. Excerpts from this testimony are included in this section to illustrate Frederick's ideas after a generation in the lumber business. The hearings, known as "The Pulp and Paper Investigation United States Congress Select House Committee Hearings," were published in 1909 by the Government Printing Office and may today be found in the University of California library. Most of the material quoted here came from Volume 4.29–35.

CHAPTER 17: "UNSER FRITZ" TAKES CARE OF THE VILLAGERS

Among the letters that surfaced when the family offices moved from the long-standing First National Bank Building (the successor of the National German American Bank where Frederick once had his St. Paul offices) were a number of early communications in German between Frederick and Sarah. Other letters were also identified in the care of a village family in modern-day Saulheim, Germany. These letters, translated through the good offices of several Saulheim villagers, provide a rich and human picture of Frederick and his German cousins. By reading the letters, both those of Frederick and those written by Peter Weyerhaeuser (the German distant cousin who corresponded most with him), we can draw quite a complete picture of the relationship. Frederick was clearly the benefactor and the villagers the recipients on the money end of things, but Frederick also drew a lot of solace from these relationships that connected him to his childhood home.

The most enduring illustration of Frederick's charity is the Sangerhalle, a formal building in which the many musical groups from the village and from neighboring communities perform. But personal relationships, passed down from father to son on both sides of the Atlantic, have carried on the connection between the villagers and succeeding generations of the Weyerhaeuser family.

Karl Heinz Appenheimer, the recently retired head of the Liederkranz (the village's male chorus), is currently the main liaison with the Weyerhaeuser family. His father, Georg Appenheimer, was also head of the Liederkranz and welcomed F. K.

Weyerhaeuser, his family, and Ed and Kay Davis in the fifties. Karl and his wife have visited Weyerhaeuser family members in the United States. Many Weyerhaeuser descendents still visit Saulheim. At one point seventeen family members from America journeyed to meet the German villagers. Several dozen descendents have visited the village of their ancestors, some more than once.

The Sangerhalle is still home to vigorous singing by a number of local choruses and even some from neighboring villages. There is, indeed, an annex to the hall at which beer, wine, and food are served, but the several restaurants operating in the village today indicate that the innkeepers of Frederick's time might have made a fuss to no good end.

In the Sangerhalle, an imposing portrait of Frederick hangs in the place of honor over the front doors, while across from each other on opposite walls are large photographs of Karl Heinz Appenheimer's father, Georg Heinz, and F. K. Weyerhaeuser. The exchange continues, with the most recent visit from family members taking place as this biography was in production.

Chapter 18: The Joys of Family

Frederick Turns Toward His Family

The story of Frederick playing games with his grandchildren is noted in F. E.'s *Record* (765), and the letter to young Fritz Jewett survives in its original handwriting in the family archives. The conversational tone Frederick takes with the grandchildren echoes the style of the earlier, gently teasing and newsy letters written to his own children when they were young, especially to Maggie, whom he chided for not writing to her absent father. The story of the little girl and the high chair search is found in F. E.'s *Record* (222), recounted to F. E. by William Irvine.

The Fiftieth Wedding Anniversary

Lonie drew from her diaries to write an account of her parents' departure on the day they left for Rock Island, and she imparted these memories to F. E. some years later. She also wrote great details of her preparations for the family to stay at the house on the hill, including providing for the very youngest of the grandchildren: Sarah Maud was only a baby, born on March 22 of that year. The letter from Frederick to his distant cousins in Saulheim is from the family archives. The car that Louise Lindeke Weyerhaeuser reports as decorated by the neighbors to take Frederick and Sarah to the boat was a 1907 Packard with a custom-made limousine body. One of F. E.'s great-grandsons who has an interest in cars traced this particular vehicle, which is reported to have been a gift of the Weyerhaeuser children to Frederick and Sarah.

The irrepressible Bancroft Hill's poem is included in its entirety as it captures, better than any summary, the celebration of the family story of Frederick and Sarah.

Chapter 19: The Final Years—The Sorrows of Loss

The letters to and from Margaret are all taken from the cache in the Greer family's possession. The quotes from Elise's diary are in F. E.'s *Record* (761).

The letter to Peter Weyerhaeuser was part of the set of letters the Saulheim villagers translated for the family in recent years. The original is now in the family archives in St. Paul, along with others the villagers were kind enough to translate.

Frederick's death is described by F. E., and some recollections are taken from Harriette's diary as well. The description of Frederick's final resting place is in F. E.'s *Record* (772).

Page 203, Scene 6: This scene is built upon the actual resolution passed at the Weyerhaeuser Timber Company board meeting on June 18, 1914, two months after Frederick's death. The resolution can be found in the company's files as well as in the family's archives and is quoted in F. E.'s *Record* (710).

CHAPTER 20: FREDERICK'S MANY LEGACIES

Conservation and Preservation

For an interesting discussion of these terms, see Char Miller's *Public Lands, Public Debates* (58–62).

The Brule River Donation

The Nebagamon Lumber Company grew out of a partnership between Frederick and Ed Rutledge, a Wisconsin lumberman and one of Frederick's closest friends. More can be found on this matter in F. E.'s *Record* (329).

A good source of information on the Brule River donation to the state of Wisconsin is in a publication by the Sigurd Olson Environmental Institute, *Pines and Paddlers: A Guide to the History of the Bois Brule River* (15–16ff are especially relevant). The institute is well on the side of environmentalists in its appreciation for donations that preserve the land.

A 1995 paper from the University of Wisconsin takes a different position on the events surrounding the donation. Joseph Cullon casts the entire affair in terms of class conflict. His views are included to illustrate how difficult it is to have a clear understanding of motives and circumstances in what ought to be a straightforward contribution to the state's forest preserves.

The Itasca State Park Intercession

Frederick's role in negotiating favorable terms on the state of Minnesota's acquisition of part of what became Itasca State Park is contained in the Brower report and the minutes of the 1892 meeting of the Minnesota Historical Society committee cited. Mr. Brower's comment on Frederick's role is in the public record of these minutes.

Fire and Loss

The detail on fire consumption of standing timber may be seen in a number of sources, including the monograph "An Introduction to Timberland and Investment" by Rick Weyerhaeuser. This paper also includes much of the background for the next section.

The Economics of Trees

Information on the Weyerhaeuser Company executive history and the forest regeneration and tree planting program is taken from its public documents, especially the 2011 annual report. An interesting take on this topic from an environmental magazine is found in the 1974 *Audubon* article by John C. Mitchell, "The Best of the S.O.B.s." The author reported on the commencement and development of the Weyerhaeuser Company's tree-planting program. He notes the change with some admiration coupled with humor and imagines what the old loggers might have thought of the new technology that enabled the company to move forward in this area. These old-timers "left such things to the Lord God almighty," and even some loyal veterans in the company might have wondered what "G. H. [George] Weyerhaeuser was trying to do—grow commercially superior trees or aim in some Strangelovian fashion for the far side of the moon."

Frederick's Charitable Gifts during His Lifetime

Although most of Frederick's charitable gifts made during his lifetime were not large, they were well considered. From the Sangerhalle in Saulheim to the House of Hope in St. Paul, they expressed his own feelings and personal connections. He seems to have set a tradition in the family whereby each of the branches (descendents of his seven children) make charitable gifts from their "branch" foundations as well as from the foundation they share in common.

Margaret's heartfelt letter to Richard expressing frustration about so many redundant charitable requests is from the Greer family letter collection. Nancy Weyerhaeuser's quote is taken from *Pebble in the Pond*, a history of the Weyerhaeuser Family Foundation published privately in 2005.

Frederick's Legacy—Family

The conversation between Frederick and Dr. Bengston of Rock Island is re-created from a news article by George Carlock that can be found in F. E.'s *Record* (754–55).

CHAPTER 21: REMEMBERING FREDERICK

The full letter from E. J. Palmer to Richard Jewett is in the family archives, and the letter from E. T. Buxton is quoted in F. E.'s *Record* (778). William Irvine's speech to the Chippewa Lumber and Boom Company in 1925 reflected the affection he had developed working for Frederick over many years when he was a young man.

Frederick's obituary cited here was published in the *American Lumberman* (April 11, 1914), a week after his death on April 4.

Bibliography

Books

Brinkley, Douglas. *The Wilderness Warrior: Theodore Roosevelt and the Crusade for America*. New York, London: Harper Perennial, 2009.

Hauberg, John H. *Weyerhaeuser and Denkmann: Ninety-five Years of the Manufacture and Distribution of Lumber*. Rock Island, IL: Augustana Book Concern, 1957.

Healey, Judith Koll. *Pebble in the Pond: A History of the Weyerhaeuser Family Foundation*. St. Paul, MN: North Central Publishing, 2005.

Hidy, Ralph W., Frank Ernest Hill, and Allan Nevins. *Timber and Men: The Weyerhauser Story*. New York: MacMillan Company, 1963.

Jensen, Derrick, and George Draffan (with John Osborn, MD). *Railroads and Clearcuts: The Legacy of Congress's 1864 Northern Pacific Railroad Land Grant*. Spokane, WA: Inland Empire Public Lands Council, 1995.

Josephson, Mathew. *The Robber Barons*. San Diego, New York, London: Harcourt, Inc., 1934.

Kohlmeyer, Fred W. *Frederick Weyerhaeuser: A Pen Portrait*. St. Paul, MN: Privately printed, 1967.

———. *Timber Roots: The Laird, Norton Story, 1855–1905*. Winona, MN: Winona County Historical Society, 1972.

Larson, Agnes M. *The White Pine Industry in Minnesota: A History*. Minneapolis and London: University of Minnesota Press, 1949.

Lindeke, Louise, and William Bancroft Hill. *Frederick Weyerhaeuser: Pioneer Lumberman*. St. Paul, MN: Privately printed, 1935.

McMahon, Eileen, and Theodore J. Karamanski. *North Woods River: The St. Croix River in Upper Midwest History*. Madison: University of Wisconsin Press, 2009.

Miller, Char. *Gifford Pinchot and the Making of Modern Environmentalism*. Washington, DC: Shearwater Books, 2001.

———. *Public Lands, Public Debates: A Century of Controversy*. Corvallis: Oregon State University Press, 2012.

Morris, Edmund. *Theodore Rex*. New York: Modern Library, 2001.

Steffens, Lincoln. *The Autobiography of Lincoln Steffens, Volume II*. New York: Harcourt, Brace and World, 1932.

245

Tweet, Roald. *The Quad Cities: An American Mosaic.* Rock Island, IL: East Hall Press, Augustana College, 1996.

Twining, Charles E. *Downriver: Orrin H. Ingram and the Empire Lumber Company.* Madison: State Historical Society of Wisconsin, 1975.

———. *George S. Long: Timber Statesman.* Seattle and London: University of Washington Press, 1994.

Weyerhaeuser, Frederick Edward. *A Record of the Life and Business Activities of Frederick Weyerhaeuser, 1834–1914.* 5 vols. St. Paul, MN: Privately printed, 1937.

Wickstrom, George. *The Town Crier.* Rock Island, IL: J. W. Potter Company (*Rock Island Argus*), 1948.

Monographs

Cullon, Joseph. "Landscape of Labor and Leisure: Common Rights, Private Property and Class Relations Along the Bois Brule River, 1870–1940." Master's thesis, University of Wisconsin, 1995.

Norton, Mathew. *The Mississippi River Logging Company: An Historical Sketch.* Privately printed, 1912. Copies in the Weyerhaeuser Family Archives.

Sigurd Olson Environmental Institute. *Pines and Paddlers: A Guide to the History of the Bois Brule River.* Ashland, WI: Northland College.

Weyerhaeuser, Frederick (Rick). "An Introduction to Timberland and Investment." May 1905.

Weyerhaeuser, Frederick (Rick), The Nature Conservancy, and James W. Giltmier. *Forest Management and Policy in the U.S.: An Historical Perspective.* Washington, DC: The Pinchot Institute for Conservation, 1997.

Weyerhaeuser, Frederick King (F. K.) *Trees and Men.* New York, San Francisco, and Montreal: The Newcomen Society in North America, 1951.

Article

Bronoagh, Whit. "North American Forests in the Age of Man." *American Forests* (Summer 2012).

Mitchell, John C. "The Best of the S.O.B.s." *Audubon Magazine* (1974).

Index

Black Hawk Wars, 13

Black River, 80

Bloedel, Andrew (brother-in-law): arrival in Coal Valley, 44; Civil War service, 59, 60; on F. C. A. Denkmann, 55; on Weyerhaeuser's Civil War conscription, 59

Bloedel, Andrew (nephew), 109

Bloedel, Anna Catherine. *See* Denkmann, Anna Catherine Bloedel

Bloedel, Elizabeth Sarah. *See* Weyerhaeuser, Elizabeth Sarah Bloedel

Bloedel, John Philip (father-in-law), 30, 44

Bloedel, Philip (brother-in-law): Civil War service, 59, 60; on F. C. A. Denkmann, 55

Bonaparte, Napoleon, 11, 23, 27–28

Bonn, Romanzo, 89

boom(s): function of, 73, 74; as term, 72–73. *See also* Beef Slough boom

brailling of logs, 74

Breaking New Ground (Pinchot), xiii

brewery, Weyerhaeuser's early employment in, 29–30, 38

Brower, J. V., 211

Brule River, Weyerhaeuser's donation of land along, 209–11

Brule River dam, proposal for, 209–10

burial: of Mrs. Weyerhaeuser, 197; of Weyerhaeuser, 199

business: and family life, 45, 57, 106; on frontier, rough-and-tumble nature of, 49; Weyerhaeuser's influence in, ix, 132; Weyerhaeuser's love of, 138, 154–55, 157

business, Weyerhaeuser's skill in: Andrew Bloedel on, 44; gift for administration, xii; gift for innovation, 39; gift for sales, 39; and success in Coal Valley, 47; teaching of to grandchildren, 188–89; tributes to, 220

business model of Weyerhaeuser: and honest associates, importance of, 59;

Weyerhaeuser and Denkmann Lumber Co. and, 54

Buxton, E. T., 220–21

C. Lamb and Sons, 84

career of Weyerhaeuser, early employment, xi, 11, 29–30, 37

Carson, William, 97, 189

Caughey, Albert, 106

Caughey, Elisabetha "Elise; Eliza" Weyerhaeuser. *See* Weyerhaeuser, Elisabetha "Elise; Eliza"

Caughey, Hugh (brother-in-law), 44, 104, 105, 198

Central Pacific Railroad, 15

Chamberlin, Clarence, 98

character, Weyerhaeuser on importance of, 188

character and personality of Weyerhaeuser: as action-oriented, xii; business, love of, 138, 154–55, 157; charitable giving as indication of, 214, 244; circumspection of, 129; complexity of, 219; concerns about personal cost of his actions, xiii; confidence of, 26, 38; diplomatic skills, 129–30; emotional isolation of, ix–x; forgiveness of others, 102; friendly, easy-going manner, 55; gift for administration, xii; gift for innovation, 39; gift for sales, 39; gregariousness of, 43; hard work, habit of, 39, 47–48, 130, 137; honesty and fair dealing, 98–99, 164–66, 219, 220, 221; impatience with dishonesty, 95; impatience with inept colleagues, 76–77; importance of family to, 37, 111, 216; importance of loyalty to, 54; leadership abilities, 3, 98, 203, 220, 221; sense of humor, 71, 107–8, 117–18, 118–19, 188–89; strength of, 163; temper, displays of, 95; tributes to, from associates, 219–20; workers, concern for, 106–7; worries, refusal to dwell on, 38. *See*

Bloedel's move to, 39–40; Third Avenue residence in, 104–5; Weyerhaeuser's charitable giving in, 214–15; Weyerhaeusers' departure from, 135; Weyerhaeuser's first journey to, 35; Weyerhaeuser's first move to, xi, 12, 31; Weyerhaeusers' return to for fiftieth wedding anniversary celebration, 189–91

Rock Island and Peoria Railroad, 37, 38

Rock Island Argus: on Beef Slough, 81–82; on floods of 1880, 90; history of, 37, 60, 233; on importance of Weyerhaeuser, 132; on Weyerhaeuser as man, 111; Weyerhaeuser interview on trusts in, 92–93; on Weyerhaeuser's circumspection, 129; on Weyerhaeuser's Senate testimony, 100–101; on Weyerhaeuser's Wisconsin timber purchases, 125

Rock Island Daily Union, 57, 61

Rock Island Millwork Company, 106

Rock Island Rangers, 13

Rock Island Republican, 37, 60, 233

Rock Island Sash and Door Works, 106

Rock River Improvement Association, 61

Roosevelt, Theodore "Teddy": interest in forest preservation, 166–67, 205, 213; Pinchot and, 17; and Second American Forest Congress, 17, 167–69; on timber industry, xii, 17, 167–69; trust busting by, 140, 173; and Weyerhaeuser, efforts to meet with, 167

Rust, Ezra, 56

Rutledge, Ed, 94, 133, 209

St. Anthony Lumber Co., 126

St. Croix Indians, timber agreements with whites, 70

St. Croix River, 80

St. Louis Boom and Improvement Co., 132

St. Louis River, and log transport, 131

St. Paul, Minnesota: importance as transportation hub, xii, 135; population in 1890, 127; Weyerhaeuser family members' move to, 135; Weyerhaeusers' life in, 136–37, 140; Weyerhaeusers' move to, xii, 127, 135–36; Weyerhaeusers' residences in, 136, 146

St. Paul and Duluth railroad line, 131

St. Paul Boom Co., 126

St. Paul Pioneer Press, 137

sales, Weyerhaeuser's talent for, 55

Sangerhalle (Niedersaulheim, Germany): current uses of, 182, 242; described, 242; dry rot damage to, 185–86; opposition to Weyerhaeuser's gift of, 180–82; Weyerhaeuser descendants' ongoing visits to, 239–40, 241–42; Weyerhaeuser's gift of, 178–80, 182; Weyerhaeuser's visit to, 156–57

Saukenuk village, 12–13

Sauk Indians: removal of, 12–13; and War of 1812, 13

Saulheim, Germany. *See* Niedersaulheim, Germany

Saunders, Edward Nelson, 210, 214

Sauntry and Tozer, 78

sawmills: methods of purchasing logs, 68–69; rise of, along route to Wisconsin forests, 70; workers, life of, 131

Sawyer, Philetus, 85

scalers, role of, 74

scaling of logs, 74, 78

scarlet fever epidemic, in Coal Valley (1869), 104

Schneider, Mrs., 37–38, 39

schools of forestry, establishment of in U.S., 16–17

Schricker, Lorenzo, 83, 84, 86

Scott, Winfield, 13

Scribner Rule, 74

scrip paid to Civil War soldiers: and opening of West, 60–61; purchase of by land speculators, 61, 72

Niedersaulheim, 30; support for Weyerhaeuser's work, 46; travel in Europe, 151–53, 153–54, 156–57; travel to join Weyerhaeuser, 110–11; Weyerhaeuser on, 26; Weyerhaeuser's appellation for, 193; and Weyerhaeuser's clerical work, help with, 43; Weyerhaeuser's mourning of, 196–98
Weyerhaeuser, Frances Maud Moon (daughter-in-law), *xvii*, 130, 148
Weyerhaeuser, Frederick: appearance of, 111; birth of, 3; childhood of, 21, 23–26, 27–28; death of, 3, 198; as German speaker, 51–52, 75, 98, 152–53; memory of, as remarkable, 39, 58; siblings of, 24; visionary insight of, 144. *See also* character and personality of Weyerhaeuser; *other specific topics*
Weyerhaeuser, Frederick (grandson, by F.W. Weyerhaeuser), 190
Weyerhaeuser, Frederick Edward "Freddie; Fred; F. E." (son), *xvii*; on Beef Slough, origin of name, 82; birth of, 43; on birth of Weyerhaeuser's children, 42–43; bond with mother, 117; childhood of, 117; correspondence, 119, 168–69; on *Cosmopolitan* article on Weyerhaeuser, 172, 173; on courtship of parents, 30–31; on early U.S. forest conservation efforts, 168, 169; education of, 117, 148; employment in family business, 123, 133, 134, 139–40, 145, 195; and family move to St. Paul, 135; on father's hard work, 48; on F. C. A. Denkmann, 55; on F. E. Ingram, 97; friendships of college years, 167, 210; on grave of Weyerhaeuser, 197; on John Weyerhaeuser's Civil War memories, 60; on life in St. Paul, 137; marriage, *xvii*, 130, 139; misbehavior at Yale, 148–50; and mother, illness and death of, 196; on mother, 45; on parents' silver anniversary celebration, 116; recollections of Rock Island family life, 105,

106; *A Record of the Life and Business Activities of Frederick Weyerhaeuser,* 117, 230; on relationship with father, 123; residence in St. Paul, 139; Roosevelt's efforts to meet with, 167; and Second American Forest Congress, 17, 167–69; as source of personal information on Weyerhaeuser, 79; travel in Europe, 151; tributes to father sent to, 219–20; on Weyerhaeuser and Denkmann partnership, 51–52; on Weyerhaeuser's accounting skills, 58; on Weyerhaeuser's beekeeping, 44; on Weyerhaeuser's business dealings, 97; on Weyerhaeuser's character and personality, 95–96, 99, 101–2; on Weyerhaeuser's charitable giving, 214; on Weyerhaeuser's enjoyment of grandchildren, 187; on Weyerhaeuser's health, 169–70; on Weyerhaeuser's policy on helping children in business, 133–34; on Weyerhaeuser's public speaking ability, 98; on Weyerhaeuser's southern trip, 138–39; on Weyerhaeusers' travels in Europe, 152, 154; on Weyerhaeuser's views on success, 216
Weyerhaeuser, Frederick King (grandson, by John P. Weyerhaeuser), 145, 239, 241–42
Weyerhaeuser, Georg (German relative), 178
Weyerhaeuser, George (great-grandson), 211–12, 213, 244
Weyerhaeuser, Harriette Louise Davis (daughter-in-law), *xvii*, 130, 139, 170, 194, 198
Weyerhaeuser, John (father), 21, 23, 24
Weyerhaeuser, John Phillip "J. P." (son), *xvii*; birth of, 43, 44; character and personality of, 45, 113; childhood of, 44–45, 112; children of, 145, 213; Civil War memories of, 60; correspondence, 115; education of, 113–14, 115;